THE JAPANESE EMPLOYMENT SYSTEM

The Japanese Employment System

Adapting to a New Economic Environment

MARCUS REBICK

OXFORD
UNIVERSITY PRESS

OXFORD
UNIVERSITY PRESS

Great Clarendon Street, Oxford, OX2 6DP,
United Kingdom

Oxford University Press is a department of the University of Oxford.
It furthers the University's objective of excellence in research, scholarship,
and education by publishing worldwide. Oxford is a registered trade mark of
Oxford University Press in the UK and in certain other countries

Published in the United States of America by Oxford University Press
198 Madison Avenue, New York, NY 10016, United States of America

British Library Cataloguing in Publication Data

Data available

Library of Congress Cataloging in Publication Data

Data available

ISBN 978-0-19-924724-0

For my family

Preface

The beginning of the 1990s brought major changes to the economic environment in Japan. The decade began with a collapse in asset prices that was soon followed by slower economic growth. Macroeconomic mismanagement and the financial crises of the late 1990s led to rising unemployment and prolonged stagnation. Japan had not experienced such a prolonged slump since before the Second World War. Given this kind of change in the economic environment, it should come as no surprise that the employment system had to adjust to adapt to this slowdown. The aim of this book is to examine what changes have been taking place in the Japanese employment system and labour markets, particularly in the past 15 years.

Although there are a number of books published in Japanese, there has so far been no unified treatment in English dealing with this important subject, although there have been edited collections of papers both in book and journal form. My aim in this book is to present a unified picture of what is taking place, putting prime emphasis on two important points. The first main point is that the employment system, despite the recent increase in dismissals of employees, has not changed in its fundamental arrangements. There are still secure jobs for regular employees, who are employed for an indefinite period up to the age of mandatory retirement. The fact that these employees can be dismissed during hard times, such as the past 10 years, is nothing new. Japanese employers have always made redundancies after prolonged downturns in business. In other words, the dismissals that we are seeing are perfectly in tune with the nature of the system in place since the 1950s.

The second main point that I wish to make is that there has been a fundamental shift in strategy on the part of firms to make greater use of atypical employees, mainly in the form of part-time workers. This strategy has been greatly helped by the fact that there is an abundant labour supply of part-time employees to be drawn from the ranks of self-employed and family workers, as well as non-working women. The move towards greater use of low-cost atypical employees has had a major impact on the labour market for young school graduates, especially those without tertiary education. Middle-school and high school graduates are finding it much more difficult to find regular employment.

Although this book places great emphasis on the two points that I have just mentioned, there are many other ways in which the employment system is gradually evolving that are also of great interest. The position of women in the labour market is changing in both legal and real terms. The system of collective bargaining, focussed in the past on a unified demand for an annual wage increase, has had to adapt to a new era of deflation. Firms are also changing their personnel management system, in part in response to the ageing of the workforce. Managerial posts have become relatively scarce and firms have had to find other ways in which to motivate their employees. The introduction of performance-related pay is one of a number of measures that are promoting a more individualistic treatment of the employee in the workplace. The rise in the unemployment rate has also led to a shift of government policy, with more emphasis being placed on programmes aimed at helping individuals to retrain for new jobs, rather than the subsidization of old jobs. All of these topics are covered in some detail over the course of the book.

For the most part, this book takes an institutional approach and is descriptive in nature. As much as possible, I try to avoid using economic jargon. Although economic arguments are used to gain insight into the changes that are taking place, there is no attempt to place exact measures on such things as labour supply elasticities. This is largely due to the restrictions on use of data in Japan, but is also because the book is an overview. The main points might easily be lost with an excess of detail.

It is my aim that the book will be read not only by economists, but also by others who are interested in the changes taking place in Japan today. The future of Japan's employment system has wider implications for Japanese society and politics. For example, the decline of the family enterprise removes a central pillar of support for the Liberal Democratic Party at the same time that it changes the nature of the family in Japan. The question of whether Japanese firms maintain their postwar tradition of providing secure jobs to men up to the age of mandatory retirement is of central importance in determining whether the Japanese are becoming less tied to their organizations and more individualistic. The increased difficulty faced by many high school graduates in finding secure full-time jobs may lead to greater inequality in the future. Broader issues such as these are raised in the book. If this book provides some help in understanding these wider issues then it will have achieved its purpose.

There are many individuals and institutions that have helped me both in the course of writing this book and in the research for it. First, I would like to thank Andrew Schuller of Oxford University Press for encouraging me to undertake this venture. My colleagues at the Nissan Institute of Japanese Studies, Jenny Corbett, Roger Goodman, Arthur Stockwin, and Ann Waswo have offered support and advice. I have benefited and learned from collaborative work with Yuji Genda and Hiroshi Ono. I have at various times been a visiting researcher at the economics departments of Nagoya University and Gakushuin University, the Social Science Research Institute at Tokyo University, the Research Institute on Capital Formation at the Development Bank of Japan, and the Japan Institute of Labour. The Recruit Works Institute has provided data used in this book. Support for travel has also generously been provided by Oxford University. It is not possible to thank everyone who has helped me along the way but I would like to acknowledge the assistance of John Benson, Scott Davis, Yoshio Higuchi, Koichiro Imano, Minoru Ito, Katsuhiko Iwata, Masuyuki Kakuho, Takao Kato, Brian Maclean, Motohiro Morishima, Hiromi Murata, Isao Ohashi, Souichi

Ohta, Yoshio Okunishi, Machiko Osawa, Hideya Sakashita, Hiroki Sato, and Toshiaki Tachibanaki. I would also like to thank Jennifer Wilkinson and Carol Bestley, my editors at OUP, and Virginia Williams, my copy-editor, for their help in producing this book. Finally, I would like to thank Bernadette Urtz and Adam Rebick for their continuing love and support.

M.R.

Acknowledgements

The author would like to thank the following for permisssion to reproduce published material: Oxford University Press (Table 6.5, Figure 10.2); the Japan Institute for Labour Policy and Training (Figure 5.1). Parts of Chapter 3 consist of reworked material from Rebick (2000) with the permission of Oxford University Press. Parts of Chapter 9 consist of reworked material from Rebick (1998) with the permission of Routledge.

Table of Contents

Part I   Introduction

Part II   Institutional changes affecting the Labour Market

Part III   Major Trends in Labour Markets

List of Tables

List of Figures

PART I

INTRODUCTION

1

Introduction

The decade from 1992 to 2002 saw major changes in the performance of the Japanese economy. The growth rate slowed dramatically from an average of 3–4% in the 1980s to just 1% through the 1990s. It is now common to refer to this period as the 'lost decade', reflecting the loss in potential growth over this period. There is also a widespread view that Japanese society has been undergoing some kind of fundamental change, although the direction in which the country is going is uncertain. Expressions such as 'Japan in transition', 'Regime-shift', or the 'end of the Japanese model', are often used to try to emphasize that the changes now taking place represent a radical break with the past.[1] On the other hand, there are sceptics who emphasize continuity with the past, arguing that reforms or changes are superficial, merely a change of clothing with the main essentials of a long-established postwar system lying undisturbed.[2] As with the economy, the Japanese 'model' of industrial relations and personnel management is said by some to be breaking down. Lifetime employment guarantees seem to be broken, as press reports appear of planned cutbacks and downsizing in major Japanese corporations. The unemployment rate, running at 2–3% for most of the postwar period has recently doubled. There are frequent reports of companies overhauling their pay systems, claiming to eliminate payment by seniority. On the other hand, more careful examination of employment practices reveals that 'lifetime employment' was not so widespread, nor did it encompass the entire career for most employees. Companies have always been able to cut staff by calling for 'voluntary' early retirement when times have been tough. Payment systems are changing, but this needs to be seen in perspective—payment systems in Japan have been undergoing change throughout the past century.

Nevertheless, Japan cannot avoid experiencing major change. It is written into the demographic profile of a population which is experiencing ageing at an unprecedented rate. At the same time, it is now apparent that the days when Japan could be said to have a superior economic performance compared to other developed countries have come to an end. Growth has slowed down. There is no more talk of Japan dominating the globe, and there is far more attention paid to the various social and economic problems that Japan faces.

THE JAPANESE ECONOMY IN THE 1990s

The last 20 years have seen the continuation of a steady shift of the economy away from manufacturing and agriculture, in terms of employment. As in other countries, it has been more difficult for Japan to raise productivity levels in the service sector as rapidly as in manufacturing, and so potential economic growth was bound to slow over the 1980s and 1990s. The shift to slower growth has not been a gradual one, however, as a very high dollar in the early 1980s and an asset price bubble in the late 1980s kept growth rates higher than they might otherwise have been. Then, action by the central bank, concerned with the extent of the asset price bubble, brought an end to the boom, and financial institutions and firms that had invested in stocks and real estate developed major problems on their balance sheets. Many firms are badly in debt to banks that were all too willing to lend money during the boom period. The banks have been reluctant to foreclose on these loans as this would push the companies into bankruptcy and the extent of the write-off would be very large. The government has tried to push the banks to reduce the number of non-performing loans, but has not forced the issue because of the fear that widespread bankruptcies would lead to a major increase in the unemployment rate. The result is a situation where banks have been reluctant to make new loans and where investment rates, especially in the small business sector, have fallen (Motonishi and Yoshikawa 1999). Since 2003 there has been some improvement, mainly due to increased demand for exports, but it is still too early to know how long the recovery will last. Although Japan's saving rate is gradually falling, it still remains well above investment rates and domestic consumption has not played a major role in the recovery so far.

Government efforts to stimulate the economy through fiscal policy have not been consistent (Posen 1998), and have also pushed the national debt to very high levels by international standards (150% of GDP (gross domestic product)). Despite the high level of government debt, the Japanese government is not at high risk of default—Japan is a net creditor nation. Nevertheless, the high level of government debt and the rapid ageing of the population have led the Japanese to conclude that there will be large tax increases and reduced old-age pension benefits in the future. The result is a demand-deficient economy that is largely responsible for the rise in the unemployment rate and the sluggish record of growth. This has been further aggravated by the development of a deflationary monetary environment with prices falling at an annual rate of 1–2% since the late 1990s.

As demand deficiency and deflation have hit the economy, there has been a loss of confidence in the institutions of the economic system. The very practices and relationships that were often given credit for Japan's high growth in the past are now held to be responsible for the poor performance at present. Prior to the 1990s, the close relationships between banks and firms and between the private sector and the government were often given credit for the ability to make long-term investments that ultimately led to better growth outcomes. Unlike the indirect, market-mediated methods of corporate control, Japanese corporate governance was exercised partly through the major banks that directly monitored the firms to which they lent. Similarly, the legislature preferred to enact vague laws that allowed for great scope on the part of government to informally provide guidance to the main actors, especially the large banks and firms. With the collapse of the bubble in 1990, however, the same close relationships and lack of clear-cut legislation have led to paralysis. The government has been unwilling to bail out the banking sector both because this would be politically unpopular and because this would add to the ballooning government debt. It has also found it difficult to aggressively force banks to foreclose on their loans, as this would lead to a number of spectacular bankruptcies.

CONTINUITY OR DISCONTINUITY

This brings us back to the issue of change in Japan. The view of those who prefer to see continuity is based on the fact that many of the underlying institutions, political and legal, have not changed much in the past two decades. The Liberal Democratic Party (LDP) has remained in power continuously since 1955 with only a brief break in 1993–4. The underlying approach of Japanese law has allowed for great leeway on the part of the bureaucracy in the enforcement of law and the making of policy and this, too, remains unchanged. Finally, there is the simple fact that the changes that have hit the Japanese economy, great as they are, have not yet had much influence on the actual standard of living of most of the population. As we shall see, the unemployment problem has not had a great impact on the male household heads who figure so prominently in the distribution of family income. The growth in income inequality that affected most industrialized countries in the 1980s has had only a slight impact on Japanese incomes as they exist today, particularly when permanent income (lifetime income) is considered.

Nevertheless, there is a major change taking place in the labour market for youth, and a shift in the balance of what I call the primary and secondary parts of the labour market. Japan provides a good case for dual labour market theory because the divisions between types of employment are fairly clear-cut. On the one hand, there is highly stable employment in medium-sized to large firms with employment security up to the age of mandatory retirement. These positions have typically been occupied by men. On the other hand, there is a much less stable, secondary sector comprised of part-time workers, young unmarried full-time women, workers on temporary contract, and workers in small-sized and family-run firms.

The main objective of this book is to show how this division of the labour market is shifting and how labour market institutions have been coping with and adapting to the changing economic environment, including the secular slowdown in growth, the demand deficiency of the 1990s, and the ageing of the population. I shall argue that the main features of the primary sector of the labour market (which is what most people have in mind when they speak of the 'Japanese model') have not changed in any fundamental sense, but have been modified in a process that long predates the 1990s. There has been a shift in attitudes and expectations about the future, but to date most of the changes have not been dramatic. The main shift that is taking place is that non-standard working arrangements (principally part-time work) have become more important as women are increasingly participating in the labour market as employees, rather than staying at home or working in family businesses. Young men, especially those with weaker records in education, are finding it increasingly difficult or choosing not to enter primary sector jobs. The dual nature of the Japanese labour market, if anything, has become more pronounced in recent years, especially if we consider youth.

Furthermore, the nature of the dualism in the labour market has changed. In the past, the division between the primary and secondary sectors of the market was between the larger firms and their subsidiaries, or the companies that subcontracted their work. Gradually, however, over the past 40 years, there has been a decline in the small business sector, especially in the numbers of self-employed and family workers and a growth in the numbers of part-time workers or short-term contract workers. These workers are found working alongside the core workers (often doing the same tasks) and so the boundary has moved inside the firm to a greater extent. The observed increase in the number of part-time workers is partly related to a decline in the number of family workers, and is thus a supply-side issue. Much of the explanation for the shift lies on the demand side, however.

DEMAND-SIDE EXPLANATIONS FOR THE RISE IN ATYPICAL EMPLOYMENT

It is possible that firms may be taking on more part-time workers as a response to slower growth. Consider a firm with full-time core workers working alongside less privileged part-time or contract workers. There are usually higher costs associated with the hiring and firing of workers in the more protected core jobs (including the loss of investment in training). The secondary workers have lower hiring and firing costs attached to their employment, but are not complete substitutes for the primary workers, generally because they are not as skilled. For simplicity, suppose there is no long-term growth in output for the firm and that labour productivity remains constant. If demand is fluctuating, the firm will usually choose to hire secondary workers during upturns and to fire them (or not renew their fixed-term contracts) during downturns. The reason for this is that the firm does not want to be saddled with too many primary workers during a downturn, as there are costs to firing such workers. As in the theory of Saint-Paul (1996) some of that cost may also be expressed in a higher (efficiency) wage that would need to be paid to core workers if there was a greater chance of being fired due to economic downturns.

Now imagine the same situation in the case where there is a high secular rate of economic growth. Under these circumstances it becomes possible to continue to hire extra core workers in an upturn since a downturn will probably only require a hiring freeze, rather than a situation where core workers need to be made redundant. The result, in effect, will be that the proportion of core workers will be higher than under the case of no growth, since core workers are, on the whole, more desirable than secondary workers.

The slowdown in growth that Japan is experiencing is partly due to the demand-deficient recession(s) of the past 13 years. It is also, however, an inevitable consequence of both the demographic situation (a declining labour force) and a structural shift to the tertiary sector where growth in productivity is likely to be more hard-won. For this reason, the long-term average potential growth rate of the economy has slowed. Consequently, it is reasonable to believe that there will be a long-term shift in the employment structure towards the secondary labour market, with a growth in the proportion of labour input that comes from part-time and other non-standard forms of labour. Furthermore, we would expect that the relative size of the large firm sector would decline in Japan, as more work is contracted out to firms in the 'secondary' sector, with their lower labour costs.

It is the rising cost of labour in Japan, a product both of the appreciation of the yen and also of the decline in the population that is pushing firms to look for lower cost alternatives to the use of regular employees. Firms are also becoming increasingly cost conscious as the nature of corporate governance changes in Japan. Where, previously, firms relied on bank loans for finance, they are now more likely to raise funds directly on equity markets. The result has been that firms have become less concerned with growth in market share and more concerned about profitability (Hoshi and Kashyap 2001).

All told, the combined impact of the decline in the family firm, slower growth, and the shrinking of the labour force will push firms towards a greater use of part-time and other forms of secondary labour. This in turn will have major implications for Japanese society as there will be an increasing number of households where no member holds full-time regular employment. This will also mean that, other things being equal, a system of enterprise-based unionism that is centred on the core workers will inevitably decline in terms of its share of employees. There are also implications for the income distribution, as much of Japan's provision of welfare comes through the firm, but is limited to core workers and their families.

CHOICE OF PERIOD OF STUDY

This study will be primarily concerned with what has been taking place over the past 20 years. There are several points during the period where it appears that the Japanese economy has faced a major change in the economic environment. This is best seen by looking at some primary economic indicators. Figure 1.1 plots the growth rate of GDP and the unemployment rate for Japan, while Figure 1.2 shows trends in asset prices. Finally, Figure 1.3 plots the exchange rate for Japan over the past 20 years. Referring to these charts, one can find several breakpoints, depending on one's viewpoint. The huge appreciation that followed the Plaza

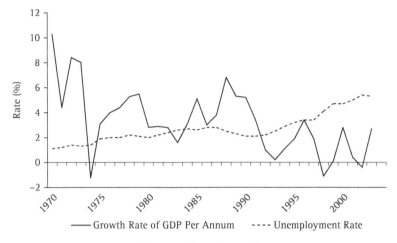

Figure 1.1. *GDP growth and unemployment rates*
Source: MHLW4 (2004), tables A1, A2.

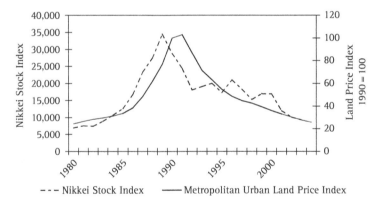

Figure 1.2. *Stock prices and land prices*
Source: Japan Real Estate Institute, The Bank of Japan, The Financial Forecasts Centre
(http://www.forecasts.org).

Accord of 1985 had a great effect on the competitiveness of Japanese exports and lowered the price of imports. If one looks at the subsequent period of the asset price bubble as an aberration, then one could reasonably conclude that 1985 represents a watershed. The doubling of Japan's labour costs on the international market led many manufacturers either to shift operations overseas, or to find sources for intermediate goods from abroad.

A second possible choice for a break would be the collapse of asset prices in 1990. This led directly to major problems in the banking sector and was the

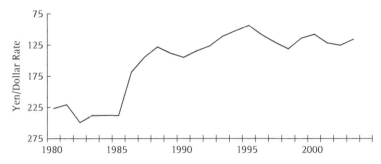

Figure 1.3. *Yen–dollar exchange rate*
Source: MHLW4 (2004), table A1.

harbinger of the slowdown in growth that was to follow. 1992 marked the first year in which the slowdown hit the real economy as the growth rate fell below 1% for the first time since 1974. The labour market reacted with a lag, so 1993 marked the start of a steady upward climb in the unemployment rate. Finally, 1998 marked a real break in the unemployment series as the unemployment rate surged to double the levels of the 1980s following the Asian financial crisis and the slowdown in Japan. As we shall see, the pace at which firms cut employment quickened noticeably after 1998.

As the forgoing list of dates suggests, unlike the crisis of the first oil shock, there is no one date that will provide a satisfactory starting-point for all of the issues that need to be covered in this book. In addition, many of the fundamental changes that are taking place in Japan have been in progress since the 1970s. For example, the growing use of part-time workers, the decline of the agricultural labour force, the growing share of the service sector in employment, and the decline in union density long predate the 1990s. Nevertheless, the changes of the last 10 years are leaving a legacy that will gradually transform Japanese society. In particular, the decline of the family-run firm and the rise of 'non-standard' forms of employer–employee relationships, including contract labour and part-time employment, especially in the youth labour market, represent a major shift in the balance of employment. The effect of these shifts will only gradually be realized in future years as new cohorts enter the labour market.

OUTLINE OF BOOK

The book is organized into three parts. Chapter 2 offers an account of the stylized facts about the Japanese labour market, as it has been analysed up to the 1990s. Readers that are familiar with these institutions should skip ahead to the next section of the book.

The second part of the book examines the institutional changes that are affecting the labour market in Japan. Chapter 3 begins this survey by examining the ways in which the treatment of the core worker has changed in Japan, looking at the introduction of new compensation systems. I will argue, however, that in broad perspective, the changes that have taken place have been minor, and their impact has not been significant. I follow this with a chapter that documents the growing use of non-standard labour (atypical employment) in Japan, looking at the trend towards part-time work and also at the decline of the family-run firm in Japan. This is the single biggest institutional change that has affected the Japanese labour market.

Chapter 5 then looks at the state of industrial relations in Japan. The main story here is the continuous decline in union density (unionization rates) since the mid-1970s. The enterprise union was once considered to be one of the pillars of the Japanese labour system, but with unionization rates at the 20% level, it is hard to make that case today. Against this backdrop of decline, the 1990s have seen the union movement focus mostly on job security, putting little pressure on wages. The end of the 1990s and the development of deflation in Japan then brought about a weakening of the famous Spring Offensive and a shift of focus away from wage issues as firms were unable to present a united demand for an across-the-board wage increase. Slow growth has decisively weakened the union movement and this, too, is partly a reflection of the declining importance of the 'core worker' in the large firm.

In the third part of the book I turn to an analysis of the major trends in the labour markets. Chapter 6 looks at the overall condition of the labour market, including the rise in unemployment and labour mobility. The widespread notion that unemployment figures in Japan are misleading is examined and put in perspective through international comparison. Some estimate is made of the cost that Japan is bearing through the inability or reluctance of Japanese firms to dismiss their redundant employees, and the problems with government policy are examined. The final part of the chapter looks at how Japan's income distribution may be widening.

Chapter 6 is followed by three chapters looking at specific labour markets where atypical employment is most common—the markets for women, older workers, and youth. In all of these markets, we see the impact of the drive towards greater use of 'secondary labour' during the 1990s. Chapter 10 then turns to longer-run issues, especially the declining labour force and the ageing of the population. The United Nations has indicated that Japan would need some 33.5 million immigrants between 1995 and 2050 (650,000 annually) to prevent its labour force from declining (Papademetriou and Hamilton 2000). Japan remains opposed to such large-scale immigration, however, and so I examine the alternatives and show that the alternative of low immigration does not necessarily lead to a gloomy prognosis for Japan. If Japan succeeds in maintaining growth in economic well-being with a declining population this will challenge many of the assumptions that policy-makers have held over the past century.

Finally, I briefly offer some general conclusions, observations, and policy suggestions in Chapter 11.

USE OF STATISTICS IN THIS BOOK

The Japanese government imposes heavy restrictions on the use of microdata on individuals by non-governmental researchers. In general, for all of the major government surveys used by labour economists, it is necessary to conduct the research in Japan, to work in an organized research group, and to work on a pre-designated topic. In practice, access is only granted to projects that meet the approval of the government. For academics, this usually means that they are working with the government on an advisory board or deliberative council (*shingikai*). No individual academic has free access to microdata from the entire spectrum of surveys that are run by the government. As a result, a book that depended entirely on using microdata would necessarily have to tackle a limited number of issues. For this reason, the fact that microdata is not used as evidence stems from practical necessity. To compensate for this, I have used two strategies. First, when it is appropriate, I make reference to the results of researchers who have used microdata. Since this is by no means comprehensive, I also make use of the published statistics provided by the government. In a couple of cases, I make use of microdata collected by private research organizations. In most cases, published statistics are entirely satisfactory to illustrate the points that I wish to make about trends in the labour market. The appendix to this chapter provides a description of the principal surveys that I have used for reference.

NOTES

1. For example, Pempel (1998) and Kuruvilla and Erickson (2002).
2. Some champions of this view for economics include Lincoln (2001) and Mulgan (2002).

APPENDIX: DESCRIPTION OF SURVEYS USED

There are four major surveys conducted by the Japanese government that I use in this book. In all cases, I have used published tables, many of them available on the Internet at the website for the appropriate ministry. The following list is hardly an exhaustive list of the surveys available and there are a number of others, including the *Population Census* and the *Survey on Wages and Working Hours*, which I employ.

1. *Wage Structure Survey* or *Wage Census* (WSS) This is an establishment-based survey conducted annually by the Ministry of Health, Labour and Welfare. The published tables consist of detailed cross-tabulations of earnings and hours worked according to gender, age, seniority, education, occupation, industry, managerial rank, firm size, and prefecture. The tables are restricted, however, in the number of cross-tabulations or cells that they can list, so for any given table separate cells will be listed for only a subset of the preceding list of variables. Furthermore, the information given in each cell may be restricted according to the table. For example, the tables with cells for different seniority groups do not provide information on hours of work, so it is impossible to calculate average hourly earnings for different seniority groups using this table.

With the exception of 1974, the data are considered to be highly reliable, sampling over 70,000 establishments and more than a million employees. Enterprises with more than five employees are surveyed, although most of the useful tables are for firms with more than 10 employees. In general, part-time workers are surveyed and tabulated separately, where a part-time worker is defined as one who is so designated by the firm, and who may be working more than 35 hours per week.

2. *Employment Status Survey* (ESS) This household-based survey is conducted every five years by the Statistics Bureau of the Ministry of Public Management, Home Affairs, Posts and Telecommunications. The most recent survey was in 2002. It provides information on the type of economic activity and status in employment and is conducted through households, thus providing complete coverage of the population. Various tables have cross-tabulations according to gender, age group, industry, occupation, and prefecture. I have used the survey primarily to look at trends in self-employment and part-time work.

3. *Labour Force Survey* This household survey, conducted monthly by the Ministry of Public Management, Home Affairs, Posts and Telecommunications, provides basic information on participation, employment, and hours of work for different age and gender groups. It is the source of the unemployment statistics used in Japan and so corresponds to the Current Population Survey in the United States or the Labour Force Survey in the UK. There is also a *Special Survey* conducted in February and August that provides more detailed information, about the unemployed, job changers, and the status of the worker (e.g. part-timer, and so on). Unfortunately, the survey is not consistent from year to year in the information it collects and reports, so it is not as useful as the ESS over longer time periods. The Special Survey has been merged with the Labour Force Survey since 2003.

4. *Employment Trends Survey* (ETS) This survey, conducted by the Ministry of Health, Labour and Welfare through establishments, provides information about separations and accessions across industries and for different age or firm-size groups. The survey also reports on the methods that new hires have used to find their jobs. The survey is conducted semi-annually, but the main reports are produced annually. Coverage is restricted to those in establishments with more than 10 employees.

2

The Japanese Employment System

INTRODUCTION–A BRIEF LOOK AT THE IMAGE AND REALITY OF JAPANESE EMPLOYMENT

This chapter provides an overview of the stylized facts about the Japanese employment system as it existed until the late 1980s. The reader should be aware that the employment system has been undergoing continuous change throughout its history and the period since the end of the Second World War is no exception. Nevertheless, there are a number of characteristics of the employment system in Japan that have been present throughout the period from 1960 to 1990. These have been well-documented in numerous books and studies, but I will review them here as there may be some features of the employment system that are unfamiliar to readers. I begin by briefly listing the features to give an overview of the entire system before discussing the explanations and rationales given for their presence.[1]

Long-Term Employment

Japanese men and women on average have longer tenure in their jobs and fewer changes of employment than their counterparts in most other countries. Table 2.1 shows average length of employment in a number of OECD countries. Only Italy, a country with very strong job protection backed up by substantial union power, has longer average tenure. Also of interest is the fact that Korea, a country often seen as following Japanese practice, shows the opposite tendency with very low tenure. One of the consequences of the long-term employment system is that much of the adjustment to the business cycle is made through hours of work, rather than through hiring and firing (Abraham and Houseman 1989; Hashimoto 1990).

Enterprise-Based Unions

Japanese labour unions are based in the enterprise, although most of these band together in industry- and economy-wide federations. Enterprise-based unions have been responsible for the fact that blue-collar workers receive similar treatment to white-collar workers in terms of pay increases and non-wage benefits. This leads directly to the next point.

Introduction

Table 2.1. *Average employer tenure by gender and age for selected OECD countries*
in 1995

Country	Total	Men	Women	Age 15–24	Age 25–44	Age 45+
Italy	11.6	12.1	10.6	2.8	9.4	19.2
Japan	11.3	12.9	7.9	2.5	9.5	18.0
France	10.7	11.0	10.3	1.6	9.0	17.5
Sweden	10.5	10.7	10.4	2.2	8.2	15.9
Germany	9.7	10.6	8.5	2.4	7.7	16.2
Spain	8.9	9.8	7.2	1.0	7.3	16.1
UK	7.8	8.9	6.7	2.2	7.0	12.2
USA	7.4	7.9	6.8	1.6	6.2	12.4
Korea	5.2	5.9	3.4			

Source: OECD1(1997), p. 139, table 5.6.

Pay Rises with Age and Seniority

The average wages of both blue-collar workers and white-collar workers show a pronounced rise with age to the age of 45. This is in contrast to most other OECD countries, where only white-collar workers display this kind of upward-sloping profile for such a long period. As a result, the average wage profile slopes more steeply in Japan, but this is largely because blue-collar workers also enjoy steeply rising wages.

High Rates of Employee Participation and Involvement in Decision-Making

The period since the end of the Second World War has seen the development of a number of institutions that have facilitated and encouraged the involvement of employees in their work. These include Joint Labour-Management Committees (JLMCs) and various forms of small group activities, including quality control circles.

Large Gender-Based Differentials and Gender-Based Segregation in the Labour Market

As shown in Table 2.2, Japan has a large gender-based wage differential by OECD standards and there are few women in the upper tiers of management.

Differentiation by Firm Size

Size matters in the Japanese labour market. Employees of larger firms are more likely to be male, more likely to have higher pay and better benefits, even after controlling for employee characteristics.

Table 2.2. *The gender wage gap for full-time employees in some OECD countries, 1998*

Country	Unadjusted ratio of female/male average hourly earnings
Japan[1]	67
USA	79
UK	80
Germany	80
France	87
Australia	91
Switzerland	76
Sweden	86
OECD average (not including Japan)	84

Note:
[1] Japanese values are for 2001.

Source: OECD1 (2002); Japanese values calculated from Wage Census Tables (MHLW1 2001).

Internal Training within Companies

Most of the larger companies prefer to hire new graduates and train them within their organization, using external training institutions only when they lack the resources to train themselves. This may lead to higher levels of firm-specific knowledge than would otherwise be the case. It may also mean that knowledge itself is organized in ways that are specific to each firm, making it more difficult for employees to undertake their training elsewhere. It also leads to the following consequence:

Age-Based Discrimination

Most of the largest firms prefer to hire new or recent school graduates rather than middle-aged employees. Job advertisements carry explicit age limits (even though prohibited by recent law). This is a feature of labour markets in other countries but is more institutionalized in Japan.

Status Differences

There is a sharp differentiation between the 'regular' employees of companies, and those who are on part-time or temporary contracts. The latter are usually given fewer benefits and lower pay and have less job security.

Widespread Use of Mandatory Retirement Systems

Most Japanese companies have a mandatory retirement system with the usual age of retirement set at age 60. Company-based pensions (often given in lump-sum form) are provided at retirement, and many firms have programmes to re-employ retired employees on a full- or part-time basis. Companies also arrange for some of their employees (especially managers) to find work in subsidiaries as they approach retirement age.

A Well-Organized Entry Market for New Graduates to Obtain Jobs

The academic year in Japan runs from April to March, in synchronization with the fiscal year. Firms generally hire new employees to start work in April and this is also the time at which most in-company transfers take place.

Internal Mobility

Internal mobility between establishments in large companies is a substitute for external mobility (Hildreth and Ohtake 1998). Temporary posting to remote locations is common practice, often requiring that men temporarily live apart from their families.

DISCUSSION OF THE JAPANESE EMPLOYMENT SYSTEM

It is my goal in this chapter to try to provide an integrated analysis of all of these features, with reference to other, supporting elements. Most models used to explain Japan's labour market focus on male employees of large companies, a minority of the labour force (albeit an important one). I will take a wider view.

Regular versus Non-regular Employment

To start, the distinction between regular and non-regular employees is crucial for understanding the Japanese labour market. The regular employee is employed for an indefinite period, while the non-regular employee has been restricted to employment for a fixed period, usually less than one year in length. This distinction is not just one of custom, but is written into Japanese labour law (the Japanese Labour Standards Law) and the restriction of the length of the fixed period contract was originally made to prevent exploitation of the weaker elements of the labour force.[2] At the same time, as discussed below, both Japanese labour law as developed through case law and company practices have led to employment guarantees being extended to regular workers. The presence of non-regular employees in the company provides the firm with a buffer, allowing it to cut its labour force without firing permanent employees. This can be done simply by declining to renew a contract upon termination.

The distinction between regular and non-regular employees is not quite as sharp as the preceding paragraph suggests, however. Many of the non-regular staff in companies are part-time workers (mostly women). These women are often employed for many years on year-long contracts that are routinely renewed on an annual basis. Japanese courts have given these employees the same kind of protection that is given to regular employees. In other words, *de facto* treatment of a worker as one on an indefinite contract provides the same kind of job protection as is given by the indefinite contract.

In general, non-regular employees do not have the same fringe benefits as regular employees. These include company housing, company pensions, company health coverage, and family benefits. The non-regular employee is also less likely to be regarded as a full member of the community that makes up the company. One of the major themes of the book is the growth in the non-regular component of the workforce and I will return to this subject in Chapter 4.

Tenure of Employment

Cultural Factors   Of all the features of the labour market, the low turnover rates and long average tenure of employees in Japan have attracted the greatest attention, admiration, and criticism, especially in the USA, where turnover rates are much higher. The Japanese go so far as to refer to this property as 'lifetime' or 'permanent' employment (*shushin koyō*) even though these terms are highly misleading. There are a number of competing explanations for this pattern. In the 1950s, some observers assumed that Japanese capitalism was still immature and that the observed patterns reflected a feudal organization of the labour market (e.g. Abegglen 1958). Employees seem to have strong loyalty to their companies and personal identity seems to spring more from company affiliation than from occupation. This tendency is still strongly shown in surveys to this day. Such ceremonies as the singing of a company song before work in the morning, and after-hours socializing with peers in the company also seemed to have more in common with a feudal, military culture than that of the 'modern' business organization.

Historians have, however, made some important corrections to the view that long tenure is a relic of Japan's feudal past. The Japanese labour market of the 1910s was characterized by very high turnover rates, and blue-collar workers deliberately moved from firm to firm to gain experience and develop their skills (Gordon 1985). It was only gradually through the 1920s and 1930s that the characteristics of the contemporary labour market began to take shape. Nevertheless, the fact that there is no direct historical link from the feudal period to the present does not mean that present-day practices have simply appeared as a profit-maximizing strategy on the part of firms. As Andrew Gordon and others have pointed out, one of the main goals of the pre-war Japanese labour movement was to have blue-collar workers included as full *members* of the organization. Unlike labour movements in Britain or the USA where blue-collar workers have sought to maintain a separate identity and class-consciousness, the Japanese blue-collar worker has been most interested in being included in the general community of the workplace (Dore 1973). Thus, the outcomes that we observe today do appear to have their roots in aspects of Japanese society that promote community attachment and group identity. It is fortunate for Japan that this goal of a shared community has been consistent with economic rationality for many of Japan's industries in the period since the Second World War. One of the major questions facing Japanese businesses today is whether such a culture is consistent with the kind of labour market needed for leading technological industries such as information technology or biotechnology.

The cultural view of the labour market that I have just mentioned is consonant with a more general social-anthropological view of Japanese society. Japanese people, it is held, derive much of their identity from group membership. Consequently, long-term work relations are more highly valued and we would expect to see longer-term attachments to the firm. For example, the psychoanalyst Takeo Doi has drawn attention to the prevalence of words connected with dependency in the Japanese vocabulary (Doi 1981). Chie Nakane has theorized that vertical (superior–subordinate) relations are more important in Japan than the horizontal relations that, in her view, predominate in the West (Nakane 1970). One must not lose sight, however, of the fact that there are Japanese who prefer not to be so dependent, even if it means accepting a much poorer standard of living.[3] Japan has had one of the highest rates of self-employment by OECD (Organization for Economic Cooperation and Development) standards and to some extent this may reflect a desire for independence. Dependency in Japan, whether or not it is a basic cultural trait, is backed up by various social and economic institutions. For example, the widespread development of company housing may have been instituted because of problems in the housing market, but it has also brought greater social control as a by-product. Dependency brings security, but at the cost to the individual of greater coercion.

Economic Factors   Economists have generally kept clear of the cultural and psychological explanations for Japanese employment tenure, focussing instead on economic incentives that keep employees in the same firm or barriers that prevent job-hopping. To use the language of Hirschman (1970) the costs of exit from the organization are very high. First, there is the practice of basing pay on seniority. Cross-sectional analysis of the wage structure in Japan indicates that pay increases with tenure at about 1% per year (Tachibanaki and Ohta 1994; Ohtake 1998). Studies have also shown that separation rates are inversely correlated with the rate at which pay increases with tenure (Mincer and Higuchi 1988). Secondly, company pension benefits do not become vested until quite late in one's career and the penalty for changing jobs prior to mandatory retirement is considerable. One estimate puts the costs of changing jobs at age 45, including both pension and earnings losses, as high as 100 million yen or close to a million dollars (Ichinose 2001). Clearly there is a strong disincentive for middle-aged Japanese to change jobs. Nevertheless, the 'tenure effect' on pay is not significantly larger in Japan than in the USA, and it is also true that tenure has tended to increase over time, while the effect of tenure on wages has fallen.

There must be other factors at work discouraging mobility and this brings me to the subject of employment protection.

The Significance of Labour Law Contemporary Japanese labour law was first instituted in the immediate postwar period during the American occupation. Apart from the requirement that 30 days' notice is required for a dismissal, the labour law itself does not provide much in the way of employment protection. The Japanese constitution, however, includes articles proclaiming a right to work (Article 27) and the right to a minimum standard of 'wholesome and cultured living' (Article 25). This part of the constitution has been interpreted by the courts to be the basis for some of the highest levels of employment protection found in the OECD. More specifically, in a series of rulings beginning in the 1950s and extending into the 1970s, the courts have decided that employers must meet four conditions before they can fire an employee:

(1) the firm is under severe duress such as facing possible bankruptcy and redundancies are unavoidable;
(2) employers have made efforts to avoid redundancies by taking measures such as cutting overtime, hiring freezes, transfers, seconding workers to other companies, or seeking voluntary retirements;
(3) they have consulted with the labour unions and employees;
(4) they have a rational selection procedure for selecting those who are to be fired.

In addition to these four tests, the courts have also stipulated that the redress for an employee who has been improperly dismissed is the reinstatement of the employee along with back pay. In other words, if the employee refuses to leave voluntarily, it is extremely difficult for an employer to dismiss him or her unless under severe financial distress. This means that it is preferable to retrain employees whose skills have become redundant rather than firing them and hiring previously trained workers.

Legal protection, of course, is not necessarily sufficient to provide protection on its own, particularly in the case of Japan where legal actions may take years to run through the courts and can be costly for the litigant. In particular, workers in small, non-unionized firms are unlikely to feel that they have much protection from the courts. Nevertheless, one of the effects of this case law has been to promote the social consensus that dismissals should only be used as a last resort. The main recourse of most employers who wish to get rid of employees is to exert moral pressure on employees, encouraging them to take early retirement or voluntarily quit the firm. This can be particularly effective if there is a consensus among the remaining employees that selected members should be encouraged to quit. Peer pressure can be very effective, especially in the tight-knit society of the Japanese firm.

Nevertheless, the costs of firing an employee in terms of legal actions, loss of reputation as a good employer, and demoralization of the remaining workforce mean that most Japanese firms will try to avoid redundancies to a greater extent than firms in countries where employment protection is not as high a social goal. Employment protection serves to reduce mobility between firms in two ways. First, it directly reduces the number of redundancies. As important, however, is the effect it has on vacancies: firms prefer to retrain their own workers rather than hire from other firms. This reduces the outside opportunities for workers in firms and thus lowers their propensity to quit.

Wage Increases with Age and Seniority

Empirical Studies   I have already mentioned that what is particularly notable about Japanese wage increases with age and seniority is that blue-collar workers as well as white-collar workers experience substantial pay increases until middle age. There is a large research literature that attempts to measure the importance of the tenure and age effects on earnings. Unfortunately, all of the data that are used come from cross-section surveys, so the importance of tenure, in particular, is open to question if those who change jobs are either inferior (or superior) to the average employee. Furthermore, if, when employees change job, there is a better match between the employee and the new job compared with the previous job, this would affect the statistical observations. The earliest published studies of the wage structure in Japan used tabulated data, primarily from the Wage Structure Survey, or Wage Census, a comprehensive establishment-based survey of wages. These studies, in particular that of Hashimoto and Raisian (1985), concluded that the effect of tenure on earnings was much higher than observed in the USA. In recent years, however, some researchers have been allowed to use microdata and their results are more reliable. It turns out that studies, such as Hashimoto and Raisian's, using tabulated data overestimated the effect of tenure on earnings, and new estimates using microdata from the same surveys show that the estimated returns to seniority or tenure are no higher than those of the USA (Ohtake 1998). This revision of the view about the importance of seniority in the Japanese wage profile has not received the attention that it deserves.[4]

Blue-Collar Careers   Despite this correction to our view of the importance of tenure in Japan, it is worth discussing the reasons why Japanese pay for blue-collar workers also rises sharply with age and seniority. Historically, the pre-war and wartime period saw the development of seniority-based pay systems as firms provided incentives to skilled blue-collar workers to remain with their firm at a time of skilled-labour shortages. Following the war, the early postwar period saw the rapid development of a labour movement that was concerned that workers be paid a 'living wage' that would meet their basic needs during a period of great privation (Gordon 1985; Ono 1987). Older and more senior workers were held to have greater need than youth because of their family responsibilities. The unions also wanted blue-collar workers to receive the same treatment as white-collar workers with regular raises and provision of fringe benefits.

Economists offered alternative explanations for the wage profiles. The best known of these is represented in the work of Kazuo Koike (1988) who argued that (1) Japanese blue-collar workers receive more training than their counterparts in other countries and (2) that because most of this training is done on-the-job, Japanese blue-collar workers follow firm-specific career paths analogous to those of white-collar workers. The first point explains why earnings rise steeply with age for blue-collar workers, while the second point explains why seniority may be more important in Japan than elsewhere—Japanese employees have relatively high amounts of firm-specific capital.[5] Hashimoto (1990), taking a more culturalist line of reasoning, claims that a Japanese upbringing makes investments in group-specific or firm-specific human capital less costly for Japanese than for others. The investments in firm-specific human capital then serve to bind the employee to the firm.

A slightly different approach to the same basic idea of firm-specific human capital was taken by Mincer and Higuchi (1988), who claimed that it was the extraordinarily high productivity growth in Japan that led to a greater emphasis on firm-specific human capital. They found that the coefficients on tenure in wage equations were positively correlated with productivity growth in a cross-industry study. With lower productivity growth after the 1960s, tenure should have become less important, and this too is consistent with their observations.

Agency Theories   The main economic criticism of the firm-specific human capital approach is that there are other plausible explanations for the observed returns to seniority in the firm. Leaving aside the issue of whether the cross-section estimates are biased, the competing theories are primarily concerned with issues of motivation. In the simplest version, the firm will underpay workers early in their career with the firm and overpay them later, in order to make it costly for them to leave the firm. A mandatory retirement date must be set, however, to prevent the latter period of overpayment from continuing indefinitely (Lazear 1979). The fact that compensation is delayed makes it more likely that the workers will be motivated to work hard. Even if they are protected from dismissal by employment law, they are more likely to cooperate and work hard if they fear the disapproval of their colleagues. Japanese employees are also aware that they collectively share in the fortunes of their firms. Free-riders will be disciplined by the comments of their fellow workers, possibly more effectively than by their employer, who is constrained from dismissing them unless their infractions are severe.

This theory has support in the observations that (1) mandatory retirement systems are ubiquitous, (2) employees are often rehired by their firms after mandatory retirement on fixed-term contracts, but at a wage rate that is only 50–70% of the wage at retirement. This suggests that they are overpaid in terms of their value to the firm (not to mention their market value) at the end of their time as a regular employee.

Thus the answer to the question of why blue-collar workers have such a steep age/seniority-wage profile remains in doubt, although it appears that the thesis that Japanese employees have higher levels of firm-specific human capital than their counterparts in other countries is doubtful. On the other hand, there is somewhat more support for the view that Japanese blue-collar workers receive more training over their careers than workers do elsewhere and this is at least part of the explanation for why their earnings increase so much with age.

The Importance of Promotion in Earnings Determination   Some refinements to the views of seniority-based earnings have come from the work of Tachibanaki (1996) and others who have shown that a large component of these earnings increases are correlated with promotion to supervisory posts and that, without them, the actual returns to age and seniority are more limited. The extent to which this alters our perception of the importance of tenure and seniority depends on how the wage increases with promotion are interpreted. If the wage increases from promotions reflect compensation for the greater ability of the worker or compensation for work actually being done in the job, then this would imply that the returns to age or seniority are actually lower than previous estimates suggested. On the other hand, if the increased pay is a reward for winning a promotion tournament, then this reward must be paid for by lower pay for the losers in the tournament. In this case the *average* return to seniority would remain unaffected by the inclusion of the promotion variable. As Aoki (1988) has pointed out, the Japanese economic system as a whole relies less on markets to provide incentives than on the provision of internal incentives within organizations. In the case of labour, these incentives are provided through tournaments to decide who is promoted first to managerial posts. There is consequently a fierce competition within firms between employees of the same cohort. At the same time, the lack of mobility in an external labour market, as well as the tendency to have general training in a wide range of skills, means that the employee's primary identity has been with the firm, not a professional group.

The research on promotions also tends to ignore one important point often made about Japanese promotions—there is usually a tacit minimum age requirement attached to most posts. In other words, no matter how bright or capable the employee is, he or she will not be promoted to a high position at a young age, and usually not to a position where he or she would be supervising many older regular employees. This is what is implied by the Japanese term, *nenkō jōretsu* system, which implies that *ranking* is based on length of service. The significance of this idea may be seen by the fact that the employees of Japanese companies are acutely aware of the year in which they entered a company, and who is in their peer group or 'entering class' (Rohlen 1974).

In one sense, the arguments about whether the observed increase in earnings with tenure is based on firm-specific training, or due to some other explanation is ultimately not particularly important from the point of view of the employee. Whatever the cause of the increase in pay with age and seniority, it would be difficult for employees to move between firms in mid-career without suffering a major drop in earnings. On the demand side, if companies are reluctant to hire employees at a lower wage rate than their age peers, there will be barriers to the mobility of labour.

Enterprise-Based Unions

Composition of the Union Movement   Japanese unions are generally organized along enterprise lines with different subunits representing different establishments in the company. The company unions in turn tend to be federated into industry associations that may be associated with a larger national association. Today, the most important national association is Rengō with 11 million members (out of a total of 17.5 million), but there are also several other federations including Zenrōren (1 million members) and Zenrōkyō (250,000 members) which are more left-wing. Rengō, founded in 1989, is a relative newcomer to the labour relations scene and for most of the postwar period there was a division between Sōhyō, which tended to push harder for wage increases and included many of the public-sector unions, and Dōmei, a more conservative and cooperative federation that aimed to keep wage increases in line with productivity improvements and was supported by many of the most important unions in manufacturing industries. Most of the unions that were formerly in Sōhyō and Dōmei belong to Rengō today and the more conservative line of Dōmei seems to be dominant in the new federation. Japan's unions are mostly to be found in the larger firms, with union density around 60% for firms with more than 1,000 employees, but less than 2% for those with under 100 employees (Tachibanaki and Noda 2000).

Docile Unions?   The fact that Japanese unions are enterprise-based has led to the accusation that they are docile company unions that don't represent employee interests. Japanese Labour Law does require, however, that unions be independent of company management, be financed independently, and managers are not allowed to be union members. Benson (1996) suggests that the reality is more complex—most unions are cooperative, but there is a minority that is not. Chapter 5 will outline some reasons for the relative docility of unions in Japan.

Benefits of the Shuntō   One of the benefits of the cooperative approach of most unions, however, is that in many cases management is willing to open its books for inspection (Morishima 1991a). At the same time, most companies have established joint consultation committees alongside the unions, and these are often used to iron out differences before conflict arises (Morishima 1992). This kind of 'corporatist' behaviour removes much of the distrust from the bargaining process and makes it easier for management to get unions to show restraint when it is needed. It also makes it easier for management to co-opt the union leadership and impede action on serious issues such as unpaid overtime.

The cooperative approach between management and labour is best shown in the wage negotiations known as the *shuntō* or Spring Offensive. The *shuntō* originated when the Sōhyō federation aimed to achieve better wage increases through coordinated bargaining, and this coordinated approach is given much of the credit for Japan's macroeconomic performance up to the present time. In particular, Japan was conspicuous in the 1970s and 1980s for its ability to cope with the first and second oil shocks without experiencing the levels of unemployment and long-term slowdown in growth observed in many other countries. One of the ways in which this positive outcome was achieved was through the wage restraint shown by labour unions at a time when higher energy costs were pushing up prices. When the monetary authorities acted to check the burst of inflation that had initially followed the first oil shock, this wage restraint reduced the impact on employment. Thus, through coordinated action Japan avoided the stagflation found elsewhere, and no small part of this was due to the organization of the Spring Offensive.

Union Role in Redundancies   In cases where some job losses are unavoidable, due to poor financial circumstances, it is often left to worker representatives to put forward the names of those who will be dismissed. This has some advantages from the firm's point of view. First, it is likely that employees whose family circumstances are such that dismissal would be an unbearable hardship will be spared. Secondly, by making the union an active partner in the process, it is more likely that the union will accept the layoffs. This latter point, however, is another reason why many observers find the unions overly cooperative.

High Levels of Employee Involvement

Japan has been a world leader in developing mechanisms for employee involvement in decision-making. Japanese employees have generally been given more responsibility for decision-making on the shop floor (Koike 1988), although the degree of autonomy should not be exaggerated (Lincoln and Kalleberg 1990). Teamwork and group responsibility are also emphasized. Shop-floor committees (SFCs) are often formed to discuss safety and health, workplace training, and to deal with grievances (Kato and Morishima 2002). Quality-control circles (QCs), small groups where employees gather to discuss measures to improve quality and work performance, proliferated rapidly after the 1960s (Cole 1979). Although Cole points out that the QCs do not always play a useful role, nor do they always imply high levels of employee commitment, there is little doubt that they played a major role in the development of high-quality manufactured goods, for which Japan became famous in the 1970s and 1980s.

In addition to the more direct attempt of QCs and SFCs to improve commitment and involvement with work, there are numerous other, more indirect methods of improving work performance. Joint labour-management committees (JLMCs), which have proliferated since the 1950s, facilitate the sharing of information about the firm's financial performance and generate higher levels of trust. Employee stock-ownership plans and other profit-sharing mechanisms linked to bonus payments are also widespread. These workplace practices can lead to higher productivity, especially when used in combination. One recent study estimates that productivity improvements in the range of 8–9% can be achieved (Kato and Morishima 2002). Similar estimates have been found for the United States (Ichniowski *et al.* 1996).

The Significance of Gender

A recent comparative analysis of the wage structure in eight OECD countries including South Korea found that gender had a greater impact on wages in Japan than in other countries (Tachibanaki 1998*a*).[6] Furthermore, Japan was the only country where gender was the single most important variable in wage determination. Similarly, OECD comparisons of the simple male–female wage gap such as that shown in Table 2.2 show that Japan is an outlier with the largest gender-based gap in earnings in the OECD.

Less Training for Women   The primary explanation for the disparate treatment of men and women is that women have not received the same levels of training as men in Japan. We can see the validity of this point by noting that although the average earnings of a full-time woman employee at age 20–24 is 89% of that of her male counterpart, this has fallen to just 60% by age 40–44. Women are not channelled into careers that are similar to those of men. The reasons for this are complex, but at least part of the reason is that women appear to have a weaker attachment to the labour force than men and are more likely to quit when they marry or have children. As we have already seen, the Japanese approach to personnel management would then make it difficult for these women to return to work since it would be difficult to fit them back into the company career structure. It is only recently that large numbers of firms have allowed women to continue working after having children. In the past, women would have been expected to resign at first pregnancy or even at marriage.

M-shaped Pattern of Participation   If we examine the participation rate of women by age, we can observe what is referred to as the M-shaped pattern of labour force participation, which illustrates the extent to which women withdraw from the labour market while bringing up young children (see Figure 2.1). Many women will return to the labour market when their children reach school age, but the majority of these take part-time positions and are not regular employees. Although part-time workers in Japan may work more than 40 hours a week, as long as they work fewer hours than the men in the same establishment they may be considered part-time workers, and thus entitled to few of the benefits given to regular workers. Their wages are often lower than the rates of younger women with full-time regular status who are doing exactly the same

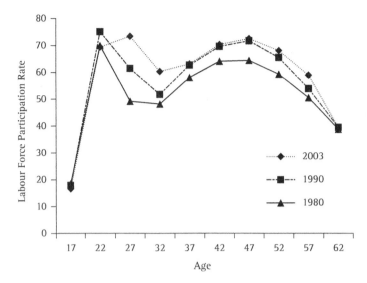

Figure 2.1. *The M-shaped pattern of participation of women, 1980, 1990, and 2003*
Source: MHLW4 (2004).

work, and this is a source of considerable discontent and even litigation (Nakakubo 2002).

The pattern of women's labour force participation has led most employers to draw the conclusion that investment in training women is risky. The result is, not surprisingly, that women are systematically discriminated against with respect to career opportunities and training. Women are also unlikely to reach the higher levels of management. It has also been the case that, until relatively recently, women had significantly lower levels of educational attainment than men. In particular, although women had slightly higher levels of high school completion, those who went on to higher education tended to attend two-year colleges, rather than the four-year universities chosen by the vast majority of men. Although there is some doubt as to how much academic learning takes place in much of Japanese undergraduate education, the decision to attend a two-year college sent a strong signal to employers that a long-term career was not being considered. Nevertheless, even those women who attended four-year universities more often than not found themselves in limited secretarial jobs. As we shall see in Chapter 7, this situation has changed in the last 15 years.

The Firm-Size Differential

Trends Japan has long seen a significant difference in the pay levels of employees in large and small firms. At the beginning of the 1990s earnings of men in firms with more than 1,000 employees were 14% higher than those of men in firms with 10–100 employees, even after controlling for worker characteristics such as age and education. The premium for women (working full-time) in large firms was even higher, at 23%. Historically, this differential first becomes noticeable in the early part of the twentieth century and seems to accompany the development of large manufacturing firms. These firms were willing to pay more highly skilled employees a premium to prevent them from leaving. They were also better able to do so financially. The firm-size differential expanded throughout the period up to the early 1960s for essentially the same reason. Pay at the lower end of the spectrum in the smaller firms was held down by the availability of low wage labour that could easily migrate from the countryside. Only after the source of this labour began to decline did the wage gap begin to shrink as wages in the small-scale sector were bid up. This decline in the firm-size gap continued through the period of rapid growth until 1973. At this point, the downturn in the Japanese economy put a halt to this trend and, as I will discuss in Chapter 6, the firm-size differential has increased in tandem with the increase in unemployment rates.

Relation to Industrial Organization   The firm-size differential is intimately related to the organization of business in Japan. Subcontracting is widespread, especially in manufacturing, leading to the pyramidal production structures known as vertical *keiretsu*. Smaller, subsidiary firms, which are often wholly owned by the parent firms, provide intermediate inputs including both goods and services to the parent firm. The quality of labour in terms of education, training, and innate ability generally declines as one moves down the hierarchical chain. Although flexibility and competitiveness may be enhanced through the use of these structures, they also have one other important role—the division of the labour pool used in the production process. The group consciousness that is nurtured by firms and enterprise unions makes it difficult to tolerate vast differences of pay within the individual firm. This means that if activities with a lower value marginal product are pushed into a separate, subordinate firm, it is easier to pay workers according to their marginal product.

New school graduates are aware of the firm-size differentials and so will generally prefer to seek employment in the larger (and more stable) companies, if they possibly can. This quality differential is not likely to be entirely captured by the usual measures of worker ability such as age and education. Consequently, even after controlling for these variables it is not surprising that some differential remains. The remaining differential after adjustments have been made (through regression or other analysis) suggests that the firm-size differential is much larger than in the USA (Rebick 1992*b*). Could this difference be entirely due to differences in the quality of the workforce? It is possible, but it is also plausible that there are strong enough barriers of movement between the different size categories of firms that segmentation of the labour market allows the larger firms to pay higher wages. It is also possible that larger firms are more concerned about making their employees work hard, while at the same time they have more difficulty in monitoring them on a daily basis. In this sense, the higher wages in large firms could also reflect an efficiency wage premium. Finally, we should recall that it is the larger firms that are unionized and perhaps they are more likely to engage in profit or rent sharing with their employees. The larger firms may also have larger profit margins per employee to offer.

The firm-size differential is larger in the case of women. While there may be a greater unmeasured quality difference between women according to firm size, a more likely explanation is that large firms have been the first to equalize pay between men and women because of (1) the presence of unions and (2) the pressure put on them by the Ministry of Labour. As I show in Chapter 7, this situation is changing.

The Firm-Size Differential's Effect on Mobility Whatever the cause of the firm-size differential, it has some effect on the pattern of mobility in the Japanese labour market. There is a tendency for employees to move to smaller firms if they change firms after the age of 50. In 1997 there were 1,670,000 employees who switched firms, and by definition total separations of these employees equalled accessions (MHLW3 1998). If we restrict our attention to firms with more than 1,000 employees, there were 192,000 separations involving inter-firm moves, but only 172,000 accessions. The main source of this 'mobility deficit' for large firms is found in the 50 and older age groups. Most companies prefer to keep an egalitarian pay structure for their regular employees, and so large firms would be under pressure to pay a mid-career recruit at a similar rate to their existing employees. We have already seen that middle-aged workers may be paid more than their marginal product to compensate for underpayment when they were younger. A mid-career employee may not be worth enough to a large firm to justify hiring at the going rate for his age. A smaller firm, however, could pay the employee a lower wage, more in keeping with the employee's marginal product without upsetting the egalitarian wage structure of the company.

Internal Training within Companies We have already seen that studies by Koike and others have emphasized the role of on-the-job training in the Japanese firm. The tendency for Japanese firms to train their workers internally is due to the fact that Japan was a late developer, and the demand for skills developed before the educational system could provide the necessary training. Companies had to learn how to do many things as they were organizing production for the first time, often by using licensed technology from abroad. Foreign advisors did help in the initial stages to train some of the employees in Japan, but eventually the Japanese themselves took over the training. If nothing else, the language barrier would have made this a necessity.

On-the-job training has turned out to have advantages, however, and the development of a more self-reliant workforce is one of them. In-house training also fosters a sharper sense of belonging to the organization rather than to a group with similar skills (professional or occupational identities). So, students may study Japanese law at university, but they will only rarely become professionally qualified as lawyers. It is more likely that they will be hired by firms or by the government to do legal work for the organization, but learn much of what they actually do on the job itself. For this reason, Japanese university undergraduate programmes are not particularly important in themselves as providers of training, with the exception of technical courses in the sciences or engineering. A further advantage of training on the job is that more time is given to passing on and developing the kind of knowledge that is not easily written into manuals or textbooks. This appears to be one of the reasons why Japanese workers are so productive (Koike and Inoki 1990).

Problems of On-the-Job Training (OJT) and the Information in the External Labour Market There are disadvantages with this approach, however, the most important of which is that it is difficult for employees to describe their skills in ways that are meaningful to other potential employers. As long as Japanese firms have been able to find enough work for their employees, this has not been a great problem, but as we shall see, this disadvantage has now become much more significant as there is a greater need for employees to move between firms.

Age-Based Discrimination

Reading a Japanese newspaper, an American or British observer might be surprised to see that job advertisements frequently contain age restrictions, usually with upper age limits.[7] Age discrimination, is of course, hardly unique to Japan, but the overt use of age limits in employment advertisements suggests that it is not only widespread, but socially acceptable. Although legislation enacted in 2001 prohibits overt age discrimination, surveys suggest that 90% of firms have a policy to restrict their hires to those under a certain age, except for special cases where particular skills are needed (JIL 2001a). The reasons for this are in part related to the issues mentioned above with respect to the returns to tenure, and the policy of most firms to try to treat their employees equally according to their age. Company surveys of job changers (MHLW12 2000) suggest that the new hires tend to be paid much the same as their peers. If this is the social expectation, then to do otherwise would invite resentment and be disruptive.

The pay structure is not the only reason given for the barriers to older employees, however. A less tangible factor is the issue of differences in the training systems between companies. If there are definite career paths (for blue-collar as well as white-collar workers), and they differ from firm to firm, then it may be difficult to fit a new employee into the training system. Managers often speak of the difficulty of fitting mid-career recruits in to their company, often complaining that they do not fit in well with the 'company culture'. This kind of attitude may reflect a genuine issue of different firm-specific socialization or training. It may also, however, reflect the likelihood that employees who leave firms in mid-career have particular personality traits that make it difficult for them to fit in anywhere.[8]

Widespread Use of Mandatory Retirement Systems

History Mandatory retirement systems are a dominant feature of the employment system in Japan. In 2000, more than 90% of companies with more than 30 employees and all companies with more than 1,000 employees set an age for mandatory retirement (MHLW4 2000). By far the most common average age for mandatory retirement was 60, young by the standards of the USA before mandatory retirement was outlawed there. The setting of the retirement age at 60 is actually a recent change from the earlier age of 55 which prevailed until the 1970s. Starting in the 1970s, the government and unions made a concerted effort to move the retirement age to 60, since public pension benefits were not available until that age. It was not until the 1980s, however, that the age of retirement finally moved to 60 for the majority of firms. In order to achieve this, firms had to negotiate agreements with unions to ensure that earnings did not continue to rise after age 50, and in some cases there were even wage reductions after age 55.

The Tenseki System The extension of the age of mandatory retirement, along with the ageing of the population also meant that a shortage of managerial posts began to develop in firms. There were a number of different approaches taken to solve this problem, but we will restrict our attention here to those that were and are related to the mandatory retirement system. One solution to the overcrowd-ing at the upper end of the age scale is outplacement to a managerial post in a subsidiary or supplying firm. Although not all firms will agree to this, many of them find it advantageous to have a strong personal link to the downstream firm. Other firms, especially wholly owned subsidiaries, are in too weak a posi-tion to refuse. This kind of action is referred to as *tenseki* or secondment accom-panied by a change of membership to the new firm. The transferred employee is generally guaranteed employment until the age of mandatory retirement in his original firm. This relieves some of the pressure for the sending firm, but of course does not help those firms at the receiving end. In addition to direct out-placement to other firms, however, in recent years there has been an increasing tendency to induce early retirements in order to reduce the number of regular employees. This tendency will be discussed more fully in succeeding chapters.

Company Pensions The mandatory retirement system also provides employees with company pensions, which supplement the pensions received from the gov-ernment. Generally, these pensions resemble severance payments that employees will receive at an earlier age, but are much larger, amounting to some three or four years of basic pay. The money is often taken in a lump sum as this is tax exempt, but the money can be easily converted into an annuity or life-insurance policy if desired. Often the lump-sum payment is used to pay off housing mort-gages or debts for children's school fees and other expenses. The trend towards taking the retirement payment in the form of annuities has increased over time, however, and often this takes the form of supplements to the public pension scheme of the government. Japanese pension rights tend to be vested very late in the career of an employee, providing another reason for staying with the com-pany until mandatory retirement.

Motivating Older Workers   The outplacement system mentioned earlier gener-ally does not affect the size of the company pension benefit to be received. The fact that outplacement is a possibility may act directly on employees as a motiv-ating device. A large company may have many different places to which it can transfer its older employees, or it may simply induce the employee to leave with an early retirement scheme. Given all of these possibilities, it would be in the employee's interest to maintain a positive attitude, even if he is passed over in promotion decisions. The weakness of the market for older employees and the existence of age barriers to hiring on the open market also strengthen the hand of the employer in this situation.

High Labour Force Participation Rate for Older Men   The fact that mandatory retirement or early retirement from the firm occurs at or before 60 should not lead to the impression that this leads to low levels of participation for older workers. To the contrary, Japan has some of the highest rates of participation for older persons as we will see in Chapter 8. The median age of retirement from the labour force was age 70 until the 1990s. There are many reasons for this high rate of participation, including the high rate of self-employment (self-employed workers tend to work longer), social attitudes, and work ethic. The outplacement and re-employment of older employees also helps to provide older workers with job opportunities that can last beyond the age of mandatory retirement. Finally, for a group of poorer Japanese, there may be no choice but to continue working, as they may not receive an adequate pension from the government. These issues will be looked at in more detail in Chapter 8.

The Port of Entry: School Graduates

Japan has an exceptionally well-organized entry market for new school gradu-ates, with intense activity taking place up to a year or more in advance of the date of graduation. In the case of high-school students or students in university science faculties, the school or faculty, often with the help of professors, plays an important role as an intermediary in the matching of students to jobs. There is a tendency for hiring relationships to persist between employers and schools or universities, and this in turn means that entry to particular schools or universit-ies becomes an important selection mechanism that can have vital significance for one's future. Japan has long had a system where entrance examinations were used extensively to determine admissions from the middle-school level upwards. Competition for entry into both high schools and universities is very heated, and the term 'exam hell' has been used to describe the period during which students prepare for entrance examinations. One result of this intense competition for entry to prestigious schools is that Japanese children tend to be very well educated in terms of basic skills, literacy, and numeracy by international standards. To the extent that there are positive externalities in the attainment of these standards, the screening conducted by educational establishments may have real social value.

High Internal Mobility

Mobility has been low for regular employees and the main movement has been at the entry level of new school graduates and the exit level around the age of mandatory retirement. On the other hand, one of the factors that compensates for the lack of this external mobility is the high mobility of employees within firms. Employees are generally rotated to different sections within the company every two or three years. Furthermore, if an establishment within the firm is shut down, the employee is usually given the choice of moving to a different location, sometimes in a different part of the country. If the move is a temporary one, then it is common for the employee to leave his family behind and live separately (*tanshin funin*) in accommodation provided by the employer close to the new workplace. In 1998, there were more than 300,000 such cases of employees living apart from their families, or roughly 1% of all male employees (MHLW6 1998).

CONCLUSION–A SYSTEM DUE FOR CHANGE?

Up to the end of the 1980s, the Japanese system seemed to have an edge over others in terms of productivity, but more than a decade of economic stagnation has exposed many of the weaknesses of the system. In particular, the lack of mobility in the external labour market becomes a major problem in a period of low growth as companies stagnate and are unable to shed unwanted labour. The education system, which has been efficient in terms of preparing graduates with a broad base of knowledge, may also be relatively weak at turning out entrepreneurs. Systems of general training within firms may not be sufficient in an age that calls for increasing expertise in technical systems. Finally, we need to consider that affluence has undone the willingness of many young Japanese to commit themselves to work for life with one firm and they are less willing to become involved in the competition within the firm. Motivation has become a more serious problem within the firm.

In the ensuing chapters of this book I will look at ways in which Japanese institutions such as firms, unions, and educational establishments have been adapting to the challenges presented by the long period of slow growth of the

1990s. Many of these changes are not very dramatic from the point of view of those who would like to see radical reform. Nevertheless, slow, incremental changes will lead over the next couple of decades to a markedly different Japanese labour system.

NOTES

1. The material in this chapter is largely based on the general literature on Japanese employment. Readers who would like to see a more complete treatment are referred to Koike (1988), Hashimoto (1990), Dore (1973), Rohlen (1974), Clark (1979), Shirai (1983*a*), Brown *et al.* (1997), and Hart and Kawasaki (1999).
2. In the past decade, the restriction to one year for non-regular contracts has been relaxed, but only in some cases.
3. For a critique of the forgoing view of Japanese society see Mouer and Sugimoto (1986).
4. Mincer and Higuchi (1988) use microdata from the Employment Status Survey and find higher returns to tenure in Japan than in the USA, but they exclude firm size from their specification. Since firm size and tenure are positively correlated, the absence of this variable may lead to an upward bias in estimates of the effect of tenure on earnings.
5. Nomura (1992), however, believes that Koike's observations, while pertinent for the 1960s may be less relevant in the 1980s.
6. Besides Japan and South Korea, the countries were the USA, the UK, Canada, France, Germany, and Australia.
7. Readers elsewhere may not react in the same way as age limits in job advertisements are common practice in many European countries.
8. A somewhat similar strain of thinking underlies some culturalist explanations of this reluctance to hire in mid-career. These employees are regarded as used goods, the argument goes, and in Japanese culture there is a tendency to shy away from such 'contamination'. In the past, it was often said that the Japanese would not buy second-hand goods for the same reason. The recent growth in second-hand markets suggests that this is not such a deep-rooted aversion as previously maintained.

PART II

INSTITUTIONAL CHANGES AFFECTING THE LABOUR MARKET

3

Changes to the Employment and Treatment of Regular Employees

I begin my analysis of the changes taking place in Japanese labour by looking at the employment and treatment of regular employees. Regular employees are full-time workers who are hired, in principle, until the age of mandatory retirement. I will discuss changes in the relative numbers of these employees in the next chapter. Here I will focus on four main areas of change—employment security, the career structure, compensation, and hours of work.

CHANGES BEFORE THE 1990s

The careers and compensation of regular employees have not remained unchanged over the postwar period, but have undergone continuous change since the 1950s. One should bear this in mind when considering the changes that are taking place at the present time. Some of the changes that have already been seen are:

- extension of the age of mandatory retirement to 60 from 55;
- flattening of the age–wage profile. As we shall see later in the chapter, most of the decline in the slope of this profile took place before the 1990s;
- increasing educational attainment of the workforce;
- a gradual drop in the number of middle-school graduates hired and a corresponding loss in the average quality of this group as the best middle-school graduates continued on to higher education;
- a gradual drop in the share of high-school graduates in management posts in the firm.

Most of these changes were related to the rapid growth in average incomes that accompanied economic growth. Educational attainment of the general population increased as parents could now afford to support their children to an older age. Pay was less likely to be tailored to employee needs as prosperity and average pay levels rose, allowing for a gentler rise of pay with age. The changes that have been given the most attention in the 1990s, however, are changes in career structures and changes to incentives offered to employees. I begin by looking at changes in career patterns.

EMPLOYMENT SECURITY

Reading the news, it is understandable that a casual observer of the Japanese labour market might be tempted to believe that the employment system is radically changing, and that, in particular, companies no longer guarantee a job until mandatory retirement. There are frequent announcements of companies making large-scale cuts in their workforce with thousands of employees being invited to take early retirement. Although early retirement in these cases is usually said to be 'voluntary', it is often the case that the company will put heavy pressure on their unwanted employees to leave the firm. In this sense, much of voluntary early retirement may be seen as the Japanese equivalent of dismissal.

To get some idea of the extent to which firms are adjusting their labour force more rapidly, we should look at statistical evidence rather than sensational cases. I begin by examining the tenure of full-time workers to see if there is any evidence that long-term jobs are becoming less common.

Trends in Tenure

Table 3.1 displays average tenure of full-time employees by age and gender for the years 1977, 1988, and 2003. It is clear that average tenure increased for all age groups except for some of the youngest between 1977 and 1988. This is even

Table **3.1.** *Average tenure by age and gender*

	1977	1988	2003
Men			
20–24	3.3	2.7	2.5
25–29	5.9	5.3	5.2
30–34	9.2	8.9	8.6
35–39	11.9	12.7	12.0
40–44	13.8	16.1	15.5
45–49	15.8	19.0	18.9
50–54	17.1	20.2	21.8
55–59	13.2	17.8	22.8
Women			
20–24	3.0	2.7	2.3
25–29	2.1	5.4	4.9
30–34	6.2	7.7	8.0
35–39	6.4	8.6	9.8
40–44	6.9	9.1	11.2
45–49	8.3	10.3	12.4
50–54	9.5	12.0	14.1
55–59	9.4	13.0	16.1

Source: MHLW1 (1977, 1988, 2003); figures for full-time workers only in firms with more than 10 employees.

more impressive when we consider that rising educational attainment would have meant that an increasing number of men and women in each age group would have started work at a later age. Nevertheless, the average tenure for men dropped between 1988 and 2003 for men aged 45–49 or younger. Some of this reduction is due to increased numbers of quits in the youth labour market, but there has also been an increase in involuntary separations. Chuma (2002), noting that average tenure increased up to the early 1990s, believes that the strengthening of case law related to dismissals is the main cause of this trend. Kato (2001), using the Employment Status Survey up to 1997, calculates the proportion of individuals who remain in the same job over 10 and 20 year periods. He also finds that there is no drop in the rate at which long-term jobs are held, except for middle-aged men who have recently changed jobs. He suggests that this may be due to a company's greater willingness to dismiss an employee who has not devoted as many years of service to the company. Kato's work, however, does not cover the years since 1998 when the unemployment rate and separation rate have increased.

Trends in Mobility

Turning now to the flip side of the increase in tenure, evidence from the Employment Trends Survey suggests, as we might expect, that separation rates have risen significantly for the younger age groups, but that they have also increased for middle-aged men in the 45–54-year-old age category (Table 3.2).[1] Higuchi (2001: 54–59) uses a simple lagged adjustment model to examine the speed of adjustment of employment to changes in the real wage and the growth rate of the economy over the period from 1960 to 1999. He estimates an adjustment coefficient that reflects the extent to which firms adjust their labour force

Table 3.2. *Separation rates by age and gender*

	1988	2002
Men		
20–29	16.0	17.6
30–44	6.7	8.1
45–54	5.8	8.2
55–59	13.9	11.4
Women		
20–29	27.5	28.8
30–44	16.4	18.0
45–54	13.0	13.1
55–59	16.8	15.7

Source: MHLW3 (1998, 2004). Computed from tables on separations and numbers of employees. Figures do not include construction workers.

Separation rate is defined as separations/employees.

to the optimal level that would be reached if there were no costs to firing (or hiring) employees. He finds that the speed of adjustment has more than doubled since the end of the rapid growth period in 1973, but he also finds that most of that increase had taken place by the mid-1980s. He also estimates the speed of adjustment in the USA and finds that US values are almost double those of Japan for the most recent period.

At least some of the increased speed in adjustment found by Higuchi may be attributed to the increase in the number of part-time workers. Miyamoto and Nakata (2002), applying a similar model to firm-level data in the retail sector, find that the presence of greater numbers of part-time workers actually lowers the speed of adjustment for full-time workers as their scarcity value increases. This is somewhat related to the argument made in Chapter 1 about the role of secondary workers in a slow-growth environment. A second explanation for the increased speed of adjustment may lie in changing methods of corporate governance. The ability of large firms to raise capital on equity markets has reduced the role of main bank monitoring and arguably made firms more sensitive to profit indicators (Hoshi and Kashyap 2001). Tanisaka and Ohtake (2003) show that stock prices do react to announcements of cutbacks in the labour force on the part of firms, so it is reasonable to expect firm behaviour to change.[2] Abe (2002) shows that firms that have less concentrated stockholding have faster adjustment rates under normal economic conditions.

Time series studies such as those of Higuchi may have missed some of the more recent trends however. Figure 3.1 shows the trends in the overall separation and accession rates from the early 1980s to 2001. It is clear that the separation rate rose to its highest level after 1999. The Employment Trends Survey, from which

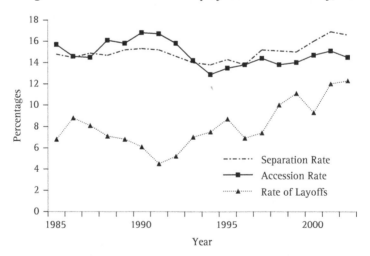

Figure 3.1. *Trends in accession, separation, and layoff rates*
Source: MHLW4 (1995), tables C-7, C-14 and MHLW4 (2004), tables C-6, C-10.
The layoff rate is defined as layoffs/all separations

these figures are taken, also surveys the reason for the separation. As the lowest curve in Figure 3.1 indicates, there has been a steep increase in the percentage of separations that are due to dismissals for economic reasons. Although the numbers cannot be taken too literally as a representation of all such dismissals, there is a clear upward trend, starting in 1998.[3] This is also the year when the unemployment rate began to increase rapidly, as accessions failed to keep up with the rise in separations.

Chuma (2002), using data on individual large firms, finds that between 1994 and 2000 large-scale downsizing of more than 20% of the workforce was promoted in most of the companies that he surveyed. In more detailed case studies both he and Kato (2001) find that the use of *shukkō* and *tenseki* outplacement, as well as reductions in hiring helped firms to avoid outright redundancies to some extent. However, as Chuma notes, there are practical limits to the numbers of employees that can be sent to subsidiary or related companies, and in the end redundancies, often encouraged through 'voluntary' early retirement incentives have been widely used.

It is, perhaps, too early to say for certain whether or not the increase in the rate of involuntary dismissals represents a major change in the behaviour of Japanese firms (Nitta 2003). As Koike (1988) points out, Japanese firms have long followed the practice of dismissing workers if poor economic conditions persist for more than two years. By that point, the firm has usually exhausted the other means at its disposal such as transferring workers between divisions, cutting back on the hiring of new graduates, secondment to subsidiaries (for large firms), and cutbacks in overtime. It is probably best to view the trends of the last few years as part of the normal operation of the Japanese employment system during a time of severe economic duress.

CAREER PATTERNS FOR STANDARD EMPLOYEES

As explained in the previous chapter, the career of the standard employee (both blue- and white-collar) in the large Japanese firm is one which sees the development of wide-ranging skills through frequent job rotation and the discouragement of specialization. The employee develops sets of skills and personal connections that are specific to his firm and not transferable to other firms (Koike 1988; Hashimoto 1990). This, along with job guarantees, is held to be the main reason why mobility has been so low in Japan. Smaller firms also attempt to follow this pattern, although their ability to guarantee employment, and the extent to which firm-specific sets of skills and interpersonal relations can develop is not as pronounced (Koike 1988).

The Growing Need for Specialist Training

There are good reasons to believe that this kind of training may be about to change. First, many of the skills that are needed in the company are highly specialized and require a great deal of in-depth training. It is unlikely that generalists, moving between departments would be able to master their briefs in the short period of three years that is typical of many job rotations. For example, many of the problems in the finance and insurance industries have been caused or aggravated by the lack of expertise in financial management in the deregulated environment that has prevailed since the 1980s. More specialized knowledge is also required in those service industries that serve the information technology (IT) and telecommunications needs of businesses and consumers.

It is difficult to document trends towards specialist careers in medium-sized and large Japanese firms. Ariga *et al.* (2000) have surveyed reports from the human resource management journal *Rōsei Jihō* and find that the development of 'multiple career tracks' has been an important development of the 1990s. Under this system, after an initial period in which all management track employees follow the same career path, there are several different career paths that one can take in the firm, rather than just a single general career path. For example, one could specialize in accounting, law, engineering, or another branch of the firm's operations. Other employees, however, might not specialize and would advance through the various ranks of management much as in the past. Specialists, while not carrying managerial titles *per se*, would have equivalent titles to indicate their level of seniority and expertise within the firm. For example, one prominent hotel in Tokyo described in JIL (1998) uses the English word 'expert' for the specialist promotion track. During the first year at the firm, new employees are rotated through various positions and their performance and enthusiasm are evaluated. They are then steered either towards the general management track, or into one of several specialties. Those who specialize may advance from 'Expert C' up to 'Expert A' and then on up until they reach 'Division-chief-rank expert'. Finally, for those whom the firm re-employs after mandatory retirement, the title 'Grand Expert' (*gurando ekisupaato*) is used!

In one sense this kind of system is not new. The management system in use by most firms provides 'qualifications' to reward employees for whom management posts are not available.[4] What is different here is that relatively early in the employee's career there is an explicit division made between the generalist and specialist tracks. In the past, some 10 years would pass before such a selection was made. While this offers both greater flexibility and the opportunity for specialization, Ariga *et al.* (2000) note that firms adopting this system are still recruiting new graduates into a common career path for an initial period and are not really opening up an external labour market for specialists. They suggest that the new system is mainly a way of creating more opportunities for promotion, particularly for the most capable employees. Other researchers, such as Imano (1998), are not as sceptical, suggesting that the multiple career track systems really are a more efficient way of training employees. Whichever view turns out to be justified, the development of multiple career track systems may open the way for the development of greater mobility in the future. Finally, it should be noted that the division of employees into various specialist groups may act to weaken the sense of unity in the firm.

Changes in the Nature of Blue-Collar Work on the Assembly Line

There may also be a growing trend towards specialization on the shop floor for blue-collar workers. It was common in the past for blue-collar workers to repair the machines and tools with which they worked. This is much less likely today, when the skills of a specialist are more likely to be required for the repair of sophisticated electronic controls. There has also been a shift in the average ability of blue-collar workers that has come with higher educational attainment. In the 1950s many able middle-school graduates were unable to afford more schooling and went to work in factories. The typical middle- or high-school leaver today is unlikely to be as able as in the past, however. This decline in ability of the blue-collar workforce implies that training is not likely to be as cost-effective as it was in the past. The combination of changing technical requirements and a changing workforce meant that even by the 1980s much of the repair work on the shop floor was being done by specialist workers (Nomura 1992).

Declining Emphasis on the Peer Group in Corporate Culture

A similar sign of weakening solidarity in the organization may be seen in the decline in the number of firms that are holding formal initiation ceremonies for new recruits. In the past, new recruits would assemble on their first day of work (usually in April or May) and be addressed by the company president and other top managers or directors. Parents of new recruits would often attend as well.[5] More recently, however, there has been a trend towards more informal ceremonies, or their outright abolition (JIL 2002). This is partly due to the fact that companies are moving away from hiring new regular employees solely in the spring, as I will discuss in Chapter 9. The breakdown of the annual hiring pattern is likely to have some impact on corporate culture. In particular, the sense of solidarity with a peer group (*dōki*) in the firm is likely to weaken.

Acceleration of Promotion

The sense of solidarity just mentioned was maintained by a management system that delayed making distinctions among employees for five to ten years after a new group was hired. This delay had several advantages. First, it allowed the firm to carefully observe employees over a long period of time and with different supervisors. This reduced the scope for opportunism on the part of individual supervisors, and encouraged greater cooperation among the employees in the peer group. It also prevented the less able employees (or those judged less able) from becoming demoralized at an early stage in their career.

Recently, however, firms have indicated that they intend to start making distinctions earlier in employees' careers. The ageing of the workforce in many companies has meant that managerial posts have become relatively scarce, and the average age of promotion has risen (MHLW7 2003: 181; Ariga *et al.* 2000). This has led to a loss of morale amongst younger employees. Voluntary separation rates for younger employees have actually risen in recent years and firms are anxious to keep their best young employees (MHLW7 2003: 182). Although the average employee may have to wait longer for promotion, firms are beginning to introduce fast-track promotions for their best young employees. This move will also weaken the sense of solidarity and increase the sense of competition amongst the younger employees. The shortage of posts is also leading to a change in the compensation system, and it is to this subject that I now turn.

COMPENSATION

I have already pointed out that the slope of the rise in wages with seniority has become flatter with time. Here I would also like to show that the direct connection between wages and seniority has weakened over time. First, however, I need to explain the structure of a Japanese employee's compensation package.

Structure of the Compensation Package

For most of the postwar period compensation in Japan has had several different components that are common to all firms. These are illustrated in Table 3.3. Roughly four-fifths of current cash compensation for regular employees comes in the form of wages paid monthly (including overtime payments). The remaining fifth comes in the form of two semi-annual bonuses paid in June and December. These bonuses are generally expressed in terms of a number of months of monthly pay, and so are directly linked to the determinants of monthly pay. In the monthly wage package (leaving overtime pay aside), some four-fifths of pay is 'basic pay' (*kihonkyū*) while the remainder comes as allowances, including family, housing, and commuting allowances. Family allowances typically account for 3–5% of monthly compensation (not including bonuses).[6] Some 80% of firms in Japan have some form of family allowance and the ratio rises to 90% for large firms with more than 1,000 employees. If anything, these ratios have risen over the past 10 years suggesting that the idea of compensating employees according to their needs is still present in Japanese enterprise policy.[7] The firm also provides compensation in the form of paying one-half of charges for national health insurance, unemployment insurance, and the national pension. These charges are expressed as a percentage of monthly pay. Finally, firms generally pay several years of severance pay at the age of mandatory retirement and these payments are also based on the employee's final year's wages. Since most of the non-cash compensation and bonuses are directly related to levels of basic pay, much of the remainder of this section will discuss the determination of basic pay (wages).

Table 3.3. *Components of compensation for Japanese employees in 2002 (%)*

Component of Compensation	
Monthly cash payments	78.9
Basic pay	67.6
Allowances	5.0[1]
Family	2.4
Commuting	0.7
Housing	0.8
Regional	0.4
Other	0.6
Overtime	6.3
Semi-annual Bonuses	21.1
Total Cash Compensation	100.0
Other expenses borne by firm	
Retirement and other severance payments	7.0
Employer's share for national health insurance	3.6
Employer's share for national pension	6.2
Employer's share for employment insurance	0.8
Employer's share for accident/injury insurance	0.7

Note:

[1] Figures for allowances are taken from JPC (2004), table C-40-1 and are based on a survey of the Central Labour Commission for firms with more than 1,000 employees and more than 500 million yen in capital.

Sources: MHLW6 (2002), tables 88 and 98 and from General Survey on Working Conditions (2002). Figures are for workers in establishments with more than 30 employees. Figures for overtime are estimates based on figures from Wage Census.

The Development of the Ability-Qualification System

Wage payments in large firms were made primarily on the basis of age and seniority in the 1950s, but during the 1960s and 1970s almost all firms adopted the ability-qualification wage payment system (*shokunō-shikaku seido*), whereby individuals in the firm are paid according to qualifications that they receive for developing skills. Payments in this system are based primarily on these qualification rankings and not on the actual post held on the factory floor or in line management. The qualification rankings themselves are common to all employees in the firm and tend to be acquired with seniority so that wages are still essentially linked to seniority, although there is some variance in the speed with which employees acquire the qualifications. Although earnings dispersion increases with age, seniority and age still have the largest effect on earnings in the Japanese firm, often acting as a prerequisite for promotion (Tachibanaki 1996).

This system's problems lie partly in its emphasis on the acquisition of general skills. Although there are many good reasons for acquiring a wide set of general skills, firms are increasingly interested in the development of specialist skills as the previous section indicated. It is also the case that the ageing of the workforce within firms has made it costlier to pay individuals for qualifications, regardless of whether they actually use them (Fujimura 2003). As a result, many firms are moving away from the skills-qualifications system to wage determination based on job content or on ability as shown through actual performance on the job, rather than potential performance on the job. Since the number of managerial posts is limited, another way in which individuals can demonstrate ability is through the acquisition and use of more intensive, specialist knowledge.

Introduction of Performance Evaluation

Firms have started to indicate that performance evaluation will now be given greater consideration in wage setting. Table 3.4 lists some of the changes that have been implemented according to surveys conducted in 1996 and 1999. It is evident that job-based performance evaluation and the introduction of an annual salary system (with pay based on job performance) that would bear closer resemblance to practices in the USA have become popular, especially with large firms in Japan. In 2001, some two-thirds of firms surveyed by the MHLW claimed that individual achievement was reflected in the earnings their employees received. At the same time, among large firms, while 80% reported that they based some component of base pay on age or seniority in the case of non-managerial workers, only half reported that age or seniority was important in managerial pay determination (MHLW6 2001).

Table 3.4. *Percentage of firms with changes to their wage and salary system implemented in the last three years*

Type of change	All firms		Large firms	
	1996	1999	1996	1999
Increase in the range of salary increases	11.9	10.5	15.7	14.1
Decrease in the range of salary increases	23.3	30.1	18.4	31.3
Abolition of the regular salary increase	3.8	10.5	6.3	11.2
Increase in job content-related pay	12.1	11.3	12.8	19.8
Increase in functional ability-related pay	15.7	15.8	24.5	28.5
Increase in results-related pay	15.0	15.5	28.2	38.8
Decrease in allowances	4.9	6.4	8.7	11.9
Revision/introduction of annual salary system	3.0	5.4	9.1	16.5
Increase in weight of the bonus	3.5	2.7	3.5	5.5

Source: MHLW6 (1996), table 127, pp. 221–2, MHLW6 (1999), table 97, pp. 198–9. Large firms have more than 1,000 employees.

The Role of the Bonus and the New Annual Salary Systems

The extent to which Japanese firms have been using bonuses as a means of sharing profits has been debated (Brunello and Ohtake 1987; Freeman and Weitzman 1987), but Imano (1998) reports that firms are increasingly adopting an explicit linkage between firm performance and bonus payments. Many firms are also linking bonuses to group performance within firms or to individual performance. Although the annual salary system introduced by many firms for upper-level management and for specialists within the firm dispenses with bonuses (and most allowances), the part of the annual salary that is comparable to the old base wage usually remains unchanged. It is the part comparable to the semi-annual bonus that is subject to greatest variation according to individual and firm performance (Imano 1998). In this sense, the introduction of the annual salary system is primarily a means of individualizing the bonus portion of compensation. While the tying of bonuses or annual salaries more closely to firm and individual performance won't necessarily affect the slope of the age–earnings profile, the introduction of greater incentives for performance may make it easier to flatten this profile without adversely affecting employee incentives.

Performance-Related Pay as an Additional Layer in the Package

To a considerable extent, however, the new performance-related pay (*seikashugi*) or PRP in Japan can be seen as adding another layer (or layers) of complexity to pay determination in Japanese firms (Morishima 2002). PRP is simply another component in the entire pay package. As Morishima suggests, Japanese firms now have some of the most complex pay determination systems in the world. Given the complexity of the system, it is understandable that there is a great deal of scepticism in Japan about the actual effect of these new compensation systems in motivating employees.

Despite the evidence that firms are formally changing their compensation systems it is not clear whether these new systems are, as sceptics would maintain, merely cosmetic changes to old practices that firms use to impress shareholders, or whether they will result in substantial changes in the actual wage received or in individual behaviour within the firm. I turn to this subject in the remainder of this section, first by looking at the flattening of the age–wage profile and secondly by looking at the increased dispersion of wages within age groups. It should be noted, however, that an increase in the weight of performance-based pay alone is not necessarily as important as changes in the criteria used to assess performance and incentives, as these will eventually have an impact on productivity in the workplace.

Flattening of the Age–Wage Profile

Figure 3.2 shows the earnings differential for basic monthly pay between 20–24-year-old and 50–54-year-old men in manufacturing who have worked

Institutional Changes

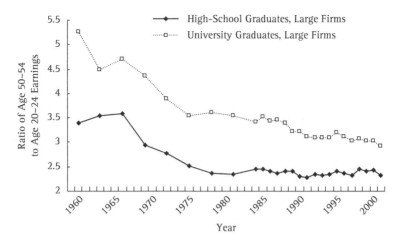

Figure 3.2. *Trends in the age differential for standard male employees*

Note: Standard employees are those employees who have been with the same firm since graduation.

Source: JPC (2004), table C-11.

for one firm since school graduation between 1967 and 1996. Separate curves are shown for large and small firms and for high-school and university graduates. The figure shows a substantial drop in this differential between 1967 and 1975 with a gentler decline afterwards. The main purpose of this figure is to show that most of the flattening of the age-earnings profile took place long before the 1990s. The rapid drop in the period from 1967 to 1975 reflects the fact that this was the period when the adoption of the ability-qualifications system became widespread; the importance of seniority in pay determination declined.

Since employees who have only worked for one firm are an unrepresentative group, it is better to look at evidence of changing rates of return to age and tenure using a broader sample. Clark and Ogawa (1992*b*) use published grouped data on male employees from the Wage Census and show that while the slope of the age–earnings profile (controlling for tenure) has remained stable during the 1970s and 1980s, the slope of the tenure-earnings profile (controlling for age) has dropped by more than 50%. The work of Clark and Ogawa has been supported by both Ohtake (1998) and Genda (1998) using microdata from the Wage Census for the more restricted period from 1980 to 1992. Clark and Ogawa (1992*a*) also use cross-industry evidence to show that the age of mandatory retirement is positively correlated with flatter wage profiles. This observation is consistent with the implicit contract model of Lazear (1979), which suggests that delayed compensation (by paying higher wages to those with the greatest seniority) can act as a disciplinary device. As the age of mandatory retirement increases, the profile would become flatter as the delayed compensation is paid out over a longer period of time.[8] As a corollary of this, we might expect that extension of the mandatory retirement age to 65, a goal of the government, would induce further flattening. It is likely that extension of employment guarantees to 65 would be accompanied by agreements to cut wages after age 60 (or even earlier) in a similar manner to what already occurs under existing employment extension programs (Rebick 1992*a*).

To extend this work into the 1990s, I use data from the published tables of the Wage Census to estimate changes between 1985 and 2003. The Wage Census is conducted every year in July by the Japanese government. This is a statistically representative survey of the actual monthly earnings and annual bonuses of over 1 million employees in Japan and is conducted through business establishments. It is the most commonly used data for analysis of earnings and earnings differentials in Japan.[9] The published Wage Census cross-tables consist of cells broken down by a number of different employee characteristics. The cross-tables that I use include information about average age, total pay (including overtime) per month, bonus payments over the past year, and an estimate of the number of employees in each cell. The cell characteristics consist of education (four categories), age group (12 categories), tenure (nine categories), firm size (three categories), gender, occupation (two categories—production workers and non-production workers—only for mining, manufacturing, and construction) and nine one-digit industries. Although there are cells for both men and women I restrict my analysis to men as I will be looking at changes in the treatment of women separately in Chapter 7. That leaves roughly 10,000 cells in any given year.[10]

I measure the effect of experience and tenure by using a standard regression model:

$$
\begin{aligned}
\text{Ln earnings} = {} & a + b_1\text{--}b_3 \text{ Schooling Dummies} + c_1 \text{ Experience} \\
& + c_2 \text{ Experience}^2 + d_1 \text{ Tenure} + d_2 \text{ Tenure}^2 \\
& + \text{ Industry Dummies} + \text{Firm-size dummies} \\
& + \text{ Blue-collar dummy} + \varepsilon
\end{aligned}
\tag{3.1}
$$

For each cell of the cross-table, the definition of average hourly earnings used is set equal to regular-time monthly earnings plus one-twelfth of the annual bonus payments.[11] Here the schooling variables are dummy variables set to 1 if the employee has exactly that level of education. Experience is 'imputed experience' and is set equal to age-education years -6 where the number of education years is set at 9, 12, 14, and 16 for each of the schooling groups.[12] Regressions use weighted least squares where the weights are the estimated number of employees in each cell. Since mandatory retirement at age 60 is often responsible for sharp drops in compensation, I exclude cells for employees over the age of 60.

The results are shown in Table 3.5. The table shows a roughly 20% decline in the effect of tenure on earnings between 1985 and 2003. Equally important, however, there has been a 20% decline in the effect of experience (age) on earnings. Thus it appears from this exercise that there has been a continuing flattening of both age–earnings and tenure–earnings profiles in Japan over the last 15 years.

Table 3.5. *Regression analysis of earnings of Japanese men, 1985–2003*

| | Dependent Variable: Log Earnings[1] | | | |
	1985	1990	1995	2003
Experience	0.050	0.046	0.042	0.039
Experience[2]	−0.0004	−0.0008	−0.0007	−0.0006
Tenure	0.026	0.024	0.021	0.020
Tenure[2]	−0.0002	−0.0001	−0.0001	−0.00009
R^2	0.94	0.93	0.93	0.92
No. of cells	8,258	8,101	7,974	7,616

Note:

[1] Earnings defined as regular time monthly earnings plus one-twelfth annual bonus.

[2] Experience defined as age-schooling −6.

Source: MHLW1. All regressions include a constant term, 8 industry dummies, 3 schooling dummies, 2 firm-size dummies and 2 occupation dummies. Age groups over 60 are excluded. Observations are weighted by the estimated number of individuals in each cell. All estimated coefficients are significant at the 1% level.

There are reasons why we might expect this trend to continue in the future. If new systems of personnel evaluation such as those mentioned above are increasingly used as a motivating device, there may be less need to rely on long-term implicit contracts and we might expect that the profile would gradually flatten over time. Okunishi (1998) using a survey of 450 firms in the Tokyo area finds that firms with steeper age-earnings profiles also tend to be firms that are most likely to use secondment and early retirement incentive schemes to encourage or force older employees to leave the firm. They are also more likely to be instituting policies to deliberately flatten the age–wage profile. What he doesn't find, however, is evidence that the slope of the age-earnings profiles is correlated with the use of any particular payment system. It is neither obvious that the new compensation systems are dramatically changing incentives, nor that the slope of the age-earnings profile has a great effect on incentives (other than to stay with the same firm).

One other aspect of the flattening of age–earnings profiles relates to non-cash compensation in the form of health insurance and both public and company pension contributions. The rate of premiums that firms must pay for public health insurance and the national pension scheme are increasing over time and this is adding to the pressure felt by firms over their wage bill. The rate of return experienced by the employee on these payments is declining with the ageing of the workforce as the number of claimants of pensions or health services rises with the ageing of the Japanese population (Horioka 2001). Most large firms operate their health insurance through company management of premiums and benefits that are kept in balance. As the company workforce ages, the cost of providing health care for employees rises. For smaller companies that participate in the national public health insurance, premiums are rising with the ageing of the population.

Company Pensions

Finally, mention should be made of the company pension schemes that I described in Chapter 2. Typically, these pension plans are defined-benefit plans that pay a lump sum or annuity that is based on the monthly wage of the employee just prior to retirement. In 1993 these averaged around 45 months of such pay.[13] Although there is a great deal of discussion of the need to reduce the level of company pensions as the company workforce ages, there is little evidence so far of changes in the number of months of pay being used for severance payments.[14] However, as the age–wage profile flattens, company pensions will automatically fall in size relative to starting wages, even if the number of months of final wages remains unchanged. This too will have the effect of making the overall compensation profile flatter.

One other way in which changes in the design of company pensions may affect the incentive to stay with the same company would be moves from defined benefit plans towards defined contribution plans or private insurance policies. Matsushita Electric has attracted a great deal of attention with its offer of current cash compensation rather than future pension benefits (or lump-sum retirement benefits) to incoming employees (Strom 1998). Matsushita has aimed the most radical parts of this offer at specialists in law or engineering, employees who are most likely to benefit from the mobility offered by a private pension plan or a defined contribution plan. As I will discuss in Chapter 8, the Japanese government has altered the pension law to allow for defined contribution plans. The development of portable pensions may, along with flattening of the wage profile, lead to greater mobility, especially for employees with skills that are not firm-specific.

Increased Dispersion in Wages

Evidence from Wage Census The Japanese government publishes tables on the dispersion of wages for various gender, education, age, and industry groups. These can be useful in seeing whether or not there has been any tendency towards increased dispersion of wages over time. Table 3.6 shows the interdecile range of monthly regular-time earnings, standardized by dividing by the median. Values are shown for a number of different age and education groups for men in 1980, 1990, and 2003. The table suggests that there has been remarkably little increase in the dispersion of wages over time, with the exception of university-educated men, and there it is most pronounced for middle-aged men who work in medium-sized and large firms. Since this group is most likely to coincide with the managerial class of employees, it suggests that there may be some effect of the new compensation schemes on the variance of earnings. The data could, of course, reflect increasing inter-firm dispersion in wages, but this begs the question of why we don't see the same increase in variance in other groups. Rather, it seems plausible that the new compensation schemes have had an effect on income equality for this sub-group within the firm.

Table 3.6. *Dispersion in earnings of men in Japan, by age, education, and firm size, 1980–2003*

	University-educated men			High-school-educated men		
	1980	1990	2003	1980	1990	2003
Large firms[1]						
Age 25–29	0.28	0.24	0.25	0.24	0.25	0.23
30–34	0.27	0.30	0.32*	0.26	0.28	0.25
35–39	0.30	0.34	0.34*	0.29	0.28	0.28
40–44	0.28	0.33	0.36*	0.35	0.32	0.29
45–49	0.30	0.28	0.36*	0.41	0.37	0.35
50–54	0.30	0.28	0.35*	0.43	0.43	0.38
Medium-sized firms[1]						
Age 25–29	0.25	0.25	0.22	0.26	0.28	0.25
30–34	0.28	0.28	0.29	0.27	0.31	0.27
35–39	0.28	0.32	0.34*	0.30	0.33	0.31
40–44	0.30	0.32	0.34*	0.36	0.35	0.35
45–49	0.33	0.33	0.37*	0.41	0.40	0.39
50–54	0.39	0.35	0.37	0.47	0.45	0.46
Small firms[1]						
Age 25–29	0.29	0.31	0.23	0.31	0.35	0.29
30–34	0.33	0.34	0.31	0.32	0.37	0.31
35–39	0.37	0.37	0.38	0.35	0.38	0.34
40–44	0.38	0.42	0.38	0.40	0.38	0.37
45–49	0.44	0.47	0.38	0.45	0.43	0.39
50–54	0.50	0.47	0.41	0.49	0.47	0.45

Note:

[1] Large firms have more than 1,000 employees, medium-sized firms have 100–999 employees, and small firms have 10–99 employees. The dispersion coefficient is defined as the interdecile range divided by the median. An asterisk indicates that the dispersion coefficient has increased by at least 10% between 1980 and 2003.

Source: MHLW1 (1980, 1990, 2003), vol. 1.

Evidence from Survey on Working Hours　More direct evidence comes from the Survey on Working Conditions conducted in 2001 (MHLW6 2001). The survey reports that some two-thirds of firms surveyed (with more than 30 employees) based at least part of compensation on individual performance. This percentage rises to 83% if we consider only large firms with more than 1,000 employees. The same survey shows that the majority of firms surveyed increase the pay of their *top* performer by less than 10%, and decrease the pay of their bottom performer by less than 10%. Nevertheless, if we restrict our attention to managers, one in five large firms will reduce the pay of the bottom performer by 10–20% or increase the pay of their top performer by 10–20%. While it may not seem from this survey that the institution of performance-related pay has had much effect on compensation (Morishima 2002), when viewed from the perspective of past practice, these modest changes are notable and may be a sign of greater change to come.

In conclusion, the structure of basic cash compensation and the criteria on which bonuses are paid is changing. There is also some evidence that the flattening of the age- or seniority-wage profile will continue in the future, with peak earnings being reached at an earlier age by the majority of employees. Accompanying this are changes in the way in which performance is being evaluated. It is possible that employees will be encouraged to acquire more specialist skills that will allow them to adapt to the changing needs in the workplace in the future. This may increase the share of investment in general human capital relative to firm-specific capital.

HOURS OF WORK

In the 1980s, Japanese had the reputation of being workaholics. According to the establishment-based Monthly Labour Survey, the average Japanese in establishments with more than five employees worked 2,132 hours during 1986 (2,236 hours and 1,954 hours for men and women respectively). This average was considerably higher than that of other OECD countries. The average annual hours of work in the USA and the UK in 1986 stood at roughly 1,930, while in West Germany and France the figure was much lower at around 1,650 (MHLW4 1988: 223). By the end of the 1990s, Japan was not looking like such an outlier, as the average in 1999 of 1,942 hours had fallen below that of the USA.

The decline had been brought about mainly through a 10% drop in the average number of hours worked during the week. In the mid-1980s, half of all firms still required their employees to work on Saturdays. This had declined to less than 10% by the end of the 1990s. It is this single factor that accounts for at least half of the decline in the number of hours worked, although there has been some decline in the average number of hours worked per day from 8.04 in 1990 to 7.72 in 2000 (MHLW4 2000). The move to the five-day work week is significant as it suggests that the decline in working hours is permanent, rather than a temporary adjustment to poor economic conditions.

There are some doubts, however, about whether the extent of the decline is as great as suggested by the preceding figures. Japanese work large numbers of unreported (and unpaid) overtime hours, a major issue with labour unions and increasingly with the MHLW. The Labour Force Survey, a household-based survey, reports that the average Japanese in non-agricultural industries worked 46.1 hours per week in 1990 and 42.4 hours in 2001 (PMO2 2001). On an annualized basis this comes to 2,392 hours in 1990 and 2,204 hours in 2001. Even if these latter figures are too high, they suggest that the Japanese are still working long hours. If the Labour Force Survey figures are to be believed, then the number of hours of unpaid overtime worked per year remained roughly constant at 260 hours per year, or 22 hours per month.

Widespread working of unpaid overtime is partly due to the weakness of the labour unions, but is also a direct consequence of the competitive tournaments that are used to determine promotions in Japan, as described in the preceding chapter.[15] Employees often feel that they cannot leave work until everyone in the office has completed their work for the day. This is sometimes said to reflect the group-based nature of work in the firm, but the more likely reason is that employees are afraid that if they leave early they will be left out when some important plans are made or that they will not be seen as hard-working by their supervisors. The recent trends towards performance-based pay will, if anything, increase this kind of rat-race pressure.

An accompaniment to the prevalence of unpaid overtime is the low rate of take-up of vacation entitlements. In 1999, the average Japanese took just 50% of their vacation entitlement, and the actual take-up rate had declined over the previous four years. The problem of unpaid overtime and vacations not taken is one that has been high on the labour union agenda for many years, with little effect on actual practice.[16]

Adjustment in hours of work over the business cycle is one of the ways in which employers avoid layoffs. By law, overtime is paid with a premium of at least 25%, but on average the premium is not as high as this, even for paid overtime. Since bonuses and fringe benefits are not directly tied to overtime, the actual cost to the employer of an hour of overtime is lower than the average cost for a core employee. When we consider that many overtime hours are not paid at all, the flexibility to employers becomes even more apparent.

CONCLUSIONS

There has not been great change in the nature of standard employment in Japan. Although there have been considerable reductions in employment in many companies, much of this seems to have been accomplished in ways that are consistent with practices during the previous major recession of the mid-1970s (Chuma 2002). There have been adjustments to the structure of compensation, especially a continuing decline in the returns to seniority and experience. Work on Saturdays is becoming a rarity. The slowdown in promotions and the ambiguities inherent in the evaluations used in payment for performance have increased what Genda (2001) terms 'a vague uneasiness at work'. The flatter wage profile, in turn, may lessen the degree of loyalty that is felt towards the firm by its regular employees. There are also signs that the sense of seniority and identity with one's own cohort may be weakening.

Although these changes are significant in themselves, the most important change that is occurring is the declining share of this form of labour in the Japanese firm, the subject of the next chapter.

NOTES

1. The fact that average tenure is increasing at the same time that separation rates are rising is explained by the rise in the unemployment rate–some of the separated men are no longer in the sample of employees covered by the Wage Census. It is also due to the fact that the tenure figures from the Wage Census only cover full-time workers. Men who move to part-time jobs are not included.
2. A sceptic would also note that announcements of cutbacks would be likely to exaggerate the real extent to which workers were being made redundant.
3. The numbers cannot be taken too literally since many of those recorded as voluntary separations may in fact have been under pressure from their firms to quit. Secondments and those returning from secondments (*shukko*) are included in the figures, but their inclusion does not affect the trends observed.
4. These concerns are not restricted to the Japanese. Oxford University uses a similar system of 'promotions' to the higher ranks known as 'titular reader' or 'titular professor' to reward scholars for whom no open position is available. There is no extra remuneration for achieving these ranks, yet many lecturers apply for these 'promotions' each year.
5. Rohlen (1974) gives an account of one such ceremony.
6. Data from the Japanese Yearbook of Labour Statistics (MHWL6) and the Japan Productivity Handbook (JPC) for recent years.
7. The allowances have been eliminated, however, for upper management who are paid by an annual salary scheme (Imano 1998).
8. In Lazear's model employees are paid less than their marginal product in their early years with the firm and more than their marginal product in their final years with the firm in order to make the threat of dismissal for poor performance have serious financial consequences for the employee. Mandatory retirement is necessary in order to limit the extent of overpayment in later years. If the age of mandatory retirement is increased, then the wage profile must become flatter, other things equal. Although Japanese firms ordinarily find it difficult to dismiss employees, they are able to pressure employees to leave the firm by assigning them to intolerable work or by social ostracism.
9. More detailed information in English about this survey is given in the Yearbook of Labour Statistics published annually (MHLW6).
10. Leaving out women avoids conflating changes in the gender gap in earnings with changes to the standard compensation profile experienced by men. The gender gap is taken up in Chapter 7.
11. Unfortunately, the published tables do not provide information on earnings during overtime hours. Since employees of managerial rank do not get paid overtime, there may be some downward bias in the data, but since I am interested in the analysis of trends, the effect should not be very great.
12. Restricting the sample to those under 60 makes little difference to the results. Similarly, estimates adding in a tenure variable do not qualitatively change the results.
13. Ministry of Labour (MHWL1), 1995, table E-39.
14. Evidence that the number of months of final wages has remained unchanged may be found in Rōmu Gyōsei Kenkyūsho (1998: 41, table 15). For an example of a proposal to cut the number of months see the same issue, p. 30.

15. A secondary reason for the use of unpaid overtime is that managerial employees are never paid for their overtime work and so their hours are not counted in the establishment-based statistics.
16. Recently, however, the Ministry of Health, Labour and Welfare has started to take a more active interest in this question.

4

The Growth in Non-standard
Employment Relations

INTRODUCTION

The growth in employment in non-standard work arrangements is the single most important change that is taking place in the Japanese labour market. The proportion of employees working in non-standard arrangements increased from 26% to 32% of the workforce between 1990 and 2001 (see Table 4.2). This is part of an ongoing trend that stretches back to the 1960s. The increase in the number of employees in non-standard contracts is significant in a number of ways. First, this is a way of increasing flexibility in the workplace without changing the guarantees of employment stability provided to regular workers. Secondly, it is a way to circumvent the growing requirement that men and women be treated equally if they are regular employees. Thirdly, this is one area where changes in the regulatory and policy environment affect the labour market. The liberalization of restrictions on using dispatched workers from an agency, for example, has led to a growth of that part of the non-standard labour force. Finally, non-standard employment allows the workplace to accommodate the diverse needs and tastes of the population over the life cycle. It has a central role to play in helping Japan respond to the ageing of its workforce and to raising or maintaining labour force participation rates in the future.

THE DEFINITION OF REGULAR LABOUR AND TRENDS IN ITS SHARE OF EMPLOYMENT

Definitions of 'standard' and 'non-standard' will vary from country to country depending upon social norms, institutional patterns, and legal norms (Ogura 2002). My definition for Japan is based on the stylized facts presented in the preceding chapter. Thus, the aim of a definition for the 'standard' worker in Japan should be to provide a measure of how many individuals are in a secure employment contract that would generate the kind of pay determination and fringe benefits, including government-mandated fringe benefits, that are considered to be the hallmark of the Japanese workplace.

I will define a standard worker to be an employee or director who *usually* works at least 35 hours per week and is on an indefinite contract. I exclude those

dispatched workers who may be regular employees by the terms of the dispatching agency, but who are working at another company. They may have some
security and even fringe benefits, but their working environment is clearly
unusual, as they are not members of the institution where they work. I will also
exclude family workers who are not paid as employees and the employees in
very small enterprises of one to four employees. Small enterprises with less than
five employees are not required to provide health insurance for their employees
(who, like the non-employed, will be covered by the government's National
Health Insurance by default). It is unlikely that these employees will have the
kind of job security and non-mandated fringe benefits available to employees of
larger firms. Social relations in such a firm will obviously be much less formal.

To determine the number of regular workers is a difficult task, despite the fact
that the Japanese government keeps many different kinds of labour statistics.
Unfortunately, statistics usually do not break down employees according to the
kind of contract that they have with the employer and statistics on hours of
work or the definition of part-time work itself may be misleading. Hours of work
data on employment are misleading because many women, especially those that
are married, work more than 35 hours a week and yet are treated as part-time
workers in terms of fringe benefits or pay determination. Another problem is
that most household-based surveys of individuals ask how many hours a person
worked during the previous week. This means that it is possible that many of
those who are listed as working less than 35 hours a week have been absent
from work for various reasons. Hashimoto (1990) observes that there is a category of employees who have done no work during the survey week who may
have been sent home on leave of absence by their employer during economic
downturns. They are still employed, but 'not at work'.

If hours of work are not the most reliable indicator, there are still various
categories of employees used by different surveys that list 'regular employees' as
opposed to 'temporary employees'. Unfortunately, definitions of regular
employee in many of these surveys include not only employees on indefinite
contracts, but also those who have stayed with the same employee for more than
one year on repeated one-year contracts. Despite this problem there are at least
two surveys that make some attempt to obtain numbers of regular employees as
I have defined them. These are the Employment Structure Survey (ESS), and the
Special Survey of the Labour Force Survey (SSLFS).[1] These are both household
surveys, but the Employment Structure Survey, run every five years, has a much
larger sample of 430,000 households with 1.1 million individuals while the
SSLFS, run twice a year, has a relatively small sample of 30,000 households with
75,000 individuals. Both surveys use two definitions of regular workers. The first
is 'Ordinary employees' (*Jōkō*), and refers to employees who are employed on an
indefinite contract or have worked for the same employer for more than one
year. Thus many contract workers and part-time workers could be 'Ordinary
employees'. The second definition, however, is 'Regular Staff (not including
company directors)' (*Seiki no shokuin/jūgyōin*). This is based on 'what the

position is called in the workplace'.[2] In 2001, some 7% of those who are labelled as 'regular staff' worked less than 35 hours during the survey week. However, as mentioned above, absentees or else workers temporarily furloughed from work may be included in this group, so I will include all ordinary employees who are regular staff in my standard worker category.[3] To these I add the directors of companies, as company directors in Japan usually fall within the career pattern of the standard worker, having been promoted from within.

TRENDS IN THE SHARES OF NON-STANDARD EMPLOYEES

Table 4.1 shows the share of the employed in Japan according to form of employment. Standard employees, as I have defined them, make up a little more than half of the workforce, a share that has barely changed over the last decade.[4] This is a surprising observation, given the attention that has been given by the government and the media to the 'diversification' of employment in Japan. Looking at the other categories in the table, we can see the reason why this level has remained constant. Although the share of standard employees has remained stable, there has been a great shift away from self-employment (including piece-work done at home) and working in a family business, while at the same time there has been a large increase in part-time work. Some of this has been due to the shrinkage of the agricultural sector, but, especially in the last decade, most of this trend is not due to changes in the industrial structure. The result has been that the proportion of the employed working as employees and directors has increased.

Table 4.1. *Share of employed by type, 1980, 1990, 2001*

Type of worker	1980	1990	2001	% male in 2001
Standard employee	–	57.7	57.2	64.5
Non-standard employee	–	19.9	27.0	35.2
Over 65, non-director	–	0.6	0.9	71.7
Regular but very small firm (1–4 employees)	–	4.4	4.7	65.9
Part-time employee	–	12.6	19.1	23.9
Dispatched worker	–	–	0.7	24.4
Full-time contract worker	–	2.0	1.6	64.4
All employees and directors	71.7	77.6	84.2	55.1
Self-employed	15.2	12.5	10.0	76.5
Family workers	10.9	8.0	4.8	19.1
Piece workers at home	2.2	1.4	0.6	5.1
Total	100.0	100.0	100.0	59.2
Share in agriculture	9.0	5.4	3.7	57.8
Unemployment rate	2.2	2.3	4.8	60.7

Source: PMO1 (1980, 1990, August 2001).

Table 4.2. *Employees by type, as a share of all employees and directors, 1990, 2001*

Type of worker	1990	2001	% Male in 1990	% Male in 2001
Standard employee	74.4	67.9	70.5	64.5
Non-standard employee	25.6	32.1	38.6	35.2
Over 65, non-director	0.8	1.1	66.7	71.7
Regular employee in small firm				
(1–4 employees)	6.0	5.5	71.9	65.9
Part-time employee	16.3	22.7	20.1	23.9
Dispatched worker	–	0.8	–	24.4
Full-time contract worker	2.5	1.9	69.5	64.4

Source: PMO1 (1990, August 2001).

If we restrict our attention to employees and directors, there has been a shift in the composition of the labour force and the share of standard employees has dropped from 74% to 68%. This shift in composition over a 10-year period has been very rapid and is mainly due to the greater use of part-time workers in firms with more than five employees. As Table 4.2 shows, there has not only been a movement away from the use of standard employees in the enterprise, there has also been a growing proportion of women among standard employees and contract workers, while there has been a slightly greater tendency for men to work part time. The move away from self-employment and family employment and the contemporaneous increase in part-time work will be one of the main topics of this chapter, but first, I turn to a brief discussion of the various categories of the non-standard worker.

TYPES OF NON-REGULAR LABOUR AND THEIR RELATIVE IMPORTANCE

Part-Time Workers

In devising a taxonomy of non-standard labour it is important to distinguish between classifications based on the attributes of the worker, including age, gender, education, and marital status and classifications according to the type of employment arrangement that is being used. The attributes of the workforce may be important in understanding issues related to the supply and demand for different types of labour contract arrangements, but they should not be confused with the nature of the arrangements themselves. The terms used in Japan are apt to be very confusing because this distinction is not observed. For example, an employee who works less than 35 hours per week may be labelled as '*arubaitaa*' if they are working on the side while attending school or keeping house, as a '*paato*' or '*paato-taimaa*' (part-timer), a term usually applied to married women, as a '*friitaa*' if they are young school graduates who are not committed to any one employer, or as '*shokutaku*', often used for post-mandatory retirement

Table **4.3**. *Definitions of part-time workers*

Survey Definitions
1. Working less than 35 hours per week (based on Labour Force Survey) [21.8]
2. Considered to be 'part-time' by their employer, i.e. paid by the hour (Special Survey of the Labour Force Survey). [19.3%] (Employment Status Survey–1997) [18.8% (including *arubaito*)]
3. Working fewer hours per day or fewer days per week than regular employees in the same firm (Survey of Employment Diversification) [20.3%]

Tax and Benefit System Definitions
1. Less than 20 hours per week (Employment Insurance)
2. Less than three-quarters of regular working hours and less than 1,300,000 yen per year. (Health and Government Pension)
3. Less than 990,000 yen per year–no tax obligation; above this taxes (residence and/or income) start to be applied
4. Less than 1,030,000 yen per year–tax exemption for dependent given to spouse; from 1,030,000 to 1,410,000 yen this tax exemption is phased out

Note: Part-time workers shown in square brackets as a percentage of the 1999 workforce.

employees who are on fixed-term contracts and who may be working part time, or as a dispatched worker (temp). Young women may prefer the term *'friitaa'* to *'paato'*, because it has a more positive connotation, suggesting a free life without too many serious commitments.

The government's own definitions are not necessarily helpful. As Table 4.3 shows, there are a number of different possible definitions of part-time workers in the surveys used by the government. There are also a number of 'policy' definitions, where taxes (including payroll taxes) and benefits are affected by either the number of hours worked or by annual earnings.

With two adjustments I will simply label all *friitaa, arubaitaa, shokutaku,* and *paato* as part-time workers, even if there are surveys that make distinctions. The two adjustments are (1) all of those who call themselves part-time workers will be included, even if they worked more than 35 hours in the survey week, as their contract will not be that of a standard employee; (2) I will exclude from the part-time category those employees who are dispatched from a temp agency, as they will be considered separately and I wish to avoid overlap of categories.

Dispatched Workers and Contract Workers

Two other categories of employee are the dispatched worker, including those who are known as temps in the USA or UK, and the full-time contract worker. The latter category includes (1) those who call themselves *shokutaku* as well as those who call themselves 'regular staff' but are on a fixed-term contract, and (2) those who are employed by the day, unless they are working part time. Day workers include a mixture of students or other young people who work casually, some dispatched workers, and the more traditional day labourer working generally on construction sites. They are a small group and it seems reasonable to bracket them together with the contract workers. For example, as Gill (2001) points out, many of the day labourers who sell their labour in the street markets of the major cities will also work for a more extended contractual period at locations beyond commuting distance of the city in question. The full-time contract worker has shown a slight decline in these surveys, but we should remember that most of the part-time workers are on fixed-term contracts.[5]

The dispatched worker is a new arrival in the Japanese labour market. In the original Labour Standards Law introduced in 1947 under the guidance of the American occupation, it was not permitted to dispatch workers from one company to work for another as it was feared that such an arrangement could be exploitative.[6] Trade unions also opposed the use of dispatched workers, as they feared that this could undermine their bargaining position. In 1986, however, Japan implemented a Dispatched Workers Law to partly liberalize the labour market. The new law made it possible for an employee to work for a contracting agency and then be dispatched for work elsewhere. The number of industries that were permitted under the original legislation was severely limited by the original legislation, but in 1996 and 1999 the law was revised to permit a wider range of industries. The current list only prohibits certain industries, including port labour, construction, security guards, health care, legal and accounting professionals, and production-line manufacturing, and the government is now about to remove the restriction on use of dispatched workers in production. There are two kinds of arrangements that are used. In the first, the employee is hired full time as a 'regular employee' of the dispatching company, but may be moved around to different companies as needed. The number of these employees stood at 300,000 in 2001 (JIL, *Japan Labour Bulletin*, April 2003). In the second, more like Western temping arrangements, the employee is registered with an agency and is then sent to various temporary jobs as work becomes available. In 2001, 1.45 million persons were registered at agencies, but it is estimated that any one point they made up only 310,000 full-time equivalents, bringing the total number in this category to some 600,000 or roughly 1% of the labour force. There have been problems with the use of dispatched workers, something that is hardly unique to Japan (Weathers 2001*a*). One of the main problems appears to be sexual harassment, an issue that will be taken up later in the chapter on women.

Piece Workers

The other categories in Table 4.1 are mostly self-explanatory, but the piece worker at home (*naishoku*) may be less familiar to some readers. These are almost entirely women who take on consignments such as sewing garments or winding coils of wire for small motors, and so on. Changes in technology, the availability of cheaper labour overseas, and the rising wage levels for part-time women employees have been responsible for the decline in this part of the labour force as shown in the table. Changing technology has, of course, reduced the demand for such manual labour, but it has also affected the supply of such labour.

Teleworkers

Teleworkers are becoming an increasingly important part of the labour force, making up some 6% of all employees according to one government survey (MHLW7 2003). Around three-quarters of these employees are men. The long commutes that many Japanese endure in the larger urban centres makes telework particularly attractive and the Japanese government is keen to develop telework in the future. The IT Strategy Division has announced a plan to have 20% of the workforce engaged in telework by 2010 (JIL 2003). While this may reflect aspiration more than realism, it does suggest that the government will be supporting the investment in infrastructure needed to promote telework. It also reflects the interest the government has in increasing the participation rate of women to manage the labour shortages of the future. Although telework is considered by some to be a non-standard form of labour, they will still be classified as employees in government surveys and their contracts may be similar to those of regular employees. For that reason, I will not treat them as a separate category.

Since most of the shift towards non-standard labour in firms is to be found in the growing use of part-time workers, the remainder of this chapter will focus on the growth in their use.

UNDERSTANDING THE SHIFTING STRUCTURE OF LABOUR CONTRACTS

I have already outlined in the introductory chapter some reasons why there has been an increase in the use of part-time labour in Japan. There are a number of other explanations that can be given for this shift and I now turn to an examination of these:

(1) demographic shifts—more women are working, and women are more likely to want to work part time. Also, after mandatory retirement, older men may prefer to work part time. In both cases, there are economic incentives that support the desire for part-time work;

(2) shifts in the composition of industries towards industries that use part-time workers more intensively;

(3) shifts in the attitudes of youth that encourage both men and women to favour working part time. This is the *friitaa* phenomenon;

(4) cutbacks in the hiring of new graduates into full-time jobs that force them into the non-standard labour market;

(5) conscious decisions by firms to employ more part-time workers in order to save on personnel costs. Firms are under more pressure in the environment of depressed demand;

(6) under slower growth, firms are more likely to want flexibility in personnel and so are pushed towards using employees who can more easily be dismissed;

(7) a movement of women away from working in the family firm as unpaid part-time workers to working as paid employees in a larger firm;

(8) changes in operations that necessitate the use of part-time labour;

(9) changes in the regulatory environment that make it easier to use non-standard labour.

I have already mentioned how the change in labour market regulations has led to the use of dispatched labour. Here, I will examine the first eight of the explanations, but I will leave much of the discussion of youth, women, and older men for later chapters.

Demographic Factors

Starting with the first of the hypotheses, Table 4.4 shows a breakdown by different age-gender groups of the different types of workers. Due to data limitations, my definition of standard worker is slightly different in this table, and includes workers in small firms with one to four employees and men over 65. There are two main points that should be clear from this table. First, the increase in the share of non-standard employees is common to all demographic groups. Secondly, the drop in the proportion of self-employed and family workers is common to all age-gender groups. These phenomena are not restricted to any particular age group. This suggests that demographic change has had a relatively minor effect on the overall trends. Another way to see this is to conduct a shift-share analysis where we hold the rates of standard employment steady for all age groups at 1990 levels and then look at what the overall levels of standard employment would be if the number of employed in each group were at 2001 levels. For women, it turns out that the rate of standard employment shows virtually no change. For men, however, this exercise shows that demographic factors should have led to a fall in the rate of standard employment, mainly due to the increased numbers of men over the age of 65 who are still working, but in non-standard employment. The fact that the rate of standard employment for men has remained steady is due to a decline in self-employment across age groups, which in turn has led to higher rates of standard employment for middle-aged men.

In conclusion, we can say that demographic factors have had only a moderate effect on the move to non-standard employment for men, while they have had virtually no effect on the rates for women.

Shifts in the Industrial Mix

Turning next to the question of whether industry shifts have had any effect, Houseman and Osawa (1998) report that industry shifts bear little responsibility

Table 4.4. *Employment rate, unemployment rate, employment types, non-agricultural employees in 1990, 2001 by gender and age*

Group	Employment/ population rate		Unemployment rate		Share that are regular employees		Self-employed or family workers		Share that are non-regular employees	
	2001	1990	2001	1990	2001	1990	2001	1990	2001	1990
Men	71.5	74.0	4.9	2.3	77.7	77.8	12.0	15.1	10.3	7.2
Age 15–24	39.0	37.4	9.8	5.8	55.6	74.6	3.5	6.1	40.8	19.3
(in school)					1.2	3.7	3.5	11.1	95.3	85.2
25–34	91.5	93.9	5.3	2.1	87.9	89.2	4.8	7.6	7.3	3.2
35–44	94.7	96.6	3.1	1.3	88.0	82.1	8.9	15.0	3.1	2.9
45–54	93.6	95.2	3.1	1.1	82.6	79.0	13.6	17.6	3.8	3.4
55–64	78.1	79.2	6.8	4.0	68.7	63.3	18.5	21.7	12.8	15.0
65+	31.1	31.9	3.7	2.1	39.7	40.4	37.6	40.4	22.7	19.1
Women	46.3	47.0	4.6	2.4	46.2	49.1	14.0	22.5	39.8	28.5
Age 15–24	40.6	38.5	8.5	5.1	53.8	75.6	2.2	3.7	43.9	20.7
(in school)					2.7	11.4	2.7	9.1	94.6	79.5
25–34	61.2	53.5	6.3	3.6	60.9	61.6	6.2	14.2	32.9	24.2
35–44	64.0	64.9	4.0	1.9	42.7	39.3	11.5	24.6	45.7	36.1
45–54	67.1	67.2	3.1	1.4	41.6	42.8	15.6	25.2	42.8	31.9
55–64	47.0	42.7	3.5	1.9	35.5	37.6	24.3	37.2	40.2	25.2
65+	12.2	13.5	1.2	0.0	28.1	26.1	52.1	59.1	19.8	14.8
Married					37.6	38.8	18.3	28.4	44.1	32.8

Source: PMO1 (1990, August 2001).

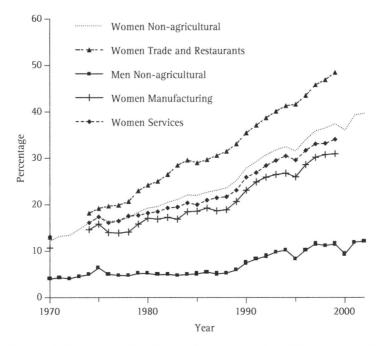

Figure 4.1. *Proportion of employees who work less than 35 hours per week*
Source: MHLW7 (2000: 518) and MHLW (2003: 379).

for the movement towards part-time work. I will show that, while this is true, there is an indirect effect that comes from the shift away from employment in family businesses. This in turn has been greatly affected by the ongoing decline in employment in the agricultural and textile industries. Nevertheless, most of the increase in part-time employment has been based on an increase within industries, with an especially rapid rise in the trade and restaurant sector. As Figure 4.1 shows, rates of part-time work have been increasing in all industries over the past 30 years. At the more disaggregated two-digit industry level, the only industries that have seen a fall in the rate of part-time work have been ceramics and metal products.[7]

The Youth Labour Market

Returning to Table 4.4, it is clear that, for men, the biggest shift to non-standard forms of employment is among young men aged 15–24, but there has also been a slight shift for 25–34 year olds. Nevertheless, the relatively low employment rates for men aged 15–24 mean that the impact they have on the overall increase in non-standard employment is moderate at three percentage points. For women, the pattern is similar to the men in that the biggest shift away from standard employment is in the 15–24-year-old group.

The question of whether this move towards working in non-standard arrangements amongst youth is voluntary is one of the most keenly debated issues in Japan and I will leave most of the discussion to Chapter 9, which is concerned with the labour market for youth. Here, I will simply note that the unemployment rates for young men and women have increased greatly and this suggests that the poor state of the labour market is responsible for much of the increase in non-standard work. Evidence from attitude surveys (Sato 1998) also suggests that, unlike the situation for older women, youth are more likely to say that they are involuntarily working part time. The downturn of the Japanese economy in the 1990s has had a particularly harsh effect on the market for recent graduates, as I will show in Chapter 9. After 1992, most firms cut back drastically on their hiring of new school graduates, and it is this, rather than a change in attitudes, that is responsible for the movement towards part-time work amongst youth. To conclude, about three percentage points of the movement towards non-standard employment for both men and women can be attributed to the labour market for youth, and it is likely that most of this movement reflects the poor state of the entry labour market for new graduates, rather than a major change in the work ethic and norms of youth.

Cost-Cutting by Firms and the Desire for Greater Flexibility

While the youth labour market does account for much of the shift towards non-standard work, the bulk of the shift in the case of women is seen in the older age groups. Here several factors may be at work. The first is that firms may prefer to hire part-time workers in order to save personnel costs or to have more flexible staffing arrangements. Government surveys provide some support for this. Responses to surveys of employers suggest that cost-cutting is a primary motive for hiring part-time workers and that the proportion of establishments indicating this has risen between 1994 and 1999 (MHLW14 1996, 2000; Houseman and Osawa 1998).

Not all of the evidence points to changes on the demand side, however. First, the increasing rate of part-time work for women is part of a long-term trend that dates back to the 1960s. Secondly, the relative compensation of part-time workers has fallen over time. Part-time hourly earnings as a proportion of full-time earnings for women have fallen steadily from 76% in 1970 to 57% in 2000.[8] At the same time, the average earnings of full-time women as a proportion of those of full-time men have risen from 0.54 to 0.66. This reflects in part the fact that more women are working at older ages, where they are likely to receive higher wages, and also the increasing educational attainment of women. The increasing full-time/part-time wage differential may simply reflect the fact that full-time workers are becoming relatively more skilled over time. To avoid this issue, we may look at the differential between women working part-time and women aged 20–24. Here we see that the differential has widened only slightly, from 0.76 to 0.70 (taking part-time hourly earnings as a proportion of full-time hourly earnings).

In a more comprehensive study, the MHLW shows that even after controlling for industry, firm size, age, and tenure, the part-time/full-time gap widened by five percentage points between 1990 and 2001. The widening of the differential suggests that the relative demand for part-time workers has not increased, but rather it is consistent with an increased supply of women who want to work part-time or women who are constrained to work part time.[9]

Another problem with the demand-side explanation is that one would expect that those industries that have had the greatest economic hardship would be turning most towards the use of part-time workers. To investigate this possibility, I have looked across industries to see if there is any correlation between (a) employment growth and share in part-time workers, (b) change in employment growth and change in the share in part-time workers, and (c) profitability and share in part-time workers and (d) change in profits and change in the share in part-time workers between 1990 and 2000. I don't find any significant correlations across industries. Indeed, the greatest increase in the use of part-time workers is found in the food-processing industry, which is the one manufacturing industry that has seen employment growth over the past decade and may be least affected by the high exchange value of the yen. This suggests that if demand-side considerations matter, they run across the board and reflect the poor state of aggregate demand across the entire economy in the 1990s.

I have already noted that young women (as well as young men) have been constrained to work part time in the 1990s, as firms have reacted to the recession by cutting back on new graduate hires. In this sense, part of the movement to non-standard labour contracts is demand-side driven as firms have cut back on their hiring of new school graduates into full-time positions. For older women, however, the shift comes almost entirely on the supply side and largely reflects the shift of women away from self-employment or work in family enterprises.

The Decline of the Family-Run Firm

A major trend in employment that is shown in Table 4.4 is the decline in the numbers of self-employed and family workers. The contrast between men and women is notable. The decline in self-employment for men corresponds to an increase in *regular* employment for the older age groups, while for women, there is a corresponding increase in non-standard employment. This is especially evident in the case of married women, where there has been a 10 point decline in the share of self-employed and family workers, at the same time as there has been a 12 point increase in the share of non-standard employment. Meanwhile, there has been virtually no change in the share of regular employees. This suggests that the increase in the share of women working as non-standard employees may be largely related to the decline in the family-run enterprise.

To examine this more closely, I begin by examining data from the Employment Structure Survey of 2002. This survey provides a cross-tabulation of job switchers showing the numbers of individuals who left a job as either a

Table 4.5. *Transition matrix for workers who changed jobs or stopped working between October 1997 and July 2002 (thousands)*

Status in 2002	Previous status			
	Self-employed or family	Regular employees	Non-standard employees	Directors
Men				
Self-employed or family	50	466	101	25
Regular employee	132	2,819	543	48
Non-standard employee	87	1,051	822	37
Directors	17	177	14	63
Not employed	465	2,534	1,356	87
Women				
Self-employed or family	43	141	157	2
Regular employee	36	912	682	6
Non-standard employee	163	1,187	2,724	14
Directors	5	20	3	6
Not employed	679	2,599	3,469	14

Source: PMO3 (2002).

self-employed or family worker and the kind of job that they moved to, if they left work after September 1997 and started their new job by mid-2002. The results of this tabulation are shown in Table 4.5. Around 80% of the women who left self-employment or family work to work as employees became non-standard workers, while most of the men became regular employees. On the other hand, women who moved from being employees to self-employed or family work were more evenly divided between regular and non-regular status.

The tabulations of Table 4.5 are suggestive, but since they don't include those individuals who are moving into employment from non-employment, they are not conclusive. One alternative way to examine the hypothesis that the decline of the family-run firm is responsible for the shift to part-time work for married women is to examine trends across prefectures. The published tables of the Employment Status Survey (ESS) for 1992 and 1997 provide breakdowns of employment type (e.g. self-employed, family worker, part-time employee, regular employee, and so on) for married women by prefecture. It is then possible to look across prefectures at the change in the share of part-time employees among married women, the change in the share of regular employees, and the change in the share of those who are family workers.

The results of simple regression analysis are shown in Table 4.6. The regression analysis of simple cross-section variation in part-time employment across prefectures suggests that 20% of the variation may be explained by the share of family

Institutional Changes

Table 4.6. *The correlation of part-time work and unpaid family work for married women, 1992 and 1997*

	Share part-time[1]	Share regular employee[1]	ΔShare part-time[2]	ΔShare regular employee[2]
Share family worker[1]	−0.81*	0.02		
	(0.24)	(0.27)		
Δ Share family worker[2]			−0.62*	−0.09
			(0.16)	(0.16)
Constant	0.46*	0.32*	0.016*	−0.002
	(0.04)	(0.05)	(0.004)	(0.004)
R^2	0.20	0.0002	0.25	0.006
Observations	47	47	47	47

Notes:
* Significant at the 1% level standard errors in parentheses.
[1] Values for 1997 only.
[2] Change from 1992 to 1997.

Source: PMO3 (1992, 1997).

workers. The share of part-time employment is generally 0.8 of a percentage point higher for each percentage point drop in the share of family workers. Furthermore, there is no relationship shown between the share of regular employees in the labour force and the share of family workers. An even stronger test of the relationship is shown in the final two columns of the table. Here I look at the changes between 1992 and 1997 in the share of part-time employment across prefectures and show that the same kind of relationship holds—part-time work increases by about 0.6 of a percentage point for each percentage point drop in the share of family workers and there is no such relationship in the case of regular workers.

The share of family workers dropped by 2.32% between 1992 and 1997. The model would thus predict that the share of part-time workers would rise by $0.62 \times 2.32 = 1.44\%$. In fact, the share of part-time employment among married women rose by 3.08% in this time period. So, this exercise suggests that the decline in the family firm explains almost half of the increase in part-time employment for married women in Japan. Of course, if we were to examine unmarried women we would be less likely to find such a relationship, as younger, unmarried women are more likely to choose to work full-time if they don't work in a family-run firm. Consequently, when this exercise is repeated including unmarried women we find that the decline in family workers explains only a quarter of the rise in the share of part-time workers.

It is not surprising that there is a strong relationship between the decline of family work and the rise of part-time work as employees. In both cases, women are working in a 'supportive' role and in both cases, hours of work can be adapted to allow for greater work in household-related activities.

The question of why the family-run firm is in such rapid decline is one that is of some importance in understanding the main trends in the Japanese economy today. Genda and Kambayashi (2002) examine this question looking at microdata from the National Survey on Income and Expenditure on the earnings of the owners of small businesses. They find that the age–earnings profile for the self-employed has become much flatter between 1989 and 1994 and conclude that the incentives to move into self-employment, especially for middle-aged men, have been dampened. Although one could speculate about what this implies for human capital investment and returns for the self-employed, it is clear that self-employment has become less profitable, and that any explanation of the decline in the family-run firm should look at why this is the case.

Table 4.7 shows changes in the rates of self-employment for selected industries in 1982 and 1997. A shift-share analysis shows that of the 11 point drop in the share of self-employed and family workers over the 15 year period, only 3.1 points, or less than one-third can be explained by changes in industry shares, and virtually all of this is due to the decline of agricultural employment. The remaining two-thirds of the drop is explained by a drop in the self- and family employment rates within industries, especially in retailing and restaurants, but also in the other industries shown in Table 4.6.

The reasons why small businesses are not so profitable seem to be related to changes in the industrial organization in Japan that have gradually put pressure on smaller enterprises. Deregulation plays an important part in this process, and in recent years, the tendency to use foreign sources for intermediate goods in manufacturing may also be playing a role. In retailing, the development of wide-spread chain-store networks has squeezed out many of the smaller independent

Table 4.7. *Share of self-employed or family workers by industry, 1982 and 2002*

Industry	Share in 1982	Share in 2002	Change 1982–2002
All industries	26.6	15.6	−11.0
Agriculture	96.7	88.0	−8.7
Consturction	21.5	18.7	−2.8
Food processing	9.4	4.1	−5.3
Textiles	38.3	28.9	−9.5
Pulp and paper products	14.7	8.7	−6.0
Publishing	14.3	7.5	−6.8
Chemicals	4.5	0.5	−4.1
Metal products	19.5	11.8	−7.7
Electrical	8.6	3.5	−5.0
Precision instruments	10.1	4.2	−5.8
Wholesale	10.7	5.7	−5.0
Food retail	51.1	19.1	−32.0
Restaurants	43.8	27.6	−16.2
Other retail	32.9	17.3	−15.5
Real estate	31.9	23.4	−8.5
Non-educational services	24.3	14.9	−9.4

Source: PMO3 (1982), table 3 and PMO3 (2002), table 19.

retailers. Deregulation of alcohol retailing is leading to the demise of the liquor specialist store, as convenience stores and supermarkets have taken over a large share of the business (Nitta 2003). Regulations such as the Large Store Act that impeded the development of larger, more efficient retail stores and protected the small retailer have been relaxed to a great extent. In a slightly different vein, hotels and motels, often part of larger chains, have replaced the more traditional family-run inn. Flath (2003) points out that the increased rate of automobile ownership has had a major impact on the retail business. Restaurants have been affected by the growth of restaurant chains, a trend that is also related to the increased use of automobiles.

Changes in Operations that Lead to Increased Demand for Part-Time Workers

Nitta (2003) points out that the convenience stores and large-scale retailers that are replacing the family-run firm are usually open for long hours (sometimes all night). This increases the demand for part-time workers.

To conclude this section, the growth in part-time employment among women over the past decade is only partly related to the decline of the family-run firm. This accounts for roughly a quarter of the rise in part-time work. Almost half of the shift to non-standard work is located in the youth labour market where there has been an increased tendency towards non-standard employment for both men and women. This, in turn, is most likely to be related to poor labour market conditions. The remainder of the increase in part-time work has taken place among older married women and is unrelated to the decline in the family firm. The case of men is much simpler. Virtually all of the three point increase in the rate of non-standard employment is located among youth.

WILL THE TREND TO NON-STANDARD EMPLOYMENT CONTINUE?

A major question that arises from the observations of this chapter is whether the movement towards non-standard forms of employment will continue. I argued in the Introduction that under slower growth there were reasons to suspect that the move to non-standard employment would be a long-term trend. Some empirical support for this view comes from the Survey on the Diversification of Employment conducted in 1999 by the MHLW (MHLW6). Of the establishments surveyed, 50% reported that they planned to increase the share of non-standard employees in their workforce over the coming three years. Of these, around half said that they would be increasing the share of part-time workers. The proportions were highest in manufacturing, trade, and services. Although it is possible that these plans simply reflect business cycle conditions, the outlook in 1999 was beginning to improve. It seems likely that firms are at least planning to maintain the proportion of part-time workers and other forms of non-standard labour that they use.

If this is true, the method that they are most likely to use is to continue to show restraint in hiring recent graduates as regular employees. Returning to Table 4.4, the sharp rise in non-standard employment for the 15–24-year-old group between 1990 and 2001 may represent a trend that will eventually spread to older groups with the passage of time. The employment protection that exists for standard employees will limit the ability of firms to change their employment structure in other ways such as through the dismissal of regular employees. Thus the youth labour market is unlikely to witness a recovery to the high demand state that was characteristic of the years up to 1992.

IMPLICATIONS AND DISCUSSION

So far in this chapter, I have looked at the various ways in which the growth of non-standard labour has expressed itself. It is natural to ask whether these changes have been positive ones, especially for the individuals involved. This is not meant to be a welfare analysis in the usual economic sense, as any such analysis would need to consider what the alternatives would be in the present economic environment. Furthermore, it is difficult to find time-series evidence concerning levels of satisfaction to make comparisons with earlier periods.

If we look at indicators of satisfaction with work, as shown in the MHLW14 survey of 1999, we find it difficult to find major differences in satisfaction levels between workers in the published data. In general, however, younger part-time workers are less likely to express dissatisfaction with the various aspects of their work than older part-time workers or regular employees (Sato 1998). It is difficult to draw strong conclusions from such studies since satisfaction as a subjective measure has as much to do with expectations as with objective circumstances. Young part-time workers working in the service sector on a temporary basis may not expect much from their work. For this reason, the evidence that 25–30% of young part-time employees would prefer to be working as regular workers is perhaps the only solid indicator that we have. Roughly the same proportion of dispatched workers feel the same way (Sato 1998).

Of more concern is the prospect for wider dissatisfaction in the future. The dissatisfaction of youth just mentioned may gradually move to older age groups as today's youth grow older, unless non-standard workers are able to move into regular employment. The dual structure of the labour market in the past was expressed mainly through the separation between employees of large firms and those in small firms and the self-employed. In the future, the most important distinction will be that between regular and non-regular employees. Since they work in the same firm, the potential for resentment on the part of the secondary workforce is greater. It is also the case that small business has had political representation through the Liberal Democratic Party, while part-time workers have no such representation for their interests.

Finally, to end on a more positive note, recent survey evidence (MHLW7 2003) suggests that the boundary between non-regular and regular employment may have become less rigid during the 1990s. There is often considerable overlap between the jobs that non-regular and regular workers do. Some 40% of firms have developed personnel management systems that allow highly motivated and skilled part-time workers to switch to full-time status (MHLW7 2003: 328). For example, in the retail sector, a part-time worker may already be acting as a store manager. Shifting to full-time regular employee status may then be a natural progression, if the employee is interested. In most cases, however, the part-time worker must be willing to relocate and accept the kind of personnel transfers that usually accompany regular worker status.

Notes

1. This is now incorporated into the general Labour Force Survey.
2. The other choices are (a) part-time worker, (b) *arubaito* (part-time work on the side of attending school or keeping house), (c) dispatched worker, (d) contract employee, and (e) others.
3. For example, 700,000 of the 'regular staff' worked less than 14 hours on the survey week. Of these, 530,000 were not at work at all during the survey week although they were on the company payroll. This suggests that they were absent from work for one reason or another and that they might well be working full-time normally.
4. Note that I have not included those standard employees who work in firms with less than five employees. The next size category would be 5–29 employees, and here we may see some form of standardized pay in the largest of these firms.
5. To make matters more confusing, there is another category of worker sometimes referred to as a contract worker. These are employees of firms that are on-site subcontractors to a receiving firm. The employees are legally under the management of the subcontracting firm, but in reality may be given instruction from the host firm. These arrangements are commonly used in production work where dispatching has so far been prohibited (Sato 2003). I do not include these employees in my definition of contract workers, and stick to the definition in the Labour Force Survey.
6. The exception allowed was in the case where a subcontractor provided work on-site at another company. In this case, however, the subcontractor directed the work at the site and was legally responsible for it as well as for the treatment of the employees. This is not temporary help in the usual sense of the term and the employees never considered themselves to be employed by the company on whose site they worked.
7. Based on figures given in the Monthly Labour Survey (MHWL6).
8. Figures in this section are calculated from Wage Census tables (MHWL1).
9. The MHLW also looked at the trend in the part-time/full-time wage differential between 1995 and 2001 after controlling for occupation, for those employees that were in specific occupations. They found that after these controls were added, the widening trend disappeared. In other words, most of the growth in part-time employment was taking place in lower-paid occupations (MHWL7 2003).

5

Industrial Relations

INTRODUCTION

Like other economic institutions, the industrial relations system in Japan has seen significant developments throughout the period since the end of the Second World War. The main features of the system were well established by the end of the 1950s, but the slowdown in growth and the need to restrain inflation in the mid-1970s led to a major change in the behaviour of the union movement. The 1980s and 1990s saw a consistent decline in union density and the deflationary period of the past few years has seen a major change of strategy of the main union federation, Rengō. At the beginning of this chapter I will sketch out some of the historical background before moving on to discuss the changes and challenges facing the industrial relations system.

JAPAN'S POSTWAR INDUSTRIAL RELATIONS SYSTEM

Japanese industrial relations did not, of course, begin after the Second World War, but the war does provide an important break with the past as liberalization and democratization took place under the authority of the American Occupation. Prior to the war, the nascent union movement had been repressed to a great extent, through legislation such as the Public Peace Law of 1900, which was used by authorities to break up strikes and other gatherings of unions. Union membership never rose above 7% of the workforce during this period. In 1938 the government outlawed unions and replaced them with factory councils known as *Sanpō* (Industrial Patriotic Associations), with representatives from management and labour. Although these councils were not always effective in managing labour disputes, they did leave a legacy for the future. Management and government did, at least, pay lip-service to the concerns of workers, and their need for dignity (Gordon 1985). The councils also forced management to sit down with labour representatives, and this provided a precedent for future cooperation. The *Sanpō* were disbanded in 1945, but a new union movement immediately sprang up in their place.

The Occupation Reforms

The American Occupation introduced a number of democratizing measures in the early aftermath of the war. One of these was the introduction of legislation to promote the development of an industrial relations system. The right to organize is explicitly laid out in the Japanese constitution as a basic human right that is 'eternal and inviolable'. The first Trade Union Law was introduced in 1945. The response to this legislation was very rapid and by the end of 1946, 46% of employees were organized, rising to a peak of 56% in 1949 (Shirai 1983*b*: 140).

The Absence of an Exclusivity Clause   To a great extent the Trade Union Law is modelled on American labour law, especially the National Labor Relations Act and Taft-Hartley Act, but there are a number of differences. Here I would like to draw attention to one in particular. American law provides for the designation of a bargaining unit for which workers can elect an *exclusive* representative by an election with a simple majority. In Japan, there is no such designation of a bargaining unit and there may be more than one unit representing any given workplace or other group of workers. This is one example of the way in which the Japanese have modified the original intentions of the Occupation Authorities. Neither employers nor the unions were in favour of an exclusivity clause in the labour legislation. The employers were against this because it obviously put the union representatives in a more powerful position. The unions tended to be against it because the union movement was divided and different groups feared that exclusivity might lock them out of the workplace. In addition, it would be difficult to establish the appropriate bargaining units as there were not the same demarcations of jobs in Japan as in other countries.

The result has been that the union movement has been left more divided than it otherwise might have been, and the unions themselves have been in a much weaker position within firms. In the event that a militant union organizes some of the workers, it is possible that a second (or third) union taking a more moderate stance will also be able to organize employees, often with the tacit approval of management. The famous strike at Nissan in 1953 is the textbook example of such a manoeuvre on the part of the employers, anxious to put down an antagonistic union (Cusumano 1985). The lack of exclusivity also made it more difficult for unions to be organized on an industry-wide basis and led to the development of more cooperative unions that were mainly interested in promoting the success of the enterprise.

The Roll-Back   The American Occupation also acted to roll back some of the provisions of the original legislation in the late 1940s. The most important change was the introduction of the Public Corporation and National Enterprise Labor Relations Law of 1948 that denied public-sector workers the right to strike. This remained a contentious piece of legislation until the 1980s, at which point most of the public corporations (railways and telecommunications) were privatized. The onset of the Cold War led to a push by the Occupation authorities to purge communists from the government. The end of the 1940s saw the introduction of tight monetary policy under Joseph Dodge, and the resulting recession gave management the opportunity to fire many of the most radical workers.[1] By the late 1950s much of the postwar industrial relations system had been established. Management and labour had struck a bargain whereby employees were given job security. In return, management had the right to allocate workers where it chose in the workplace, and the kind of job demarcations that are characteristic of other industrial relations systems did not develop. Needless to say, part-time workers were not included in this bargain.

The Labor Relations Adjustment Law   Along with the trade union laws, the Labor Relations Adjustment Law of 1946 (amended in 1949 and 1952) is of central importance to labour relations in Japan. Although grievances can ultimately be taken to the courts, the first route to settlement is through Labor Relations Commissions, established in every prefecture and at the national level under the Trade Union Law. These bodies act as conciliators or mediators in disputes, helping parties to resolve differences without recourse to litigation.

The *Shuntō*

The development of the postwar system reached completion with the introduction in 1954 of the 'Spring Bargaining Offensive' or *shuntō*. Starting with a core of left-wing unions in the Sōhyō federation, the movement quickly blossomed, incorporating some 4 million workers by 1961 (Koshiro 1983). In the *shuntō* process, unions in leading industrial sectors set the pace early in the year, asking for a common wage increase, to which employers respond with a counter-offer. Other industries then follow suit and although there may be some deviation from the common proposed wage increase, it serves as a useful benchmark. During the first 20 years, different industry groups were responsible for taking the lead in making settlements, but since 1975, the unions in the metalworking industries (IMF-JC) have set the pace. The IMF-JC unions have tended to be the most moderate and cooperative in their approach, as their industries must compete in the international market. In general, their approach is to push for wage increases that are based on productivity gains, and critics maintain that they have not pushed hard enough.

The union movement has been divided throughout the postwar period. At the most basic level, collective bargaining takes place at the enterprise level, although pattern bargaining does lead to coordinated settlements. Enterprise unions are in turn organized into industry federations which may, in turn, be subsumed under a national federation. There have been many different national federations over the past 50 years and Figure 5.1 traces their development and genealogy. The complexity of the diagram reflects the degree of disunity and weakness of the various federations. Since 1989 there has been greater stability. Today, the main federation is Rengō with over 7 million members out of a total of 11.5 million union members. Two other, more left-leaning federations are Zenrōren with roughly 1 million members and Zenrōkyō with roughly a quarter

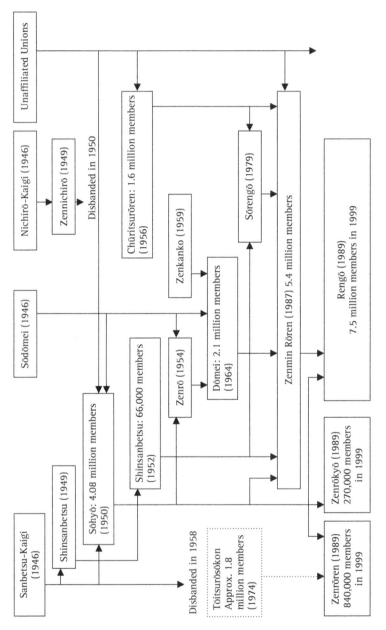

Figure 5.1. *The development of postwar labour organizations in Japan*

Source: Adapted from JIL (1992: 50–1).

of a million members. Rengō was formed by the merger of two different federations, Dōmei, which was the more centrist federation, comprising many of the manufacturing industries that have taken the lead in the *shuntō*, and Sōhyō, a more left-wing federation to which most public-sector unions belonged. In general, public-sector workers have tended to be most left wing in their approach, and since they are not under competitive pressures, they also tend to argue for higher wage settlements. The same can also be said of private sector workers working in industries such as railways that don't face international competition.

The Relations with Political Parties

The relationship of the union federations to the political parties has also had a mixed history. Sōhyō was heavily allied with the Japan Socialist Party, while Dōmei tended to favour the more moderate Democratic Socialist Party. After the founding of Rengō in 1989, Rengō tried to develop its own political party, similar to the labour parties of other countries, but without success. Recent attempts by the Democratic Party, the leading opposition party in Japan, to get support from Rengō have not been successful. Again, one has the impression of weak cohesion within the union movement.

THE DECLINE OF UNIONS SINCE 1973

Union density has been in decline in Japan since the oil shock of 1973, falling from 35% to less than 20% of non-agricultural employees by 2003. The decline in enterprise unionism is one of the main ways in which the employment system is changing. There are a number of explanations for the fall in density and here I will briefly point to some of the factors that have been important.

Change in the Composition of the Labour Force and the Structure of Industry

The decline in manufacturing, the increase in the number of women working as employees and the increased use of contract and part-time workers may all have contributed to the fall in density, if we assume that the propensity for any type of worker to be unionized remains constant. Table 5.1 shows that the drop in unionization rates between 1975 and 2002 has taken place within every industry except for construction. If we hold the industry unionization rates of 1975 constant and look at the change in the share of each industry in employment we find that only 3.3 percentage points out of the total 13.6 point drop can be explained by shifts in industrial composition. The remaining 10.3% drop must occur within industries, partly as a result of the feminization of the labour force and even more as a result of the greater use of part-time workers (most of whom are women). In order to account for these trends, I conduct a more comprehensive shift-share analysis to derive a counterfactual density that accounts for

Table 5.1. *Change in unionization rates by industry, 1975–2002*
(in per cent)

Industry	1975	2002	Change
All	34.5	20.2	−14.3
Construction	18.4	20.7	+2.3
Manufacturing	40.1	26.9	−13.2
Trade	11.2	8.6	−2.6
Finance, insurance and real estate	62.5	37.1	−25.4
Transportation and communications	65.8	35.7	−29.9
Utilities	71.2	57.1	−14.1
Services	26.2	11.7	−14.5
Government	67.6	58.7	−8.9

Source: MHLW2 (1975, 2003).

(1) changes in industry structure, (2) changes in the proportion of employees that are women, and (3) changes in the proportion of employees that work part time.[2] The result is that overall density should have fallen from 34.5% to 27.9% if the propensity of full-time workers to be unionized had remained constant. So consideration of all three factors now accounts for 6.6 points, or nearly half of the 13.6 point drop.

There are some other minor factors that will also have led to a decline in union density. For example, the ageing of the workforce has meant that firms have tended to increase the number of managerial posts per employee in order to maintain morale. Japanese union law prohibits employees of managerial rank from being members of unions, so this may have had a minor impact on total union density. A second factor that has had some influence is the decline in the proportion of employees that work in large firms. These two factors combined should account for less than one percentage point in the drop in density. Around half of the decline in the unionization rate remains unexplained.

The Decline in the Rate of New Union Births

The explanation for the remaining part of the drop in union density lies in the fact that new unions are not being organized. Figure 5.2 shows the numbers of union members in new unions and their share of all employees. It is clear from the chart that organization of new unions fell off dramatically after 1975. In fact, since a decline in union membership has been taking place at the same time (partly due to the dissolution of unions) the rate of unionization has dropped consistently since then.

A number of explanations have been put forward to explain this decline in the organization of new unions. Freeman and Rebick (1989) attribute the decline in

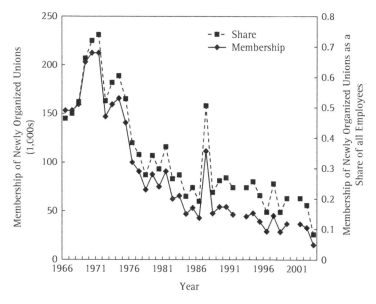

Figure 5.2. *Membership of newly organized labour unions and
share of employees 1966–2003*

Source: New members: MHLW2; employees: PMO2.

part to management resistance to the formation of new unions as profit margins have fallen since 1975. This is likely to be only part of the story, however. Another equally, if not more, important factor is that there is little interest in unionization when it does not deliver much in the way of better pay or working conditions (Tsuru and Rebitzer 1995). Most of the non-unionized firms follow the larger, unionized firms in determining their pay settlements. The result is, that, once firm size is taken into account, there is no discernible union-wage differential (Tachibanaki and Noda 2000).[3] Japanese union dues are relatively high at 2–3% of monthly pay and this also discourages potential members from joining.

Alternatives to Unions

The absence of unions does not necessarily mean that workers have no voice in the workplace. One such institution is the joint labour-management committee (JLMC) which exists in both unionized and non-unionized firms. Kato (2003) reports that some 80% of publicly traded firms had JLMCs in 1993. Among smaller firms these institutions are found in 90% of unionized firms, but in fewer than half of non-unionized firms (Sato 1997). The JLMC is primarily used for information-sharing and as a means by which management can consult with employees on a range of issues, including layoffs, fringe benefits, working hours, and pay. Management will often 'open its books' to the employee representatives, sharing information on sales, production, and even on plans for new product development. In unionized firms, these practices can smooth the bargaining that takes place before the annual *shuntō* (Morishima 1991*b*) and can raise labour productivity (Morishima 1991*a*). Kato (2003) notes, however, that there has recently been much less consultation in non-unionized firms on transfers, layoffs, and pensions and he suggests that unions may prevent JLMCs from becoming dormant, or else simply venues for management to announce personnel policy. If this is the case, then the decline in unionization rates will also weaken the role of JLMCs across the economy.

In addition to JLMCs, or as an alternative, many firms have non-union employee organizations. Surveys of employee organizations in small and medium-sized firms show that although they are often formed to organize leisure activities, roughly one in five non-unionized firms appears to have an organization that will discuss substantive workplace issues with employers (Nitta 1992; Sato 1997). In the majority of these cases, the main issues discussed are working hours, holidays, and safety and health.

One final alternative voice mechanism is to approach one's supervisor, possibly over after-hours drinks. Morishima (1999) notes that one of the problems facing the union movement is that this is the preferred method of dealing with grievances, even in unionized organizations. He cites one survey where 60% of employees indicated that they preferred to talk with their supervisors to air grievances. Only 15% would approach their labour union or employee organization.

CHALLENGES OF THE 1990s

The 1990s have brought additional challenges to the union movement as the long recession has made it difficult for unions to gain much in wage settlements during the *shuntō*. Table 5.2 shows that the average *shuntō* settlement for large firms has not declined in real terms over the past 10 years. The average wage settlement in the 1990s showed a 2.5% increase: not much lower than the average of 3.1 in the 1980s. Bonuses tell a different story, however. There has been an average decline in real terms in bonus payments over the past decade. In the case of both the wage increase and bonus increases that are reported, the figures show the average wage increase (increase in the wage bill divided by the number of employees) for the firm. For firms that have an ageing employee structure, this wage increase will largely be eaten up by the increases in wages that tend to accompany age and seniority. Thus, the actual increase from the point of view of the employee's lifetime earnings tends on average to be about 2% lower.[4] The average real increase in the 1990s for large unionized firms was around 0.5% per annum, and bonus payments fell by more than 2% per annum in real terms, once age- and seniority-based rises are taken into account.

The union membership has, however, been far more concerned about job security than pay, and willing to make major concessions (especially in bonuses). Again, unions in the export industries have been at odds with the public-sector

Table 5.2. *Annual wage and bonus increases for large firms, 1991–2003*

Year	Nominal wage increase	Real wage increase	Standardized interquartile range[1]	Rate of increase of bonus (real)[2]
1991	5.65	2.3	0.08	1.2
1992	4.95	3.3	0.11	−0.1
1993	3.89	2.6	0.12	−1.9
1994	3.13	2.4	0.12	−1.2
1995	2.83	2.9	0.10	1.3
1996	2.86	2.8	0.10	2.9
1997	2.90	1.1	0.11	1.0
1998	2.66	2.0	0.12	−1.0
1999	2.21	2.5	0.15	−4.7
2000	2.06	2.8	0.14	0.8
2001	2.01	2.7	0.15	3.0
2002	1.66	2.6	0.15	−4.2
2003	1.63	1.9	0.16	2.8

Notes:
[1] The standardized interquartile range is the difference between the third and first quartiles, divided by twice the median.
[2] Average of summer and winter bonus increases.

Source: Wage increases from JPC (2004), table C-33. Values for approximately 290 of the largest, listed, unionized firms. Bonus figures from MHLW4 (2004), table E-8, large firms only.

unions. Towards the end of the 1990s, the solidarity of the *shuntō* was broken both by individual firms and by industry federations. For example, Weathers (2001*b*) points out that the Federation of Steel Workers had no wage increase in 1995 and only token increases in the next two years. The electronic workers' federation Denki Rengō also began to delink its wage settlements from other sectors as firms began to individualize pay settlements. Finally, for the Spring Offensive of 2003, Rengō announced that it would no longer seek a unified wage increase, but would allow individual industry federations the freedom to negotiate separate wage settlements. Instead, the federation has now embarked upon a new strategy of 'minimum standards'.

Minimum Standards and the 2003 Spring Bargaining

The minimum standards advocated by Rengō are mainly based on the first decile of the wage distribution in 2002. Using the age- and seniority-earnings curves, standards are set for age levels up to age 35 and tenure up to 17 years. In addition, targets are set based on the average levels of 2002. Some examples of the minimums and targets are shown in Table 5.3.

The minimum for 'standard employees' with the maximum number of years of seniority is determined by looking at the first decile of wages reported by member unions. The minimum for newly hired employees is based on the average of the minimum earnings in existing collective agreements. The targets for 'standard'

Table 5.3. *Rengō's minimum standards and*
targets—Spring Bargaining of 2003

Age	Seniority	Minimum	Target
18	0	148,000	159,000
25	0	167,000	
30	0	185,000	
	12	216,000	264,000
35	0	205,000	
	17	245,000	305,000

Source: Rengō Internet web page.

employees are based on the average of wage settlements for skilled production workers in the unions surveyed.

The most important feature of this scheme is the desire on the part of the unions to maintain the wage curve up to age 35, including the seniority component. This seems to be the most important concern of employees. At the time of writing it remains to be seen whether or not this strategy will be successful. In addition to specifying minimums for standard employees, minimums and targets are also given for part-time workers. At 790 and 900 yen per hour respectively, they are substantially higher than the minimum wage mandated by the government, which is highest in Tokyo at 708 yen per hour. Part-time workers are barely represented in Japan (only 3% were organized in 2002), but the increasing use of part-time workers by firms means that standard employees must also take account of their wages.

The unions are also pressing for limitations to the use of unpaid overtime work and for increased use of vacation days by employees. Although working hours fell in the early part of the 1990s recession, unpaid overtime has increased as firms attempt to cut labour costs. It is very difficult for firms to force employees to go home if they feel that their career (or even their job security) with the firm depends on putting in extra work. In part, this problem is also related to the nature of work organization. Teamwork may mean that employees may need to wait for others to finish before their own work can be completed. This also makes scheduling vacations more difficult as any individual's absence may have a major impact on the work of others.

TRENDS IN LABOUR'S SHARE

One way to gauge the overall effectiveness of the labour movement is to look at trends in labour's share of national income. Figure 5.3 shows trends in the proportion of distributed national income that is in the form of employee compensation. Since the self-employed sector is in decline, we would expect this rate to be rising, other things equal. Therefore, I also show an 'adjusted labour share'

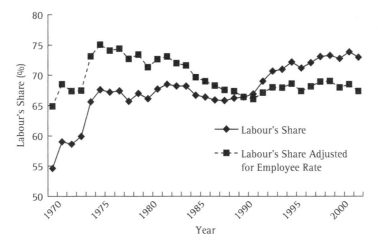

Figure 5.3. *Trends in labour's share of national income, 1970–2002*

Notes: Labour's share is the proportion of distributed national income that is paid to employees. This is divided by the proportion of employees among those employed to get an adjusted estimate of labour's share. This attributes the same average level of labour income to non-employees as to employees.

Source: JPC (2004), table A-1.

Table 5.4. *Trends in the number of labour disputes*

Year	Number of disputes	Number of participants	Percentage of disputes where no industrial action was taken
1970	4,551	9,137,473	17
1975	8,435	10,261,209	10
1980	4,376	5,455,560	15
1985	4,826	3,249,173	12
1990	2,071	2,026,232	18
1995	1,200	1,206,733	43
2002	1,002	1,004,833	70

Source: MHLW4 (2004), table I-12.

which divides the ratio by the proportion of employed who are employees, normalized at unity in 1990. Using the adjusted series as a guide, we see that labour's share rose rapidly in the early 1970s, a period of intense activity on the part of the labour movement (Table 5.4). Since 1975, however, and the advent of the more cooperative Dōmei unions, labour's share fell until 1990 before levelling out. It has risen slightly since 1990, more as a reflection of poor profit levels than of any real gains on the part of labour.

TRENDS IN WORKER DISPUTES AND COURT CASES: GREATER INDIVIDUALISM

Industrial relations have been quiet in the past few decades and the number of disputes has fallen sharply in the 1990s, reflecting the weak state of the labour market. The weakness of labour's position is reflected not only in the falling number of disputes, but also in the fact that a rising percentage of disputes are settled with no action taken on labour's part. The last few years of the 1990s also saw a fall in the proportion of disputes concerned with wage levels and a relative increase in those concerned with the firing of workers (Table 5.4).

The fact that unions have been quiet does not reflect the true state of employee–employer conflict, however, as there has been a steady increase in the amount of litigation that has taken place, mostly reflecting individual law suits over dismissal. The increase in such litigation may be seen as a reflection of the declining role of the Central Labor Commission and of labour unions in dispute resolution. Most of the increase in civil litigation has occurred within the category of the 'regular procedure', which involves a fuller treatment and is regarded as more serious than the preliminary injunction process (Nakakubo 1996). Most of the cases are brought by individuals, and most relate to wages, but dismissals also feature prominently.

Civil litigation is a cumbersome way for disputes to be resolved and the average time needed for a court decision in the first instance is more than one year. If the case is taken all the way to the Supreme Court, the entire process can take decades. The increase in the numbers of new cases began with the downturn in the economy in 1992, but, as indicated in Table 5.5, the growth has continued

Table 5.5. *Civil suits initiated in district courts under the regular procedure, 1990–2002*

Year	Number of suits
1990	647
1991	662
1992	892
1993	1307
1994	1507
1995	1552
1996	1525
1997	1656
1998	1793
1999	1802
2000	2063
2001	2119
2002	2309

Source: Hōsō Jihō (1995, 2003).

throughout the last decade. Given the difficulties involved in bringing a suit to the courts, this increase is probably a reflection of much greater levels of underlying dissatisfaction. It may also reflect the ongoing individualization of labour contracts and the decline of the importance of unions in general.

Although the introduction of individualized performance-related pay is a cause of considerable anxiety for employees, labour unions have not been very successful in influencing managerial decisions concerning the implementation of these plans. Morishima (1999) suggests that unions need to take the initiative by actually promoting the introduction of pay-for-performance schemes, but in a manner that allows for the greatest transparency in the evaluation process and that prevents abuse by managers. He admits, however, that this will not be easy, as the increasingly white-collar workplace has a greater diversity of employee interests than in the past, in part due to greater specialization of employees.

CONCLUSIONS

Enterprise unionism was held to be one of the central pillars of the Japanese industrial relations and employment system. Although it is still a presence and the *shuntō* hobbles on in modified form, the rise of individual grievance cases in the courts suggests that, as in other industrialized countries, the ability of unions to successfully fight downsizing in the current economic climate is limited. Furthermore, unions have had little success in organizing part-time workers. The increased use of part-time workers undermines the bargaining power of the union movement in addition to its effect on union density. Finally, on the positive side, it should be noted that the union movement continues to provide considerable wage flexibility. Although there are some critics who believe that high wages may bear some responsibility for the recent rise in unemployment, labour's share declined in the 1980s to levels not seen since the early 1970s. There are other, more convincing explanations for the rise in unemployment. It is to this subject that I now turn.

NOTES

1. It was this kind of action that led directly to the courts providing better job protection. The development of the four required conditions for dismissal (see Chapter 2) was intended to prevent firms from undertaking this kind of purge in the future.
2. I compute how much the total density would have dropped if we assume that part-time workers have a unionization rate of zero and then compute the male and female union densities for full-time workers separately for each one-digit industry for 1975. As Labour Force Survey data is used, full-time is defined here as working more than 35 hours per week. I then apply these 1975 densities for full-time workers to 2002 figures for the numbers of full-time men and women in each industry and compute the 'counterfactual' number of union members that would exist if the industry-specific full-time worker densities had remained constant. This figure is then divided by the total number of employees to derive a counterfactual density that accounts for (1) changes

in industry structure, (2) changes in the proportion of employees that are women, and (3) changes in the proportion of employees that work part time.

3. There is evidence that unions do have an effect on benefits and working conditions (Tachibanaki and Noda 2000; Nakamura *et al.* 1988), but this may not be generally well understood.

4. JPC (2001, table C-38) makes it clear that expected rises contributed about 2% on average to wage increases in the 1990s.

PART III

MAJOR TRENDS IN LABOUR
MARKETS

6

Rising Unemployment and Inequality

Japan's postwar economic expansion was admired not only for the high rate of economic growth, but also for the low rates of unemployment and the egalitarian income distribution that appeared to accompany it. The 1990s have seen not only the destruction of the myth that Japan would continue to outperform the other OECD economies in terms of growth, but also a rise in the rate of unemployment to American and British levels, and a growing debate about the extent of inequality. This chapter looks at both of these issues, starting with the recent move to what the Japanese call 'high unemployment'.

THE RISE IN UNEMPLOYMENT

No single change to Japan's labour market has been as startling as the rise in the unemployment rate in the late 1990s. Japan has been blessed with close to full employment since the end of the 1940s. As Figure 6.1 illustrates, the unemployment rate had been rising slowly since the early 1970s, with a major dip during the bubble period of the late 1980s and early 1990s. It then began to rise more rapidly after 1992, with a very rapid increase after the Asian Financial Crisis of 1997–98, reaching almost 6% in late 2002. This latest climb has been shocking

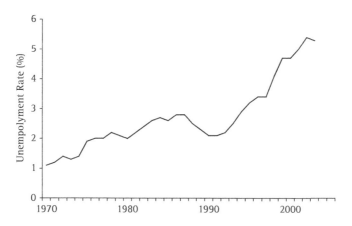

Figure 6.1. *The unemployment rate*
Source: MHLW4 (2002), table A-2.

to a society used to very low unemployment and has led to much discussion about the appropriate policy response. I begin my analysis of the unemployment situation by examining the definition of unemployment in Japan.

IS JAPAN'S UNEMPLOYMENT RATE UNDERESTIMATED?

Taira's Criticism

There is a general misconception in the wider public that Japanese unemployment figures are underestimates.[1] Whatever the shortcomings of the unemployment measures, it has become common practice to use the International Labor Organization definitions of unemployment for purposes of international comparison. Table 6.1 shows the differences between the ILO definitions and those used in Japan, the USA, and the UK. In 2000, the government's published rate and the ILO-adjusted rate were both 4.7% (OECD1 2001; PMO2 2000).

Taira (1983) opened the debate about Japan's unemployment figures by claiming that the Japanese unemployment rate was undercounted relative to the American rate. Taira noted that there were three differences that contributed to an undercounting of the Japanese rate.[2] In Japan, individuals who have been offered a job and are waiting to take up that job are not counted as unemployed, whereas in the USA until 1993, they would be considered to be unemployed until they took up the job in question. Taira used data from the Special Survey of the Labour Force Survey taken in March of the years from 1977–80 to show that there was a large number of individuals in this category in Japan. The second of the differences was that in Japan there are a large number of individuals who remain employed by their companies, but are sent home (usually at reduced pay) on a temporary basis. These individuals are not counted as unemployed in the Japanese statistics, but Taira felt that they should be. Thirdly, Taira noted that one is counted as being in the labour force and employed if one works just one hour per week in Japan, whereas one needs to work 15 hours in the USA. There was a substantial number of women family workers who worked less than 15 hours per week in this period. In all, Taira estimated that the Japanese unemployment rate was undercounted by between 1.04 and 1.86%. The differences for women were the most striking—their unemployment rate was undercounted by up to 6%.

Taira's work came under immediate criticism (Sorrentino 1984; Kurosaka 1988). First, it was pointed out that March is the month when many students finish their studies and it is common for students to take a vacation together with their classmates, recognizing that once they start work with a Japanese firm, their ability to take such vacations will be severely limited. Critics of Taira argue that it would be unreasonable to count such individuals as unemployed as they are really just taking a planned vacation. Secondly, there was criticism of Taira's decision to count workers sent home on a temporary basis as unemployed. Unlike laid-off workers in the USA, the Japanese employees were guaranteed

Table 6.1. *Unemployment definition–some international comparisons*

ILO	Japan	USA	UK
• Not at work • Able to work during survey period • Looking for work during survey week or waiting to take up job	• Not at work • Able to work during survey week • Looking for work during survey week	• Not at work • Able to work during survey period • Searched for work during previous month	• Not at work • Able to work • Want to get paid work • Registered at an employment office on day of survey
• If on temporary layoff may be unemployed even if not looking for work	• If waiting to learn results from search activity taken prior to survey week then unemployed even if not searching actively	• Workers on temporary layoff are unemployed whether or not searching for work.	• Military personnel are excluded from labour force
• Unpaid family workers are considered to be at work	• Unpaid family workers are considered to be at work, if worked at least one hour	• Unpaid family workers working less than 15 hours a week are not considered to be labour force participants	
• Unpaid family members are considered to be at work no matter how many hours are worked	• Military personnel are considered part of labour force	• Military personnel are excluded from labour force	

Note: In all cases the unemployment rate is calculated by dividing the number of unemployed by the labour force (sum of unemployed and those who are at work).

Source: PMO1 (August 2001).

a recall under the Japanese system. This criticism, however, begs the question of what the unemployment rate is supposed to indicate. As a measure of human discomfort, it would seem to be inappropriate to count these employees as unemployed—they may suffer some loss in pay and inconvenience, but they are still employed and receive payment from their employer. On the other hand, if one's interest is in the state of the economy and the use of resources, they should surely be counted as unemployed. In total, if we accept the objections to counting the new graduates and the employees not at work, the differences between the Japanese and American rates become minimal. If one considers the employees sent home as unemployed, then the difference is somewhat larger—around half of a percentage point.

Labour Hoarding

If the main concern is with the extent to which labour is under-utilized, then even the correction for the numbers of workers sent home will be an underestimate of the problem. Darby *et al.* (2001), for example, use deviations of output per worker hour over the business cycle to show the extent to which Japanese firms hoard labour during recessions. They estimate that, according to these measures, the unemployment rate may be two or three percentage points higher. Since they also find that labour hoarding of roughly 2% of the labour force occurs in the USA and UK, it is not clear whether Japan needs to be singled out for special treatment on this issue.

A somewhat different approach may be taken using the quarterly survey known as the Survey on the Labour Economy run by the MHLW. The survey samples 5,400 establishments and asks whether various measures of business activity are expanding or contracting. One of the questions is whether the firm believes that it holds a surplus or a shortage of employees. An index can be generated from the results of this question showing the percentage difference between the firms that claim to have a surplus versus those that claim a shortage. Although this index is quite crude it is useful for econometric estimation of the extent of the surplus labour problem. One method used is to regress the difference index against labour's share of income in the national economy. The equation used is:

$$DI = \text{constant} + a \times DI_{-1} + b \times \text{Labour's Share} + \text{time trend}, \qquad (6.1)$$

where DI is the difference index. Using the estimate of b (>0), one then calculates how much labour's share would need to fall to bring the DI back to 0. If one then assumes that all of this drop would be accomplished by firing employees, one can get an estimate of the extent of excess employment. Using this method the Cabinet Office (formerly the Economic Planning Agency) and the research centres of various banks have produced estimates for the years 2000 and 2001 ranging from 1.4 to 3.3 million employees or 2.3 to 5.5% of employment. There are other methods of estimating the levels of excess employment, but in general most estimates are in this range (MHLW7 2001). If the upper bound of these estimates is accurate, then the extent of this problem is comparable in magnitude to the official unemployment problem and greater than that measured by Darby *et al.* (2001). If all of these employees could be used more efficiently, there might be substantial benefits to the Japanese economy. Using a simple Cobb–Douglas production function for the economy, and taking labour's share at 0.7, the various estimates just mentioned imply that production could be increased by up to 4%.

Hidden Unemployment and Underemployment

One other criticism of the unemployment rate comes from those who point out that there are a large number of individuals who are not in the labour force, but would like to be working, usually referred to as discouraged workers. Genda (2001) uses data from the Special Survey of the Labour Force Survey (SSLFS) to show that the numbers of those individuals who are not in the labour force but who would like to work, and have actually looked for work in the previous year are roughly the same as the number of unemployed. More systematic studies have been done to arrive at essentially the same conclusion using a time-series approach (Hart and Kawasaki 1999; Rebick 1994). Fluctuations in the labour force participation rate away from long-term trends are analysed to show that 'hidden' unemployment of this sort can match the unemployment rate in downturns and that this is especially evident for middle-aged women.

To gain some idea of the conditions in 2001, I have followed the practice of Genda (2001) and used the SSFLS from February 2001 to look at the extent of hidden unemployment or underemployment (PMO1, 2/2001). The figures are shown in Table 6.2. Although women have a lower unemployment rate than men, the extent of the hidden unemployment problem is greater in their case. The second row of Table 6.2 shows that non-employed women roughly comparable to

Table 6.2. *Unemployment and underemployment in 2001*

Category	Numbers expressed as a percentage of labour force		
	All	Men	Women
Unemployed	4.8	4.9	4.6
Not in labour force but wish to work	14.7	6.2	27.1
Have already graduated from school and looked for work in the previous year	2.8	0.9	5.6
Working 1–35 hours per week and would like to work more than 35 hours per week	1.8	0.8	3.2
Employed but not at work due to bad business condition	0.2	0.2	0.1

Source: PMO1 (February 2001).

a quarter of the female labour force would like to work. Much of this may be wishful thinking, however, if they are actually constrained by household responsibilities. I also report the numbers that have actually sought work in the past year as a better indicator of the extent of hidden unemployment. Here we can see that although the numbers of men only represent some 1% of the labour force, women in this category make up 5.6% of the labour force, greater than the number of unemployed (4.6%).

Along with those without work, we should also consider those individuals who are underemployed. The figures for those working less than 35 hours a week who would like to work more hours show that while the numbers of men are relatively small, the number of underemployed women is much higher. The numbers of men and women who are employed but not at work because of bad economic conditions at work are relatively small.

The significance of these facts must be taken in international perspective, however. All countries experience the same kind of discouraged worker effects if the International Labour Organization (ILO) definition of unemployment is considered, and in some countries such as the UK the extent of 'hidden' unemployment is much greater. OECD1 (1995) considered both the discouraged worker effect and the numbers of workers who are working part time on an involuntary basis. They found that, even with these factors taken into account, Japan still had the lowest levels of labour market slackness in 1993.

Summary

To summarize the discussion so far, although Japanese unemployment rates do not depart too much from the standard ILO definitions (and may even be too high), there is today hidden unemployment or underemployment comparable in magnitude to that stated in the official figures. This is consistent with the findings of other researchers for the period prior to the 1990s. There is also a prevalence of labour hoarding that may be comparable in magnitude to the official figures on unemployment.

EXPLAINING THE RECENT RISE IN UNEMPLOYMENT

Why has the Japanese unemployment rate risen only in the late 1990s, rather than earlier during the decade? The previous section indicated that the rise in separation rates is the proximate cause of the increase in the unemployment rate. In this section, however, I look at reasons why the accession rate was not able to rise to absorb the unemployed.

The Role of Structural Shifts

If we look first at the structural shifts that have taken place in the labour market, we can get some insight into what has taken place. Table 6.3 shows the

Table 6.3. *Changes in the industrial structure of employment, 1992–2002*

Industry	Employment (millions)		
	1992	1997	2002
Agriculture, forestry, fishing, mining	4.17	3.57	3.01
Construction	6.19	6.85	6.18
Manufacturing	15.69	14.42	12.22
Utilities	0.33	0.36	0.34
Transportation and communications	3.85	4.12	4.01
Trade	14.36	14.75	14.38
Finance, insurance and real estate	2.62	2.53	2.41
Services	14.81	16.48	18.04
Government	2.04	2.15	2.17
Total	64.36	65.57	63.30

Source: PMO2 (1992, 1997, 2002).

number of employees in major industry groups between 1992 and 2002. The most striking fact is that employment in manufacturing has dropped by almost 3 million between 1992 and 2001 with 55% of the drop taking place in the four years since 1997. Manufacturing has dropped from 24% of the labour force to just 19% over this 10 year period. There has been a massive amount of new investment in this period in other Asian countries, especially China, in response to the relatively high labour costs in Japan. According to the Economic Planning Agency (now the Cabinet Office), the share of manufacturing activity in Japanese firms that took place overseas rose from 3% in 1985 to 14% in 2001 (MHLW7 2002).

Along with the decline in jobs in manufacturing, we should also note the contribution of construction, transportation and communications, and trade to the rise in the unemployment rate since 1997. Table 6.3 indicates that employment in these three industries grew until 1997 and then declined. In the case of construction, the 1990s saw numerous attempts by the government to increase aggregate demand through public works, but pressure from the rapidly increasing government debt has seen cutbacks in this area (MHLW7 2002). As Higuchi (2001) points out, Japan has very high levels of spending on public works relative to GDP by international standards, and Keynesian fiscal policy through public works spending has been applied during downturns for most of the postwar period. By the late 1990s, however, the size of the government debt (approaching 150% of GDP) had limited the willingness of the government to use fiscal policy in this manner, and Prime Minister Koizumi, in particular, has tried to cut public works spending, even during the downturn of 2001–2.

The trade sector, including eating and drinking establishments, has been affected by sluggish demand, but also by deregulation, which has led to an exodus of family-run firms from this sector, as explained in Chapter 4. Ohta and Genda (1999) show that falling employment in the construction and small-firm sectors has been correlated with the increase in unemployment. The importance of the small-scale sector becomes evident when we look at the employment losses due to business failures over the past few years. For example, the job losses due to the closing of establishments in the manufacturing, construction, and retail trade sectors were of far greater importance than downsizing within establishments in determining the fall in employment in these industries (MHLW7 2002). Although not all establishment closures are due to business failure, most of the job destruction due to business failure has occurred in the small firm sector. Out of some 19,000 bankruptcies in 2001, 98% occurred in firms with a capital stock of less than 100 million yen (METI 2002). The fact that new start-ups failed to keep up with bankruptcies puts most of the blame for the fall in employment on the poor performance of the small-firm sector.

The extent of the sectoral shifts gives us another clue to the rise in unemployment—mismatch in the labour market, as those who lose jobs in manufacturing and construction find that they lack the skills needed for work in other industries.

Increased Mismatch in the Labour Market

The Outward Shift of the Beveridge Curve   If we look solely at the vacancy figures for the early 2000s we find that there have been other periods when the vacancy rate has been as high without such high unemployment. For example, the vacancy rate in 2001 was almost as high as that of 1988, at the start of the bubble period. Figure 6.2 shows the Beveridge Curve for the years from 1963 to 2001. The Beveridge Curve made a shift to the right between 1974 and 1978, but it is after 1997 that we see a major outward movement. The earlier shift can be explained in part by the expansion of welfare benefits that occurred in Japan in the mid-1970s (Nickell *et al.* 2003). The more recent shift is probably due to a mismatch of the supply and demand for skills in the market. The Japanese government in its White Paper on the Labour Economy for 2002 (MHLW7) defines frictional/structural unemployment in recent years as that unemployment which lies above the Beveridge Curve as it was located in the years 1990–93. Under their estimates, frictional unemployment would have been minimal during those years, but rose rapidly, reaching 4% by the end of 2002 (MHLW7 2002). This seems to exaggerate the extent of frictional unemployment, since the years 1990–93 are, as Figure 6.2 indicates, somewhat unusual in that the Beveridge Curve has actually moved to the left. If we consider the years 1983–90 as our reference point, for example, we would reduce the frictional component to be somewhere between two and three percentage points.

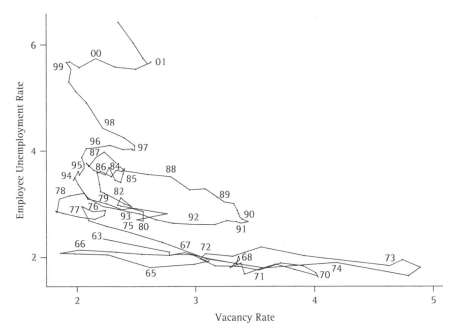

Figure 6.2. *Unemployment versus vacancies by year*

Notes: The employee unemployment rate is defined as the number of unemployed divided by the sum of the unemployed and employees. The vacancy rate is defined as the number of unfilled vacancies divided by the sum of the number of unfilled vacancies and employees.

Source: MHLW7 (2002), suppl. p. 38.

METI–Recruit Study A study by METI and the organization Recruit in 2001 provides more direct evidence of the extent of the nature of the mismatch problem. They surveyed a large number of businesses and job-seekers across 60 occupational categories and found that while the aggregate numbers of vacancies and job-seekers in their sample were approximately equal at 690,000 and 740,000 respectively, there were wide variations within occupation categories, with the ratio of vacancies to applicants ranging from 9.95 to 0.05 (METI-Recruit 2001). A major problem highlighted in the same study was the lack of necessary qualifications and/or prior work experience of job applicants, especially in some of the more specialized occupations such as IT-related work. The same report noted that the flow of information must be improved so that individuals (or outplacement departments) might improve the quality of the skill training provided in order to resolve the mismatch problem.

Information Problems in the Labour Market

The provision of information on both sides of the labour market needs greater development in Japan (Ono and Rebick 2003). The fact that most training occurs internally within companies, and the relatively poor development of specialized skills, means that many workers are unable to describe their skills in a way that is helpful for a potential employer.[3] Outplacement services and other labour market intermediaries are being developed, but employers continue to complain that they do not have enough information about potential mid-career hires. It is not just the labour supply side that provides weak information. Employers also find it difficult to tell employees exactly what will be required at their new job, since job definitions are so flexible in Japan. Misunderstandings can easily develop in such situations and the possibility of mismatch increases. The solution to these problems is not easy. On one level it seems that there should be greater encouragement of private labour market intermediaries that can specialize in the placement of unemployed workers. But the very nature of the Japanese personnel management system will always present a problem in this kind of labour market.

To summarize the discussion so far, it appears that the early to mid-1990s was a period where there was some compensation for the decline in employment in manufacturing because vacancies were being filled in some of the service industries and construction, presumably in jobs that did not have high skill requirements. In the late 1990s, however, there appears to have been a shift in the nature of the vacancies that have appeared and skill requirements have increased for many of the new job openings since 1997. The decline in employment in construction and the trade sector must also be contributing to the mismatch problem, as skills acquired in these industries would not necessarily be useful elsewhere. Information problems plague the Japanese labour market, but it is not clear to what extent these are intrinsically related to the closed nature of the training system and to what extent they might be helped by the development of better employment counselling services.

THE EMPLOYMENT INSURANCE SYSTEM

The Japanese government refers to its unemployment benefit programme as 'employment insurance' since the government's stated aim is to keep individuals in employment as long as possible, even if subsidies are required. For unemployed workers, the scheme pays out benefits equal to between 60 and 80% of the individual's wage rate. The length of the period for which benefits are paid out ranges from 90 to 330 days and depends on (1) the number of years that one has been insured, (2) the age of the employee, and (3) whether the separation from the last job was voluntary or not. The employment insurance system also provides benefits for child-care leave and for older workers whose wages drop more than 15% after the age of mandatory retirement.

Funding

The insurance system is funded through a combination of payroll taxes and employer contributions that averages 1.75% of base pay.[4] The large

Table **6.4.** *Spending on labour market programmes for five OECD countries, 1999–2000*

Country	Spending on active programmes (% GDP)	Spending on passive programmes (% GDP)	Total
Japan	0.28	0.54	0.82
USA	0.15	0.23	0.38
UK	0.37	0.58	0.94
France	1.36	1.76	3.12
Germany	1.23	1.89	3.13

Notes: Active labour market programmes include public employment services and administration, labour market training, subsidized employment, and measures for the disabled. Passive labour market programmes refers to unemployment compensation and early retirement programmes.

Source: OECD1 (2001).

increase in unemployment in the late 1990s has put the system under pressure, as the total level of general benefits (i.e. benefits that aren't targeted at special groups such as the disabled) has risen from 670 billion yen in 1990 to nearly 2 trillion yen or 0.4% of GDP in 1999. This does not represent the entire expenditure of the programmes however, which total around 0.54% of GDP according to OECD estimates. The size of the overall spending by the Japanese government is not large by OECD standards, although it is higher than that of the USA. Table 6.4 gives some comparisons. Japan does not spend as much as Germany and France, but this is partly because its unemployment problem is smaller.

Training Programmes

There are a number of programmes that provide for retraining of unemployed workers and for those who complete a study and training course approved by the Ministry of Welfare, Health and Labour, 40% of fees up to 300,000 yen are reimbursed. This is a relatively recent innovation, as previously support for retraining was given to companies to encourage them to retrain their own employees. The new approach aims to avoid the misuse of these funds as individuals shop around for the best courses on offer. Furthermore, the level of these benefits is not very high and may be inadequate for providing the level of training needed to make a difference in the job market (Higuchi and Kawade 2003).

Changes in the Targeting of the Programmes

The move towards the targeting of individuals, including those with special needs is part of an ongoing trend away from the employment policies of the 1970s as shown in Table 6.5. Starting in 1975 and facing the first major recession since the early 1950s, the government implemented the Employment

Table 6.5. *Trends in budget allocations for employment stabilization and other labour market programmes (as a percentage of total)*

Programme	1978	1988	1998
Employment maintenance	83.6	14.6	16.4
Persons with special difficulty finding work	–	46.7	28.6
Elderly workers	–	16.2	20.5
Regional employment development	–	8.6	4.1
Human resources development	0.8	3.7	10.5
Small and medium-sized companies	1.5	0.7	1.7
Job creation	–	–	2.7
Labour mobility without unemployment	–	–	2.0
Other	14.1	9.5	13.5

Notes:
1. These programmes are only part of all government expenditure on labour. For example, unemployment and injury insurance payments are not included.
2. 'Employment maintenance' represents employment-adjustment policies.
3. 'Persons with special difficulty in finding employment' represents grants for employment development for specified job applicants, provided to expand opportunities for persons with special difficulty in finding employment.
4. 'Elderly workers' represents funds provided to expand employment opportunities for elderly workers, and to encourage diverse modes of work.
5. 'Small and medium-sized companies' represents support for employee acquisition and the improvement of the employment environment in small-and medium-sized companies.

Source: MHLW7 (1999).

Adjustment Subsidy system that provided subsidies for firms which avoided dismissing their employees. The subsidies were to be used for retraining, for the secondment of redundant workers to other firms, or to send workers home on a temporary basis. Critics of this approach noted that the subsidies probably had little direct effect on the unemployment rate, and were mainly transfers of public funds to the firms concerned (Shinotsuka 1985). To the extent that they helped struggling firms survive, they might have helped the unemployment problem, but they would also have impeded the mobility of labour out of sectors that were in long-term decline.

The shift in the 1980s in employment policy was towards targeting particular groups that had problems such as older workers, the disabled, single mothers, or the repatriated war-displaced Chinese orphans of Japanese parentage. Since the late 1990s more emphasis has been placed on skill development and retraining. Firms are encouraged to retrain redundant employees before dismissing them so that there can be 'job mobility without unemployment'.

There are, however, other types of public policy on employment that are not managed by the Ministry of Health, Welfare and Labour. An indirect form of employment-stabilization policy may be found in the reluctance of the government to push for a rapid resolution of the problems in the Japanese financial sector, as well as its continuing reliance on public works projects to maintain demand (largely in construction). Prime Minister Koizumi has promised voters that he will tackle these issues, even if higher unemployment results. Nevertheless, his ability to make meaningful reform in these areas has been mostly blocked by his own party, as many LDP politicians are heavily dependent on contributions from the small business and construction sector. This is one of the principal ways in which government policy operates to prevent high unemployment. More rapid resolution of the bad loan problem and more rapid deregulation of the service sector and distribution system would undoubtedly lead to higher levels of unemployment, at least in the short run. Proponents of structural change argue that the economy would rapidly adjust to a low unemployment equilibrium, but the experience of European countries (which share a number of institutional features in the labour market with Japan) suggests that this may not necessarily be the case.

Finally, as pointed out earlier, Japan has always relied heavily on public works spending as a means of ensuring full employment (Higuchi 2001). The opportunity to work is considered to be a basic right that is written into the Japanese constitution, and this may be part of the reason why governments feel they must create jobs if none are available in the private sector. A much more important factor, however, is the role that public works spending plays in Japanese politics and in financial support for the ruling Liberal Democratic Party in particular. This can be seen in the fact that much of the public works spending is concentrated in the rural constituencies of LDP politicians.

CONCENTRATION ON DEMOGRAPHIC SUB-GROUPS

Despite the relatively gloomy picture of unemployment in Japan, the worst problems are concentrated among youth and men over the age of 60. If we restrict our attention to married men who were heads of households and whose wives were under 55, the unemployment rate in 2001 was only 2.0% (PMO1 Feb. 2001), while the employment–population ratio was 96.7%. Thus, the rise in unemployment is unlikely to have a great impact on social stability. Single youths and older couples are better situated (at present) to cope with unemployment. Older couples have pension support while youth are able to cope by living with their parents.

Nevertheless, unemployment in both groups is likely to pose a more severe social problem in the future. The movement of the age at which public pension benefits are first received to 65 will create problems for men who become unemployed after the mandatory retirement at age 60 and don't find a second job. The youth problem is of even greater importance for the future of Japanese society. First, fertility is depressed since marriage decisions will be delayed if there is no steady income (especially for men). Secondly, many of the unemployed may suffer longer-term problems in the labour market. This may lead to a gradual increase in income inequality, a subject to which I now turn.

TRENDS IN INCOME INEQUALITY

The last five years have seen a debate among researchers in Japan about whether or not there has been a rise in income inequality in recent years. There are several different strands to this debate and I will consider them in turn, beginning with the debate about changes in disposable income.

Increasing Inequality?

Japan, according to recent studies (Tachibanaki 1998*b*; Ohta 2000), falls somewhere in the middle of OECD countries in its level of inequality. Tachibanaki (1998*b*), in a widely read book, argues that Japan has experienced a large increase in after-tax income inequality, with a rise in the Gini coefficient from 0.314 in 1980 to 0.365 in 1992. Much of this increase can be attributed to one factor—the huge rise in land prices over the 1980s, leading to great disparities in wealth according to whether or not one owned property. If implicit rents are considered part of income, then some of the rise can be explained by the bubble in land prices and is not directly connected to the labour market. Furthermore, much of this contribution to the rise in inequality would have been reversed since land prices have since fallen by more than 50%.

Ohtake (2000), using different data, comes to a similar conclusion about the size of the increase in inequality in after-tax income.[5] Ohtake has analysed the increase in inequality and finds that approximately one-third can be attributed to ageing of the population—the Gini coefficient for specific age groups increases with age. How much one worries about this factor depends on one's viewpoint. In so far as it does not reflect a fundamental change in the Japanese wage pattern, but is a demographic outcome, it can be discounted. It could be argued, however, that more effort should be made to reduce the inequality amongst the older part of the population.

Ohtake finds two other factors at work in the increase in inequality. The first is that there has been a rise in the share of single-person households, and their average (adjusted) income tends to be lower. Secondly, there has been increasing inequality among married couples of working age. In the 1960s and 1970s, women married to high-earning men tended to remain out of the labour force after marriage, but in more recent years the participation of these women has risen. In other words, the income effect from their spouse is not having as much of a dampening effect on their labour supply. The result is that overall family income has risen for a group that was already high in the income distribution, and this has also contributed to an increase in the Gini coefficient.

The Contribution of the Labour Market

The labour market's contribution to rising inequality has, as Ohtake has pointed out, come largely from ageing of the population. Table 3.6 shows the extent to which dispersion in earnings increases with age. It is natural for there to be greater disparity in the earnings of older employees as the Japanese pay system, like pay systems elsewhere in the world, will make greater distinctions as more is learned about the employee and as some employees are promoted ahead of others. Since this increase in disparity with age has always existed and is likely to be important as a motivating device in the firm, the increase in inequality due to ageing is unlikely to become the concern of public policy. Furthermore, if we consider lifetime income, the dispersion in expected income remains stable.

Nevertheless, there is a perception in Japan that inequality is growing. One reason for this may be that some groups, such as middle-aged managers, are experiencing greater dispersion in earnings as pay systems change, as discussed in Chapter 3. Another source of growing income dispersion, however, comes from the growth of the differential in earnings according to the size of the firm. Rebick (1992*b*) notes that the firm-size differential in average hourly earnings for men increased by over 10% between the early 1970s and the late 1980s, showing a reversal of the narrowing trend of the 1960s.

In order to investigate more recent movements in this differential, I use a procedure similar to the one that I used in Chapter 3 to investigate changes in seniority and age profiles. Using published cross-tables from the Wage Census, I estimate the following equation for men.

$$
\begin{aligned}
\text{Log Earnings} = a + b_2\text{--}b_4 \text{ Education Dummies} + c_1 \text{ Experience} \\
+ c_2 \text{ Experience}^2 + d_1\text{--}d_8 \text{ Industry Dummies} \\
+ e_1 \text{ Blue-Collar Dummy} + f_1 \text{ Large Firm} \\
+ f_2 \text{ Medium-Sized Firm} + \varepsilon \quad\quad (6.2)
\end{aligned}
$$

The large firm dummy is set to 1 for groups in firms with more than 1,000 employees, and the reference group is small firms with between 10 and 100 employees. Medium-sized firms fall in the 100 to 1,000 employee range. The sample is restricted to those cells that are for ages under 60.[6] The estimates for coefficient f_1 for the period 1982 to 2002 are shown for two different measures of earnings in Figure 6.3. The first is total monthly earnings including one-twelfth of annual bonuses and overtime pay. The second is average hourly earnings, calculated by taking total annual earnings divided by average hours worked per month.

The differential in average hourly earnings shows the same countercyclical behaviour that was documented for the 1970–87 period in Rebick (1992*b*). The differential in total earnings is also procyclical, but of greater significance is the fact that it has shown a net increase of 10 points over the two decades, converging with the differential for hourly earnings. The main cause of the convergence has been the adoption of the five-day work week among small firms. In the 1980s, employees in large firms worked roughly 180 hours per month and this declined to 175 hours per month by the end of the 1990s. Employees in small firms, however, worked an average of 203 hours per month in the early 1980s and this fell to 183 hours per month by the late 1990s. This reduction in the hours differential for small firm employees has come at

Major Trends

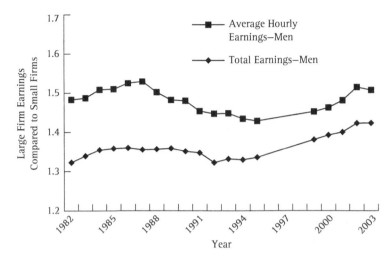

Figure 6.3. *Adjusted firm size differential—men*

Source: Computed from MHLW1, various years. For calculation method see text.

a price—their earnings have not risen as rapidly as those of large firm employees and, in fact, have fallen in real terms since 1992.[7] Thus, the 10% increase in the firm-size differential for men in total earnings may be another reason why Japanese have perceptions of growing inequality.

Turning to the movement in the firm-size differential for full-time women, Figure 6.4 shows that this has narrowed. This narrowing of the firm-size differential is related to the narrowing of the gender gap in smaller firms over this period, a topic that will be given fuller treatment in the next chapter. Although the narrowing of this differential is substantial, the numbers of full-time women workers are relatively small, so their impact on overall earnings inequality is likely to be small.

The widening of the firm-size differential for men is somewhat ameliorated, and the narrowing for women augmented, by a decline in the shares of men and women working in firms with over 1,000 employees or in those with 10–99 employees and a rise in the number of those working in firms with 100–999 employees (see Table 6.6). This movement towards the middle is responsible for the fact that most of the increased dispersion in earnings comes from ageing, rather than from movement in the firm-size differential.

Other Differentials One of the major changes in the US economy in the 1980s was the expansion of earnings differentials according to educational attainment. In particular, the earnings of college-educated men rose by 14% relative to those with only a high-school education (Katz and Revenga 1989). In Japan, by contrast, there has been little change in this premium. My estimates of the

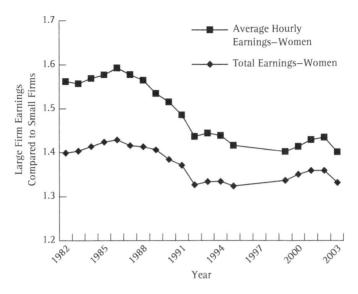

Figure 6.4. *Adjusted firm size differential–women*
Source: Computed from MHLW1, various years. For calculation method see text.

Table 6.6. *Shares of full-time employees by firm size, 1982 and 2003 (%)*

	More than 1,000		100–999		10–99	
	1982	2002	1982	2002	1982	2002
Men	35.2	30.0	31.2	36.0	33.7	33.9
Women	26.9	23.9	32.4	40.3	40.7	35.8

Source: MHLW1 (1982, 2003).

college/high-school earnings differential using regression analysis similar to that used earlier in this chapter suggests that this differential has increased by 2% over the last 20 years. Similarly, the white-collar/blue-collar differential has widened by about 2%. Of much more concern than the educational differential in earnings, however, is the relative concentration of unemployment among the less educated.

The Relation of Schooling to Unemployment   Table 6.7 shows unemployment rates according to education level for the year 2000. The table shows that unemployment rates are higher for those with lower levels of schooling. Japan is not unusual in this respect, and indeed, the education-based differential in unemployment rates is smaller in Japan than in most other OECD countries (Higuchi 2001). Nevertheless, this aspect of labour market performance is acting to increase inequality.

Table 6.7. *Unemployment rates by education level in 2000*

	Middle school	High school	Junior college	University
Men	7.9	5.5	4.4	3.0
Women	4.5	4.4	4.1	3.4

Source: PHPT (2000).

To summarize this section, the labour market has largely contributed to increased inequality through the ageing of the population. In addition, the last 10 years have seen an increase in the firm-size earnings differential and the increase in unemployment rates has been concentrated among the less well educated. Although this has not yet led to a major increase in income inequality, the perception of unfairness may well have increased as a result of these trends.

Trends in Social Mobility

Murakami's Thesis   The other main strand of research on inequality in Japan focuses on social mobility between generations. This is particularly important to sociologists who are interested in class structure in Japan, but it also has implications that will interest economists. Class consciousness has always been weak in Japan, in part because of the weakness of the labour movement. During the postwar period, however, the idea took hold that all Japanese were 'middle class'. In some opinion surveys, 90% have described themselves as middle class (Vogel 1979). In a widely read article, Yasusuke Murakami (1981) described Japan as having a 'new middle mass' politics.

These views receive support from research using the Social Stratification and Mobility Survey (SSM) of the University of Tokyo. For cohorts born in the late nineteenth and early twentieth centuries, the chances that one could attain a white-collar managerial position were very slim unless one's father came from the same background. On the other hand, for cohorts born after 1925, the relative chance that someone from a poorer background could rise to the top was much greater than it had been. This observation fitted in well with the view that since higher educational attainment was now available to all, the selection process whereby one entered better white-collar jobs in both the public and private sectors was essentially meritocratic. Large prestigious firms and the government appeared to select their candidates from the top-ranked universities and since entrance to these universities was determined by a written examination, everyone had a realistic chance of becoming part of the social elite. In other words, although there were great distinctions in status between high-level managers and bureaucrats and the rest of society, there was equality of opportunity for all.

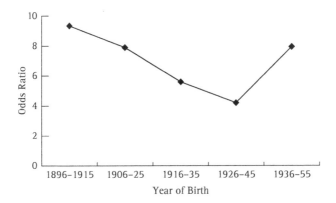

Figure 6.5. *The effect of parental background on likelihood of becoming a manager*

Note: The odds ratio represents the relative chance that an individual at age 40 has the same occupation as his father compared with individuals whose father did not have that occupation.

Source: Adapted from T. Sato (2000*a*).

Sato's Study using 1995 data In 1995, the SSM survey showed, however, that there had been a reversal of the trend that had been seen up to the mid-1980s. T. Sato (2000*a*, 2000*b*) examined the relative shares of managerial white-collar workers according to their father's occupation for different cohorts of men in their forties. Figure 6.5 adapted from Sato (2000*a*), illustrates his main argument. Here we see the following odds ratio calculated for different cohort groups. For the managerial occupational group j, we have

$$I = \frac{\text{men in j whose fathers were in j}}{\text{all men whose fathers were in j}} \div \frac{\text{men in j whose fathers were not in j}}{\text{all men whose fathers were not in j}}$$

(6.3)

This index is a measure of the relative degree of social mobility to the social elite. As the figure shows, the rate of mobility for the white-collar managerial class declined from the cohorts born in the late nineteenth and early twentieth centuries to the cohort born in 1926–45. However, the index rises again for the white-collar group thereafter, reaching the levels seen in the early twentieth century.

The primary cause of this change has been the shift in the occupational structure in Japan over the course of the twentieth century. In particular, Japan has seen a great movement out of agriculture in this period, and the number of managerial positions grew rapidly before stabilizing in the 1980s. Indeed, researchers have concluded that there has not been much of a change in class fluidity in Japan, once changing occupational structure has been taken into account (Ishida 1993). It is also worth noting that researchers find that social mobility in Japan is no greater, and may even be lower than in other industrial societies (Marshall *et al.* 1997).

Explaining the Trends   Given Japan's meritocratic selection to the white-collar and professional class, why has this reversal in mobility rates occurred? There are a couple of factors that may help to explain these facts. First, there is relatively low movement from the self-employed group between generations, as many Japanese men take over their father's business or have also tended to stay as self-employed.[8] Secondly, and perhaps more important, is the role of private education in raising the chances of entering a good university. Around 30% of Japanese children attend private high schools, and these tend to be children who were not accepted by the highest standard public high schools. This leaves a bimodal distribution of ability in the public high-school sector, with either very strong or very weak schools. Many of the private schools pride themselves on their abilities to get their graduates into the most prestigious universities. At the same time, most Japanese children attend privately run schools known as *juku* after school, which also help with examination preparation. A significant number of students who fail to be accepted at university spend an extra year attending such schools to prepare themselves for entrance examinations. The cost of all this private education can be substantial, and so the meritocratic system is biased towards those from a more affluent family background on cost grounds alone. It is also the case that the children born into the managerial class are likely to be given better support and early childhood education at home. The result is that, in Japan, as in other countries, class mobility is much more limited than suggested by the 'middle mass' concept, and with a slowdown in the growth of positions in the elite, the chances of progressing up have also declined.

Shifting Perceptions of Fairness   The SSM survey results cited in Sato (2000*a*) suggests that, there has been a shift of opinion in recent years, with those whose fathers are not in the managerial/professional class more likely to say that society is basically unfair (*amari kōhei denai*). Sato (2000*a*) also observes that, in the past, many blue-collar workers could look forward to leaving their company to set up their own small business, often as a subcontractor to their old firm. With the decline in the self-employment, however, this possibility is much reduced, and this may also have a demoralizing effect upon this group.

Future Prospects   It is in the future, however, that the possibility of a real increase in income inequality is of most concern. We have already seen that unemployment rates are highest among those without post-secondary education. Among youth, those without post-secondary education are also having the most difficulty finding regular employment. If this situation persists, there is a chance that over time a sharp division will arise between those households that have at least one member in regular employment (with all of the fringe benefits that are implied), and those that do not. The emergence of a substantial number of young men in non-standard employment is potentially preparing the ground for the development of a group of men without good career prospects. As in the USA, the worsening prospects of less-educated men have come at the same time as the prospects and treatment of women have improved. I now turn to look at the changes in the labour market for women in more detail.

NOTES

1. I base this statement on the number of questions that I get on this particular issue from those who are not labour specialists.
2. There are also differences that would tend to decrease the Japanese rate. Individuals who are not looking for work, but are waiting for the results of searches undertaken in the previous month or earlier, are counted as unemployed by the Japanese government, but would not be considered unemployed on either the US or the ILO definitions.
3. There is a running joke in Japan about the middle-aged job-seeker who, when asked in a job interview what skills he has, replies: 'I can be a kachō (section chief)'.
4. From October 2002. Employment insurance rates vary across industries from 1.55% to 1.85%.
5. There is some dispute as to whether or not one ought to consider public pension income as pre-tax income or not. Tachibanaki (2000) takes the view that public pensions are part of an overall tax and transfer system and so should not be considered. Ohtake (2000) argues that they should be counted in the interests of compatibility with US and other methods of calculating pre-tax income. My view is that if international comparisons are being made, the definitions need to be uniform. It is not clear what use there is in a measure of inequality that does not consider pensions. In a rapidly ageing society with a growing share of pensioners, there is a danger that one could exaggerate the extent to which inequality is increasing over time if pensions are ignored.
6. Inclusion of age groups over 60 does not substantially change the results.
7. We should remember, however, that hours of work in establishment-based surveys such as the Wage Census are understated in Japan, and that hours of work as measured by household surveys such as the Labour Force Survey do not indicate that hours have fallen to the same extent. So total earnings, rather than hourly earnings, are a more reliable measure.
8. This is less true today as self-employment is in decline.

7

Women in the Labour Market

The position of women in Japanese society is gradually changing. It is misleading to look only at the numbers of women taking the top management positions in firms, or to focus solely on income differentials. We must also appreciate the choices that are open to women today in Japan that did not exist in the past. I begin my discussion by discussing the changes in family formation that have taken place over the postwar period, focussing on the most recent developments.

THE CHANGING JAPANESE FAMILY

The position of women was described briefly in Chapter 2. There I noted that Japanese urban society has been characterized by a marked division of labour between men and women, with men more likely to work as employees or as self-employed managers of businesses, while women were more likely to work as unpaid workers in family enterprises or in the household. The 1950s and 1960s saw the development of patterns of urban family life that showed an extreme division of labour. Women who worked outside the home typically retired from their jobs at marriage, or at the birth of their first child, and then re-entered the labour market as part-time workers after their children had reached school age. Men worked long hours, six days a week, and socialized with their colleagues or business associates after work, returning late in the evening. Women did virtually all of the work in the household and children spent little time with their fathers.

Japan completed its demographic transition early in the postwar period with the total fertility rate dropping rapidly from 3.65 in 1950 to 2.04 in 1957 (Ogawa and Retherford 1993). The period of the late 1950s and 1960s was one of stable fertility and the variance in the age of first marriage has been low by OECD standards. Even by the late 1980s, 80% of all marriages for women occurred in their twenties (Brinton 1993). The traditional Japanese household held three generations, with the eldest son inheriting the responsibility for looking after the oldest generation. The younger siblings tended to move out to form separate households. Since the young parents of the 1950s and 1960s were born before the demographic transition, they tended to have several siblings. This meant that, even if the three-generation household survived, large numbers of 'nuclear families' were formed, often in the rapidly growing cities (Ochiai 1997). Nevertheless, the three-generation household continues to be an important feature of Japanese society, making up 10% of all households and 28% of all households with persons over the age of 65 in 2003 (MHLW2 2003).

Fertility Decline

The pattern of urban-nuclear family formation continued after the end of the rapid growth period, but starting in 1973 the fertility rate of women began to decline, falling steadily until the present. The total fertility rate in the year 2003 stood at 1.29, well below replacement (2.08). According to Retherford, *et al.* (1996), this decline in the marriage rate can be attributed to two main changes. First, the numbers of women who never marry has increased from 3% to 10%. Since out-of-marriage births are rare in Japan, this has been responsible for almost half of the decline in fertility. The other important factor is that the age of first marriage has risen over the last 30 years and this has led to a decline in the number of births within marriage, even though the desired family size reported in surveys has not fallen so rapidly. The low levels of fertility now mean that the Japanese population will decline after 2006, barring any changes to fertility or to immigration policy. I take these issues up more fully in Chapter 10.

CHANGES IN THE LABOUR MARKET

Participation and Employee Rate

The period since 1973 has also seen major changes to the market for women's labour. Table 7.1 shows the main trends in selected labour market indicators. Labour force participation rates have risen since 1980 by some seven points to reach the OECD average of 60%, although levels are some 10 points lower than those observed in the USA. This trend has continued throughout the 1990s, despite the poor economic climate. Higuchi (2001) notes that the tendency for women to withdraw from the labour market during downturns (the discouraged worker effect) has declined since the 1970s. Using panel data from the 1990s, he finds no evidence for either an added-worker or discouraged worker effect for women. Japanese women have developed greater attachment to work than in the past. This is also reflected in the delay in the age of marriage that I have just mentioned.

More remarkable than the change in participation, however, has been the rise in the percentage of women who are working as employees. This has risen by some 27 points since 1980, roughly one point per year, and is matched by the increase in the proportion of women who work part time. As I explained in Chapter 4, these two trends are both related to the decline in the number of family (and self-employed) workers in Japan. Finally, we can observe that the wages earned by part-time workers have fallen in relative terms since 1970. Part-time workers now earn a little more than half of what their full-time counterparts earn on average. This widening of the gap in hourly earnings between full-time and part-time workers is related to the narrowing of the gender gap for

Table 7.1. *Labour market indicators for women in Japan, 1970–2003*

	1970	1980	1990	2003
Labour force participation rate	52.9	52.4	57.1	59.9
Employees as a percentage of the employed	54.7	63.2	72.3	83.8
Women full-time workers' average hourly earnings as a proportion of men's	0.54	0.58	0.59	0.67
Part-time/full-time differential in average hourly earnings	0.76	0.69	0.56	0.55
Percentage of women employees who work part time	12.2	19.3	27.9	39.7[1]

Note:

[1] Figure is for 2002.

Source: MHLW4. LFPR computed for women aged 15–64. Wage differentials computed from MHLW1.

full-time workers—full-time women workers are earning more. Before I look at this trend, however, it is necessary to review some significant changes in the legal environment that have a bearing on this trend.

The Role of the EEOL and Japanese Labour Law

A number of landmark court cases in the 1970s established the rights of women to fairer treatment in the workplace (Upham 1987). The Equal Employment Opportunity Law (EEOL) of 1986 made it more difficult for firms to openly discriminate against women in hiring and promotion decisions. One should not put too much emphasis on the passing of this law, however, as it had several problems from the start. The Law lacked teeth in the sense that there were no penalties for violations. Many of the larger firms sought to get around the law by instituting a dual-track system of hires. 'General work' (*ippanshoku*) was distinguished from 'comprehensive work' (*sōgō shoku*) and this allowed women to self-select into the secretarial and clerical jobs that offered limited career prospects.

A problem of a different nature came from confusion about the purposes of the Law. As Hanami (2000) points out, equality was confused with protection. Japanese women are given protection under Japanese labour law from working late at night, working at heavy lifting, and so on. The original EEOL left these paternalistic restrictions in place, allowing employers to continue discriminating against women in some cases. In 1997, the EEOL was revised and most of these provisions were removed. Nevertheless, the revised Law is still weak on enforcement. Settlement of disputes is to take place by mediation, but there is no obligation on either side to accept the terms given by the Mediation Committee (Hanami 2000).

The preference for mediation over judicial settlement is characteristic of much of Japanese conflict resolution, and is an important basis for the Labour Relations

Law of the 1940s. This method of dispute settlement ultimately puts the responsibility for social change on the parties involved and in the case of the power imbalance between employers and their female (often non-unionized) employees this generally favours the status quo. Much of the change that does occur comes through the action of courts interpreting existing law.

It is difficult to measure exactly how much impact the EEOL has had on the market for women's labour. As I will discuss in more detail in Chapter 9, there has been a shift in the enrolment of women in higher education away from two-year college programmes to four-year university courses, and much of this shift occurred after 1986 (Edwards and Pasquale 2003). This shift in part reflects greater career aspirations on the part of women, and may have been stimulated by the EEOL.

Changes in Relative Earnings–The Gender Gap

The increase in the relative earnings of full-time women employees is partly responsible for the increased labour force participation of women–demand for their labour has risen. It is also true that the educational attainment of women has increased over this period. In 1950 only 37% of women went on to high-school education after completing middle school, and only 5% of women went on to tertiary education (MOE 2003). This means that many of the middle-aged and older women in the population today only have middle-school levels of educational attainment. By the end of the 1990s, however, the share of those with some secondary and tertiary education had risen to over 95% and 45% respectively. These rates are actually higher than the corresponding rates for men. About half of the women in tertiary education are attending two-year women's colleges, while the men overwhelmingly attend four-year universities. Nevertheless, it is undeniable that young women today are more highly educated and likely to have different attitudes to work than their older counterparts.

In order to consider the effects of improved schooling for women it is useful to estimate the trends in the gender differential after controlling for schooling, age, and the size of the firm. To do this, I again make use of the published cross-tables of the Wage Census. I measure the gender differential by using a model similar to that used in Chapter 3:

$$\text{Ln Earnings} = a + \text{Gender Dummy} + b_1\text{–}b_3 \text{ Schooling Dummies}$$
$$+ c_1 \text{ Experience} + c_2 \text{ Experience}^2 + \text{Industry Dummies}$$
$$+ \text{Firm-Size Dummies} + \text{Blue-Collar Dummy} + \varepsilon \qquad (7.1)$$

For each cell of the cross-table, the definition of average hourly earnings used is set equal to total monthly earnings plus one-half of the annual bonus payments, divided by the total number of hours worked. Here the schooling variables are dummy variables set to 1 if the employee has exactly that level of education. Experience is 'imputed experience' and is set equal to age-education years −6 where the number of education years is set to 9, 12, 14, and 16 for each of the

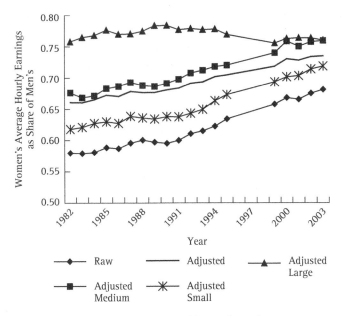

Figure 7.1. *Gender differential trends*

Source: Computed from MHLW1, various years. For calculation method see text.

schooling groups.[1] Regressions use weighted least squares, where the weights are the estimated number of employees in each cell. The sample is restricted to age groups under 60 to avoid any influence of mandatory retirement on earnings.

The results for the years 1982 through 2003 are shown in Figure 7.1. The gender gap narrows by from five to ten points when we account for age and education.[2] The figures also indicate, however, that of the 10 point narrowing of the raw gender gap between 1982 and 2003, roughly half can be attributed to ageing (i.e. greater potential experience) and increased educational attainment in the labour force. The four to five point narrowing of the gender gap from increased educational attainment and experience may seem small, but the improvement of the average human capital stock in the workforce only occurs incrementally as new cohorts of women enter the labour market and older women leave.

Some insight into the unexplained part of the narrowing of the gender gap can be obtained by looking at the adjusted gender gap separately, according to the size of the firm. Figure 7.1 shows the trends in the gender coefficient of equation (7.1) when the regressions are repeated separately for each firm-size category (without the firm-size dummy variables). The trend in the overall unadjusted gender differential is included for reference.

Several points can be made from this figure. First the adjusted gender gap is inversely related to the size of the firm. Secondly, there is convergence in the gender gap across firm-size sectors. Thirdly, there is no evidence here that the

EEOL had much direct impact on the gender gap in Japan. The narrowing of the gap seems to have been on a steady upward trend long before the law was enacted, and mainly occurs in the small and medium-sized sector. Indeed, the large-firm sector shows an expansion of the gender gap between 1986 and 2003. Although the EEOL may not have had much direct impact on the gender gap, Japanese legal precedents and gradually changing social norms may be forcing the smaller firms to adjust their practices to be more in line with those of large firms.[3] A more likely explanation, however, is that firms have begun to substitute (cheaper) full-time women workers for more expensive men in the medium-sized and small firms, but there is a limited supply of women who are able to work full time. By contrast, there is a very elastic supply of women willing to work part time, and this would explain why the part-time/full-time wage gap has widened.

The Full-Time/Part-Time Earnings Gap

The widening of the gap in earnings between full-time and part-time workers has become a major concern. It is often the case that older, married, part-time workers are employed to do exactly the same tasks as younger, unmarried full-time workers, but for much lower pay. This can generate a great deal of resentment in the workplace (MHLW7 2003: 166) and even lead to legal disputes. In just such a case, a judicial precedent was established in 1996 when a district court ruled that the discrepancy in pay between part-time and full-time factory workers at Maruko Alarms was too great. The court recognized that there were legitimate reasons for paying part-time workers less. For example, they would usually not be asked to work overtime. Nevertheless, the court ruled that the part-time workers should be paid 80% of the full-time wage in the interest of 'public order'. This judicial precedent has been very controversial, both because of the arbitrary setting of the 80% mark, but also because of its argument that equality of pay is a fundamental principle of 'public order' (Nakakubo 2002).

The Maruko Alarms precedent is unlikely to have a major impact on the payment of most part-time workers as it represented a special case. The MHLW is trying to promote better treatment and career development for part-time workers (MHLW7 2003). It is most likely, however, that the part-time/full-time wage differential will only be narrowed when the labour market for part-time women workers becomes tighter. As I will explain shortly, the Japanese tax and benefit system acts to increase the supply of part-time workers relative to full-time workers. Changes in legislation could lead to a more balanced labour market with a narrower full-time/part-time differential.

WOMEN'S POSITION IN THE FIRM

Management

As Table 7.2 suggests, there is a dearth of women in management positions in private Japanese firms. Nevertheless, there has been some change since 1982, with

Table 7.2. *Percentage of women in management posts*

Rank	1982	1995	2003
Division chief (*bucho*)	1.0	1.3	3.1
Section chief (*kacho*)	1.5	2.8	4.6
Supervisor (*kakaricho*)	3.4	7.2	9.4

Source: Computed from MHLW1 (1982, 1995, 2003).

the proportion of women at each level tripling between 1982 and 2003. The low proportion of women managers seems to be at odds with the views of researchers such as Wakisaka (1997) who believe that women do not face much discrimination in the workplace. The explanation for this paradox lies in the fact that women are much less likely to be working full time in the firm, and only full-time employees are likely to hold management posts. In other words, the low percentage of women managers may have two sources: (1) a shortage of candidates for management positions and (2) discrimination against women in promotions. Distinguishing between these two factors is important, especially for any public policy that attempts to rectify the gender imbalance.

In 2003, if we restrict ourselves to firms with more than 100 employees, 16% of full-time women aged 35–54 with university education held a managerial position at the lowest *kakarichō* level or higher. The corresponding figure for men was 47%. Thus the chances of men attaining a managerial position seem on the surface to be about three times as great as for women.[4] While this does not suggest equal opportunity, it is a much better ratio than that suggested by Table 7.2, and is probably not so different from the situation found in many other OECD countries. In other words, *the main reason why there are relatively few women managers in Japan is that there are relatively few full-time women employees at any given age level.* Critics who believe that Japan should have more women managers need to focus their criticism on the high rates of part-time employment, in addition to discrimination in promotion policy, although the latter is also a factor.

The Discovery of Sexual Harassment

To an outside observer, one of the most salient characteristics of the Japanese office is the distinctive appearance of the uniforms worn by the women. Most of the women in the Japanese offices of large companies wear uniforms, as compared with men, who at least have freedom in their choice of suits. Women are expected to serve tea and perform other kinds of tasks that further mark their (inferior) status in the workplace. Most women office workers are known by the term OL (or Office Lady in English), a term that strikes the Western observer as condescending and paternalistic.

Although there has been little change in the status of women in the office, one area where there has been a significant change in attitudes is in the area of sexual harassment.[5] The concept of sexual harassment and the rights of women have only just become established in Western countries, so the recent developments in Japan do not lag so far behind. As in the USA, feminists, especially those in the legal profession, have largely led the advance in the rights of women. According to Wolff (2003), the benchmark year for Japan was 1989 when the English term 'sexual harassment' or '*seku hara*' came into widespread use in the Japanese language. The event that triggered this development was the first court case in Fukuoka, involving a woman editor in a publishing company and her boss. The mass media focussed on this case, and, not surprisingly, there was a great deal of public interest in it and in other cases that followed. As a result, there was considerable discussion in Japan about the definition of sexual harassment and growing awareness that there was a 'problem'. The controversy over charges of sexual harassment during the confirmation hearings for Justice Clarence Thomas in the United States also attracted a great deal of attention in Japan. Finally, Japanese firms became much more interested in the entire subject after a class action suit was brought against Mitsubishi Motors in the USA, which resulted in a great deal of adverse publicity and a settlement of $34 million.

A Japanese government survey in 1997 found that more than 60% of women claimed to have witnessed sexual harassment in their workplace. Sixty per cent also claimed to have been the recipient of unwanted speech or actions (usually from a superior) at some point (Tomita 2000). Some idea of the growing consciousness concerning sexual harassment may be seen in the fact that while in 1994, there were some 850 cases of women coming to their local Young Women's office for a consultation about sexual harassment at work, by 1998, the number had risen to more than 7,000 (Tomita 2000). Social attitudes and expectations had changed over a brief period.

Until 1999, the main basis in Japanese law for sexual harassment suits came from provisions in both the Japanese constitution and in Japanese civil law that grant equality for women and the right to be treated with respect. There have been more than 100 cases brought before the courts since 1989. Although the courts did side with the plaintiffs in many cases, damages have tended to be small. For example, in cases where the plaintiff felt it necessary to quit her job because of harassment, damages of approximately 1 million yen were awarded—less than £5,000. More worrying perhaps is the fact that most decisions were based on a paternalistic view concerned with the protection of women, rather than a view that emphasized women's rights (Wolff 2003). In this sense, the treatment of sexual harassment has been consistent with the approach to equal opportunity framed in the EEOL.

The courts have also recognized counter-suits in some cases, where the defendant in a sexual harassment suit was able to successfully sue for defamation of character. In addition, some court decisions have refused to recognize sexual harassment, because the woman did not object vocally at the time when unwanted advances were made. Finally, there have been some cases where women have argued that the disparate treatment of women in the office (serving tea, and so on) constitutes sexual harassment since it violates the respect due to women, but the courts have rejected this wider extension of the concept of sexual harassment.

The Ministry of Labour was slow to take up this issue, but eventually provision was made in the revision of the Equal Employment Opportunity Law of 1997. According to Article 21 of the revised law, 'employers are required to give necessary consideration, from the view point of employment management, to ensure that their women workers do not suffer any disadvantage in their working conditions by reason of their responses to sexual speech and behaviour in the workplace, and that their working environments do not suffer any harm due to such sexual speech and behaviour'. As in much of Japanese law, however, the prohibitions are not explicit, and the law is to be enforced by social sanction. In other words, companies are given the responsibility for dealing with the problem.

Companies are understandably concerned about litigation (in no small part because of the great publicity these cases attract) and they have reacted according to ministerial guidelines along three dimensions. The first is to establish and advertise the firm's sexual harassment guidelines. This is done through a number of different means, including the distribution of pamphlets, posters, inclusion of harassment policy in the company's official work regulations, memos, and announcements at the morning meetings that are routinely held to discuss the day's business. The second dimension is to establish a consultation service where employees can bring their concerns without concern about their privacy. The third dimension is to have policies in place to deal with actual cases of sexual harassment as they arise. A recent government survey cited in Tomita (2000) suggests that about a third of companies surveyed had instituted all three of these, with compliance rising with the size of the firm. Among large firms with more than 1,000 employees, some 70% had instituted all three plans, while in firms with less than 100 employees only 10% had.

Despite the action taken by firms, evidence from surveys suggests that most women prefer to deal with harassment by either ignoring it, or by trying to make a joke of it. There is still a gap between men and women in the perception of the problem.

INSTITUTIONAL FACTORS THAT LIMIT WOMEN'S CAREERS

Set against these changes in attitudes and law, there are a number of institutional factors that have acted to keep women in part-time jobs or in positions that have lower wages. The two most important of these are the tax and benefit systems in Japan and the closed internal labour market of the Japanese firm. The latter impedes re-entry into the labour market should one take a career break to raise a family. I begin by examining the tax and benefit system.

Tax and Benefit System

Taxes Japan has had one of the most progressive systems of income taxation in the OECD, with top rates still at 88% up to 1987. Today, the top rates, including local taxes, still reach the 65% mark. Since a fair distribution of income has been one of the goals of tax policy in the postwar period, the head of the household has been given several tax exemptions for dependent family members. The one that affects the labour supply of women the most is the exemption for a spouse that totals 760,000 yen as long as the spouse earns less than 700,000 yen. This is then smoothly phased out as the spouse's earnings increase until the spouse earns 1.41 million yen, at which point it is not given.[6] The current law is an improvement on the law in existence prior to 1987 where net family income could actually decline if the spouse worked part time. Nevertheless, the marginal tax rate experienced by the family will usually be 45% if the spouse earns between 760,000 and 1.4 million yen, as there is both taxation of the spouse and the removal of an exemption.

Benefits This is not the only problem, however. The benefit systems in use in Japan also have an effect on women's labour supply. Part-time workers are exempted from making contributions to pension and health insurance as long as they work less than three-quarters of the hours worked by full-time workers. Married individuals who work part time are covered for social insurance if their spouse works full time. Once the part-time spouse's income reaches 1.3 million yen, however, a lump sum tax of around 200,000 yen, depending on the municipality, will be levied for social insurance coverage. Deductions for unemployment insurance are also not made if one works less than 20 hours per week.

Finally, the provision of many non-statutory fringe benefits to the families of full-time workers in the workplace is predicated on the assumption that women will not be working full time and thus do not receive these benefits. At the same time, part-time workers do not receive these benefits through employment as they are assumed to be dependent on a spouse who is in receipt of them. Family benefits are provided by 80% of companies in one survey, usually between 100,000 and 200,000 yen per year (Higuchi 1995). The majority of these companies will terminate these benefits to dependants if the spouse is earning more than a set amount, usually around 1 million yen. In this sense, the company benefit system functions much like the tax system to discourage full-time work.

Nagase (2002) reports that Japanese accountants advise women not to increase their hours of work to earn more than 1.03 million yen unless they can earn more than 1.7 million yen. Japanese companies often advertise positions based on the 1.03 million-yen threshold. There is some debate about whether the income threshold acts to depress the wage rate for part-time women workers (Abe 2002), but it is clear from a number of studies including Abe and Ohtake (1997) as well as Nagase (2001) that married women alter their labour supply in response to this feature of the tax code. There is discussion about doing away with this exemption, but this is likely to be politically contentious.

The Closed Internal Labour Market

Studies examining the labour supply of married women find that it is the university-educated women who are less likely to return to work after children reach school age (Higuchi *et al.* 1997), although this tendency disappears once the youngest child reaches age 18. In general, the personnel management systems in most companies do not offer highly skilled jobs on a part-time basis to mid-career hires. Consequently, it is not surprising that many such women decline the opportunities to work that are available. This is not a problem that is unique to Japan, but it is one that is exacerbated by the kind of highly internalized labour markets found there.

One result of the institutional problems mentioned above is that there is an increasing tendency for women to postpone marriage, or having children. Women are aware that marriage will probably mean that they will be unable to return to a fulfilling job if they take a break to have children. The only way of avoiding this problem would be to remain employed while their children are still young. This, in turn, usually depends on two things: the availability of day-care and the cooperation of their spouse, who would have to take on more of the work in the household.

GOVERNMENT POLICY TO HELP MOTHERS STAY AT WORK

The Japanese government has long recognized this problem and instituted a number of programmes to make it easier for women with children to work. The government instituted a Child Care Leave Law in 1992, allowing one parent to take leave from a company for up to one year after the birth of a child. Since 1995 this law, renamed as the Child Care and Family Care Leave Law, has applied to all establishments. The employer is not required to pay any support, but the government will provide up to 40% replacement of earnings if the worker has insurance and has worked for two years prior to taking the leave. Around 57% of women took some leave in 1999 but less than 1% of men (JIL Japan Labour Bulletin, vol. 41, no. 1, Jan. 2002). Nevertheless, Higuchi *et al.* (1997), using data from the period when the law only applied to firms with 30 or more employees, found that women who worked in firms that were covered by child-care leave were twice as likely to return to work at the same company as those who were not, with 80% returning after a break.

In addition to the provisions for maternity leave, the law also allows women to take leave to look after a sick family member for up to three months. This leave can only be taken once, however. As with child-care leave, Employment Insurance will provide 40% of earnings during the leave. Women with pre-school-age children or a family member in need of care may also ask to be exempted from night work between 10 p.m. and 5 a.m., although there are restrictions on the use of this exemption. Again, women with pre-school children may ask to be exempted from working more than 150 hours of overtime over the course of a year.

In 1994 the Japanese government instituted a policy known as the 'Angel Plan' which was a major initiative to increase the number of day-care centres, including those with extended hours (necessary for women who work full time) and after-school clubs. Day-care in Japan is heavily subsidized and considered to be of high quality (Roberts 2002). This initial plan had a number of problems, especially the shortage of facilities in some urban areas and a shortage of extended hours day-care centres. The government has increased the support with a 'New Angel Plan' initiative in 1999, greatly expanding the number of centres available by the year 2004. Japan now has some of the best, and least expensive, day-care provision in the OECD.

Despite these initiatives, a majority of women are still leaving work after the birth of a child and very few men are taking paternity leave. While there are undoubtedly many women who would prefer not to work while their children are very young, the government is also trying to dispel the common view that putting a child into day-care before the age of 3 is bad parenting. One of the reasons why so few men take any paternity leave is that, even though they cannot be fired for doing so, their career prospects and relationships with co-workers may be damaged.

Recently, businesses in Japan have begun to develop some 'family-friendly' policies in their workplace to make life easier for working mothers. These include shorter working hours, flextime, exemption from overtime, provision of a crèche at work, or financial assistance for day-care. A government survey in 1997 found that the last two provisions were implemented in less than 1% of workplaces, but about a quarter of establishments had implemented some of the provisions mentioned. In the case of larger establishments with more than 500 employees, this rose to three-quarters of workplaces (H. Sato 2000). Firms may have similar provisions to help women with ailing family members, but these are less common.

One of the most important family-friendly policies is simply to have personnel systems in place that are attuned to the Child Care and Family Care Leave Law. These include methods of covering for absent employees and help for returning employees so that they can smoothly re-enter their former jobs. Women are more likely to take leave if these systems are in place (Wakisaka 2002).

Finally, as mentioned in Chapter 4, many firms are developing personnel management systems that allow some of their part-time or temporary employees to move to regular worker status, usually with the provision that they must be willing to accept job changes at work. This bears some similarity to developments in the USA, where firms often use temporary help as a way of screening individuals whom they might wish to hire on a permanent basis.

CONCLUSIONS

Women have gained greater equality in the workplace, although the number of women in high managerial positions has not yet risen. Since many women choose to withdraw from the labour market at childbirth, the disruption of their working career usually means that they will find it difficult to find satisfying full-time regular employment. The closed nature of the employment system in Japan makes it more difficult (although not impossible) to re-enter at a later stage. This is not just a problem for women, but also for men who either quit, or are forced to leave, jobs after age 35. This group is the subject of the next chapter.

NOTES

1. Restricting the sample to those under 60 makes little difference to the results. Similarly, estimates adding in a tenure variable do not qualitatitively change the results.
2. Controlling for tenure would narrow the gap still further. Estimates using a different table suggest that the order of magnitude would be about two points.
3. I did not include tenure in the analysis. There has been a substantial increase in the tenure of women, but the increase in tenure has been greatest in the large firms. Therefore, the increase in tenure should have widened the difference in the gender gap between large and small firms.
4. It should also be noted that the positions the men held were on the whole higher ranked than those held by women.
5. This section draws heavily on Wolff (2003).
6. This applies only to when the primary wage earner earns less than 10 million yen per year.

8

Middle-Aged and Older Workers

Casual perusal of Japanese job advertisements on the Internet or in the print media suggests that it is more difficult to find work after age 40. For the purposes of this chapter, I will consider a worker to be older if they have reached the point where most companies impose age limits on new hires—age 40. Within this group I will make a further division, at age 55, chosen in line with published statistics, because the 55–59 year-old age grouping is the first one where the labour force participation rates of men begin to drop substantially below the prime-age rate of 96%. I will cover these two groups in reverse order, as it is easier to foresee some of the problems experienced by the younger group by first seeing what lies ahead.

MEN AND WOMEN OVER AGE 55

Trends in Participation and Employment

Employment of both men and women over the age of 55 is an important component of the Japanese labour market. Japan has some of the highest employment/population rates for older workers in the OECD. Table 8.1 shows these rates according to age for a number of OECD countries. Although Japan does not have the highest labour force participation rate overall for the 55–64 age group, men in Japan rank first in the OECD in both participation and employment. Furthermore, the widespread implementation of mandatory retirement means that this age group

Table 8.1. *Employment/population ratios for persons aged 55–64, 2003*

Country	All	Men	Women
Japan	62.1	77.4	47.5
Sweden	69.0	71.2	66.8
Korea	57.8	70.8	45.4
USA	59.9	65.6	54.5
UK	55.5	65.0	46.4
Germany	39.0	47.1	30.9
France[1]	39.3	44.2	34.6
EU-15 average	42.3	53.2	31.8

Note:
[1] Figures for 2002.

Source: OECD1 (2004), appendix table C.

Table 8.2. *Employment/population rates by gender and age, 1980–2003*

Year	Men		Women	
	55–59	60–64	55–59	60–64
1980	88.4	74.2	49.8	38.4
1985	86.8	67.4	49.9	37.8
1990	90.0	69.2	53.1	38.9
1995	91.6	69.3	56.0	38.7
2000	90.0	65.0	56.9	37.7
2003	88.8	64.6	57.0	37.7

Source: Calculated from MHLW4 (2004), tables B-5 and B-12.

is one in which a large proportion of the participants take post-career jobs as non-standard employees or become self-employed.

Table 8.2 shows trends in the employment/population ratio by age group and gender. The ratio has actually risen for the 55–59 year-old groups and the rise for women aged 55–59 is especially notable. The fall in the employment/population ratio for men aged 60–64 can be attributed to a fall in the participation rate as well as to rising unemployment. Rebick (1994) uses monthly time-series analysis to show that the employment/population ratio for both men and women aged 55–64 is about five times as responsive to economic conditions as that for men aged 30–39 in Japan, and this is divided almost equally between movements in the participation rate and the unemployment rate.

As we will see in Chapter 9, the conditions for the youth labour market have been dismal in the 1990s, so it is surprising that the situation is not worse for the older groups. The persistence of high employment/population rates for older Japanese may be attributed to a number of factors including:

1.   Japanese life expectancy is the highest in the world. In general, health tends to deteriorate in the few years prior to death, so Japanese can expect to be fit enough to work to an older age. Life expectancy is continuing to rise in Japan, and we might expect this to increase the participation rates of older Japanese.

2.   Job protection to the age of mandatory retirement means that many Japanese can expect to work to the age of 60. I will take this issue up in more detail later in the chapter. Here I will simply point out that separation rates for older Japanese have not risen, suggesting that firms continue to honour their employment commitments, except in the case of bankruptcies.

3.   Although Japanese pensions at present have a replacement rate of earnings that is about average by OECD standards (40%), the self-employed have much lower benefits and are consequently more likely to need the income. Recent changes in the pension system have reduced the levels of benefits and so this will tend to increase the participation rates of older men.

4.   In Japanese opinion surveys such as the Survey on Older Persons (MHLW5), the majority of respondents who are working after the age of 65 respond that

Table 8.3. *Older Japanese workers' reasons for working by age and gender, 2000 (%)*

Gender/age group	Financial reasons	To stay in good health	To keep active and participate in society	I was asked to, I had the time
Men	81.5	4.1	5.7	4.9
55–59	93.9	0.3	2.5	0.5
60–64	76.1	5.7	7.3	6.9
65–69	61.8	10.2	10.7	12.0
Women	67.2	5.5	11.4	9.1
55–59	74.6	2.7	10.5	6.6
60–64	65.3	6.0	11.6	9.8
65–69	51.8	11.6	13.3	14.5

Source: MHLW5 (2000).

they are working for financial reasons, although the rates are higher for men than women and for younger age groups (Table 8.3). This suggests that, although basic needs are met by the pension system, the additional income is still a dominating motivating factor. One survey conducted by the government asks the question, 'What is the minimum income necessary in order to be free from worry?' The answer to this question is quite consistent across all groups of employees except for the highest-ranking managers and comes to 350,000 yen per month, well above the level of pension income for most Japanese (AEDSC 1997). The high savings rates of older Japanese reported by many researchers (Dekle 1990; Yamauchi 1997) also suggest that concerns about the future will weigh heavily in the determination of the answer to this question.

5. After mandatory retirement, firms have been willing to continue to offer work to older Japanese at a lower pay rate. It is possible to work part time and still receive a pension. Many men also use their severance payment to set themselves up as a self-employed subcontractor for their old firm. Thus, the Japanese labour system has institutionalized means of finding jobs for older workers after mandatory retirement. Although the market for older workers has deteriorated, it is still highly effective in finding jobs for this age group.

In order to fully understand why participation rates remain high for older Japanese, it is necessary to look at pension arrangements in Japan and how they have been changing.

Pension Systems in Japan

Public Pension in Japan   The public pension for private sector employees is composed of two main parts (see Figure 8.1). A flat rate pension, known as the Basic Pension (*Kiso Nenkin*), is paid to all citizens who contribute for at least 25 years and the benefit is based on number of years of payments. This part of the pension can normally be taken at age 65, but it is possible to take the pension

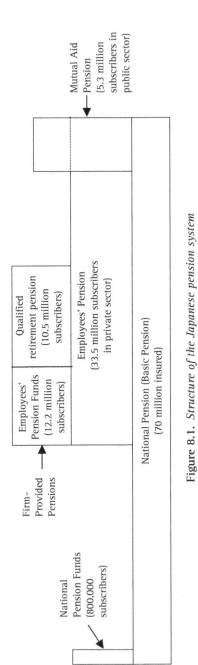

Figure 8.1. *Structure of the Japanese pension system*

Source: Adapted from National Institute for Population Research (2003) (http://www.ipss.go.jp/index–e.html).

at an earlier age, with a corresponding reduction in the annual payment, or later than age 65 with a corresponding increase. The amounts are not large—the average recipient in 2000 received just 51,000 yen.

The second main part of the pension, the Employees' Pension (*Kōsei Nenkin*), is for private sector employees and is based on earnings along with years of contributions. This portion of the pension tends to be much more substantial, on average 200,000 yen per month for men and 100,000 yen per month for women. This part of the pension previously provided benefits from age 60, but from 2013 this age will be increased gradually until it reaches 65 in 2025.[1] Contrary to common belief outside of Japan, these pensions are currently reasonably generous by OECD standards, comprising some 40% of the peak income that an employee receives (including bonuses). Pension benefits are earnings-tested as I will explain in the next section.

The self-employed are enrolled for the basic flat-rate pension, and recently have also been allowed to make voluntary contributions towards the equivalent of an earnings-related pension in what is known as the National Pension Fund. At present, however, there are only 720,000 subscribers out of nearly 20 million self-employed. Public employees are covered under similar arrangements to private sector workers except that in place of the Employees' Pension Insurance they are enrolled in Mutual Aid plans that provide benefits in the same way.

One issue that is of great importance to the question of whether the pension provides for basic needs is the variance in the level of pension benefits that can be received. Here the government does not publish information on the variance in benefit payments, but it is possible to estimate the levels that would be received for individuals with different earnings using the pension benefit formulas that the government provides. Here we are concerned primarily with men since they most likely to be the main earner in the household. My estimate for the first and ninth deciles of total pension income for a couple is 245,000 and 371,200 yen per month respectively.[2] The lower amount of 245,000 yen per month (around 235,000 after taxes are deducted) may well be higher than the actual first decile as there may be many individuals who have not contributed for a full 40 years. This level of income, while not high, is likely to meet basic needs. In the case of the self-employed, basic needs are unlikely to be met since the combined Basic Pension for a couple will only amount to roughly 90,000 yen and this is clearly not enough to provide minimum support. Furthermore, not all of those who depend on public pensions have paid into the system for the full 40 years required to receive the maximum benefit. Statistics from a special survey of older Japanese indicate that the first decile in the income distribution for fully retired men is less than 50,000 yen (MHLW5 1996, table 18, p. 168).[3] It is likely, then, that financial need is one of the main reasons why the self-employed continue to work well after age 60. The other main reason, of course, is that they work because they have the (self-provided) opportunity.

The government has been under considerable financial pressure given both the ageing of the population and the drop in tax revenue since the beginning

Table 8.4. *Employment rates and employment categories for older Japanese, 2000*

Gender/age	Employees	Full-time workers as % of all employees	Part-time workers as % of all employees	Self-employed or family worker	Company directors
Men	58.4	84.7	14.5	24.7	12.8
55–59	70.0	96.9	2.5	16.5	11.8
60–64	53.2	72.6	26.5	27.7	13.7
65–69	40.1	60.2	38.5	38.8	13.8
Women	51.9	56.7	42.7	32.7	5.1
55–59	64.0	64.7	34.6	24.6	4.0
60–64	46.4	46.4	53.1	37.4	6.3
65–69	30.4	39.5	60.2	45.3	6.1

Source: MHLW5 (2000).

of the 1990s, and benefit levels are being reduced in response. The age of qualification for pension benefits is increasing, as mentioned, and the indexing of the
benefits has been switched from a wage index to the consumer price index,
although there is no reduction for deflation. In 2004, the government introduced
a pension reform that will gradually lower the level of benefits by 15% over the
next 12 years.

The Earnings Test and Part-Time Employment   Most full-time employees see
a drop of some 30% in earnings after age 60, with average annual earnings of
men dropping from 6.6 million to 4.6 million yen (MHLW1 2000). This can be
attributed to the effect of mandatory retirement as explained in Chapter 2. Also,
many men who work after age 60 work part time as shown in Table 8.4. This can
be partly attributed to supply-side factors, especially the presence of earnings
tests for pension recipients. The earnings test for those who are aged 60–64 cuts
the pension by 20% up to the point where earnings (including pro rata bonuses)
and the pension total 220,000 yen per month. (This 20% cut will be abolished
according to the reform of 2004.) Thereafter, the pension is cut at a rate of 50%
of the increase in earnings until work earnings reach 370,000 yen per month, at
which point the pension is cut entirely. There is therefore effectively an extra 50%
tax on earnings over this interval. There are similar earnings tests for those who
are over 65, but the levels permitted are much higher: pensions are not cut until
the sum of earnings and the pension reach 370,000 yen and then are cut at 50% of
the increase in earnings above that point. As mentioned earlier, 370,000 yen
is about the level of income that most Japanese say they need to be free from
worry.

A recent government survey suggests that nearly two-thirds of those between
60 and 65 who are receiving a pension while working and hence earned less
than 370,000 yen per month are working part time (AEDSC 1997). It is likely that

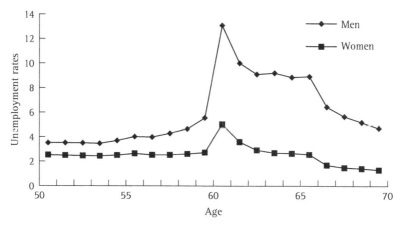

Figure 8.2. *Unemployment rates by age*

Source: PHPT (2000).

more employees will prefer to work full time as the age at which the pension may be received moves to 65. The decline in lifetime wealth itself will be one factor pushing them to do so. Maintaining full-time employment opportunities for employees after age 60, including the extension of the age of mandatory retirement to 65, or its outright abolition is thus a major policy goal of the government.

Unemployment Benefits: The 'Second Pension' Unemployment benefits also have a major impact on the labour market, especially at the age of mandatory retirement. Figure 8.2 graphs unemployment rates according to age in Japan for the year 2000. There is a notable spike at age 60, the age when many Japanese reach mandatory retirement. Although there are ways in which these employees will be helped into post-retirement jobs, many of them will be unemployed. In addition, unemployment insurance acts as a 'second pension' as it is possible to collect both a pension and unemployment insurance. The total can easily exceed the income from employment.

The Japanese government is aware of this problem and has taken two measures to tackle it. First, it has altered the period during which unemployment benefits are available. Prior to 2001, a worker that reached mandatory retirement and who had worked for 20 years for his employer was eligible for 240 days of benefits. After 2001, only workers who had 'involuntarily' lost their jobs are eligible for this period, and mandatory retirement is not considered to be 'involuntary' from the point of view of the benefit system. The result is that mandatory retirees are only eligible for 180 days of benefits.

The government has also tried to directly subsidize the employment of workers after mandatory retirement through the introduction of a subsidy for earnings if they drop more than 15% after age 60. As we shall see, this encompasses the vast majority of employees who reach mandatory retirement. Both of these changes to the employment insurance system should act to increase the employment/population rate for this age group.

Company Pensions   Both government and private sector employees normally receive pension benefits above and beyond the mandated benefits described. In the case of private firms, additional contributions may be made towards the Employee's Pension Fund that translate into higher payouts after retirement, or else the firm can provide a pension from its own 'qualified pension fund'. Government workers have a similar arrangement except that the additional pension is run directly through the Mutual Aid Pension scheme. The firm-based pension was traditionally given as a lump-sum payment to retiring employees and nearly half of all firms still provide their pension in this manner. These lump-sum payments are tax exempt and often used to pay for major expenses such as home mortgages and school loans. The amounts are substantial, averaging almost four years of base pay (not including bonuses or allowances) (MHLW8 2000).

As in other OECD countries, private pension schemes have come under a great deal of pressure. The collapse in asset prices and the low rates of interest have meant that many of the tax-qualified private pension schemes are now greatly underfunded. The Japanese government is phasing out the tax-qualified pension system over the next decade and replacing it with a system where employers that offer defined benefit plans must make sure that they are fully funded.

The move away from the 'qualified pension' system is part of a major shift in policy on private pensions by the government. The government introduced a framework to allow for defined contribution pensions in October 2001, and around 700 firms had introduced these plans covering some 650,000 employees by January 2004, with the numbers growing rapidly (MHLW9 2004). The hope is that the portability of these pensions will help to improve labour market mobility. The scheme is barely off the ground, however, and most of the firms that are using such plans continue to provide the traditional defined benefit plans alongside the new plans. Furthermore, as I will discuss below, pensions are only the tip of the iceberg in assessing the financial costs of mobility for older workers.

In conclusion, the changes in pension scheme provision and in employment insurance benefits will probably act to maintain or even increase Japan's high rates of labour force participation. I now turn to the mandatory retirement systems that place employees in 'second jobs' to see how they have fared in the 1990s.

Mandatory Retirement Systems

In 2000, roughly nine out of ten firms with more than 30 employees had a mandatory retirement system and by far the most common age of retirement was 60, although age 65 was also used by some of the smaller firms (Table 8.5).

Table 8.5. *Mandatory retirement ages by size of firm, 2003*

Size of firm	% with MR system	Less than 60 (%)	60 (%)	61–64 (%)	65 or higher (%)
5,000 or more	100	0	98.4	1.3	0.3
1,000–4,999	99.8	0	97.2	2.0	0.9
300–999	99.4	0.2	93.3	3.1	3.5
100–299	98.0	0	90.8	3.5	5.7
30–99	89.6	1.6	88.0	2.4	8.0

Source: MHLW4 (2004), tables C-22, C-23.

The Japanese government would like firms to increase the age of mandatory retirement to 65, since the age at which most public pension benefits become available is gradually being increased to that age. Nevertheless, the government's own surveys suggest that very few firms are planning to do this (MHLW4 2000).

Finding Jobs for Older Workers Despite the reluctance of firms to extend their mandatory retirement age, roughly two-thirds do provide employment opportunities for some of their employees after mandatory retirement through either 'employment extension' (*kinmu enchō*) or re-employment systems (*saikoyō*) (MHLW4 2000). If an employee is offered employment extension or re-employment, they are usually kept on until age 65, but at a lower wage rate.[4] Using 1980s data from the Survey of Employment of Older Persons (MHLW5), I estimated that employees who remain with their old employer see a median wage drop of 20–25% (Rebick 1992*a*). The rate at which firms offer work to their own employees in this way varies according to the size of the firm, and it is the smaller firms that are more likely to offer these options.

The other way in which firms find work for their older employees is to transfer them to other firms, usually subsidiaries in the case of the larger-sized firms, but sometimes trading partners. Firms do not necessarily wait until the age of mandatory retirement, moving many of their employees out well before that point as indicated in Table 8.6. In most cases, the career firm partly or fully supplements the earnings the employee receives from the new firm so that there is no loss in earnings until the age of mandatory retirement. In this sense, firms honour an implicit contract made with the employee to maintain their employment until age 60, although the conditions of employment may change.

There are several motivations for use of these transfers, related to the industrial organization of Japanese industry and the kinds of long-term relationships that are characteristic of the Japanese economy. As in the case of younger, temporary secondments, transferred workers can be used to facilitate the flow of information and to bring fresh skills to the new workplace. They can also help to consolidate corporate groups or trading relations, as employees will have many contacts and friends in their old firm. The group structures in Japanese industrial

Table 8.6. *The extent of mandatory retirement and outplacement by age and gender, 2000[1]*

Gender/age	Have experienced mandatory retirement	Retired from career firm prior to mandatory retirement age	Have not retired from career firm
Men	38.8	17.5	43.3
55–59	3.7	14.9	80.7
60–64	56.8	17.5	25.3
65–69	65.1	20.9	13.7
Women	23.7	27.9	47.8
55–59	3.1	16.9	79.4
60–64	33.2	32.0	34.0
65–69	42.9	39.5	16.9

Note:
[1] Table shows percentages of those who were employees at age 55 according to their experience of mandatory retirement or outplacement.
Source: MHLW5 (2000).

organization thus provide a special role for older employees as conveyors of information and skills. The attitude of recipient companies towards the trans-ferred workers is not always positive, however, and they can become a burden if too many of them are forced on subsidiaries. In the most extreme case, the receiving company is referred to as '*ukezara*' or receptacle, often for unwanted employees from the parent firm. The recent introduction of consolidated accounting in Japan will force companies to include their subsidiaries in their overall accounts. This should reduce the tendency to move older employees out simply to 'get them off the books'.

According to Rebick (1995), these assisted employees are likely to have higher earnings than those who find employment through other means, and this also sug-gests that such transfers can be used to motivate employees: more cooperative workers may get better positions, other things equal. White-collar workers who have reached the mandatory retirement age in large firms will generally have pen-sion benefits that cover the basic needs requirement of 350,000 yen mentioned above, and so these labour market arrangements, and the higher earnings that they offer, are particularly important in keeping these workers in the workforce.

Japanese companies generally promote from within, but one major exception to this occurs in the subsidiaries of large companies. High-ranking managers who are not promoted to be directors of their own companies are often sent to be directors or managers in one of the subsidiaries. The rationale may be similar to that of transferring rank and file employees, except that in this case there is a stronger opportunity to exercise influence and monitor firm behaviour from the parent firm. These posts can also be seen as rewards that can be used to motivate employees who recognize that they will never be promoted to the board of directors in the parent firm. The company may have difficulty in finding placements for its least able employees, such as those who have failed to gain any managerial responsibility. These are often the employees who remain with the firm until the age of mandatory retirement, although increasingly they are also likely to be encouraged or forced into taking early retirement. As Rebick (1995) shows, employees who do not find new jobs with the help of their former employer tend to suffer from greater loss of income, other things equal.

In the public sector, there is a corresponding movement of high-ranking bureaucrats to the directorships of private firms, commonly referred to as *amakudari* or 'descent from heaven'. In the typical pattern, bureaucrats who fail to be promoted to the next level resign from the ministry and are either placed in private firms, or are placed in subsidiary public-sector organizations. As in the private sector, such moves open up posts that more junior members of the organization can fill. Just as in the case of private sector firms there is a positive aspect to this movement in that the flow of information between firms and the government bureaucracy is enhanced. On the other hand, these practices have recently been blamed for the inability of the bureaucrats to satisfactorily regulate and discipline the firms that fall within their jurisdiction, as they may not wish to antagonize their future employers.

The combination of transfers and re-employment and the fact that directorships are almost universally reserved for older Japanese provide job opportunities that would otherwise not be available. The transfer and re-employment systems obviate the information problems that might otherwise make it difficult for employees to find work. The reduction in earnings that is allowed under Japanese labour law at mandatory retirement is also essential in supporting the demand for their labour. If age-discrimination legislation of the kind seen in other OECD countries was introduced, it could lead to a sharp drop in employment prospects for this group.[5]

To see whether this system is breaking down, I look at the number of employees between the age of 55 and 64 who found jobs with the help of their employer or through direct transfer as a proportion of all employees who separated from their jobs in 1989 and 2002. The tabulations are shown in Table 8.7. In 2002, roughly

Table 8.7. *Separations and accessions by age for Japanese men in 1989 and 2002*

Year	Separation rate	Accession rate	Percent of accessions that are transfers or help from former employer
1989			
55–59	12.3	7.6	17.2
60–64	35.6	14.6	16.8
2002			
55–59	11.4	5.9	20.3
60–64	35.2	10.9	24.7

Source: Calculated from MHLW3 (1989, 2004). Figures exclude construction workers.

one in four male recruits between the ages of 55 and 64, got his job either through a direct transfer or with the help of their former employer. (These kinds of interventions are much less common in the case of women.) In the case of large-firm white-collar workers the proportions are much larger—around 40% (AEDSC 1997).[6] This was an increase from 1989. The cohort size for both age groups has doubled over the decade, so the direct action of employers is actually finding more than twice as many jobs today for older workers as it did in the past. At the same time, separation rates have actually declined for men in the 55–59 year-old group, suggesting that this group is not nearly as insecure as is sometimes claimed. It seems fair to conclude that Japan's mandatory retirement system is continuing to promote Japan's high rate of employment for older workers.

Self-Employment

We have already seen in Table 8.4 that self-employed and family workers make up more than 30% of employment for those over age 55. This is substantially higher than the average of 15% for the entire working population. This high share of the self-employed can be analysed as stemming from both an age effect and a cohort effect. Today's older self-employed developed their businesses during the period prior to the 1990s when the self-employed sector was larger than today. Thus the cohort effect reflects the persistence of this kind of employment in this age group. We can see from Table 4.1 that in 1980 the average rate of self-employment was much higher than it was in 2001. The age effect reflects the fact that many Japanese start their own businesses after they retire as employees, using their lump-sum retirement payment and often with some capital input from their former employer.

Table 8.8 shows the changing pattern of employment for three cohorts of men over the period from 1981 to 2001.[7] The main point of this table is to show that, although the share of self-employed has risen for the cohorts that were 60–69 years old in 2001, the absolute number of self-employed and family workers has dropped. It is likely that the increase in the share of the self-employed has more to do with their lower likelihood of retirement at any given age than with any large-scale movement from employment to self-employment. This seems to be

Table 8.8. *Self-employment and family worker shares for fixed cohorts of Japanese men*

Age of cohort in 2001	Self-employed and family workers (1,000s)		Share of all workers (%)	
	1981	2001	1981	2001
55–59	690	510	16.8	14.4
60–64	740	540	19.1	24.1
65–69	750	430	20.6	31.6

Source: PMO2 (1981, 2001).

confirmed by the independent research by Genda and Kambayashi (2002) referred to in Chapter 4. They observe that older men are less likely to be self-employed than in the past. The numbers of employees who move on to self-employment after retirement from their career firm are limited, and self-employment no longer seems to work so well as a buffer for older workers who wish to continue working.

THE MARKET FOR WORKERS AGED 40–55 (MIDDLE-AGED)

In Chapter 2, I discussed the age discrimination faced by middle-aged Japanese who wish to get standard employment. These difficulties, possibly more extreme than those of other countries with more open labour markets, deter mobility for this age group. One of the main problems faced by this age group is the loss in both earnings and pension wealth that can come from changing jobs.

Japanese company pensions are typically vested very late in the worker's career with the company, much of the vesting taking place just before mandatory retirement. Figure 8.3 illustrates the vesting pattern for university graduates in a survey of the Central Labor Commission for 1997. Since a university graduate typically begins employment with the company at age 22 at the earliest, it is clear that leaving a company in one's early fifties would normally entail a loss of around 10 million yen from the lump-sum pension alone, since any pension from a second employer would be very small or non-existent. For this reason, the early retirement packages provided by companies offer amounts of between 5 and 10 million yen in addition to the normal severance payment to workers. This generally compensates for losses in pension income, but the losses in terms of earnings may be far greater if the employee fails to find a job with comparable pay. Ichinose (2001), using published tabulations of earnings according to age and seniority from the Wage Census, estimates that up to 100 million yen in

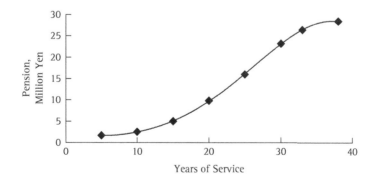

Figure 8.3. *Model severance payments as a function of years of service, university-educated men, 1997*

Source: MHLW8 (2000).

lifetime income may be lost by employees if they are pushed into early retirement from their firm and are forced to take a job at much lower pay. In general, the younger the age at which the employee changes jobs, the greater are the potential losses in lifetime income. In this sense, the issue of job loss is much more serious for the 40–54 year-old age group, than for the older group discussed in the first part of this chapter.

The main exception to this comes from those job changes that are direct transfers initiated by the first employer. As in the case of older workers over 55, a significant number of employees in the 40–54 year-old age bracket are transferred out, usually to a smaller, subsidiary company. In this case, the sending company will usually ensure that the employee's move does not involve losses in earnings and pension wealth.

How many workers are suffering these kinds of losses? The Employment Trends Survey for 2000 (MHLW3 2000) shows that in the 45–54 year-old age group roughly one in four of newly hired men suffered a cut in pay of more than 10%. This is an increase from the rate of one in six that prevailed in 1989. The poor state of the labour market also leads to higher levels of worklessness. Separation rates for men in this age group have risen, as shown in Table 3.2, and accession rates are not keeping up. It is premature to conclude from this that the Japanese employment system is breaking down. As I explained in Chapters 2 and 3, Japanese firms have fired employees when under pressure in the past. If the economy makes a full recovery, we can expect these separation rates to fall.

CONCLUSIONS

Older workers in Japan have been affected by the slump of the past 10 years, but not nearly as much as might have been expected. The direct outplacement of many employees, either before or at the point of mandatory retirement, as well as the re-employment of mandatory retirees on non-standard contracts, has been able to cope reasonably well with the downturn in demand. Unemployment rates have risen proportionately with the general rise in unemployment to double-digit levels for men in their early sixties, but the rates for younger men remain low by OECD standards. Nevertheless, the increase of the age at which pension benefits become available from 60 to 65 will present a new challenge that older workers will soon face. At the same time that this is taking place, the 'dankai no sedai' (literally, generation of the clump), Japan's baby-boom generation, born between 1947 and 1950, are rapidly approaching their early sixties. This will undoubtedly place a major strain on the ability of the system to find jobs for this age group. The government would like to encourage the extension of the age of mandatory retirement to 65, or even its outright abolition. If such steps are taken, this will have major implications for the entire compensation system, as firms will almost certainly have to flatten their age-earnings profiles further, and they will probably have to find other ways to remove their least productive older employees.

NOTES

1. As in the USA, it will be possible to receive the pension from an earlier age, but at a lower level. Also, for employees only, the flat rate portion may be taken at age 62, but this is gradually being raised to age 65 by 2013.
2. If we assume that the pension recipient has the maximum of 40 years of payments in the scheme then their benefits will be as follows:

    Basic Flat Rate Pension (National Pension) $2/3 \times 804,200/12 = 44,677$ (1)

    For a couple aged 60 there will be two of these amounting to 89,354.

    Earnings Related Pension (Employees' Pension)
    = Flat rate + 0.31 × Average Basic Monthly Earnings + Dependent Spouse
    Amount 80,000 + 0.31 × Average Basic Monthly Earnings + 19,300 (2)

    So adding up the flat amounts from (1) and (2) we have approximately:

    179,000 = 0.31 × Average Basic Monthly Earnings.

    The first and ninth deciles of basic monthly earnings for men aged 55–59 were 214,200 and 632,000 respectively but there is a 620,000 yen cap on the top level. This leads to total pension income of 245,000 and 371,200 per month (before taxes) for the first and ninth deciles respectively.
3. Assuming that they are not destitute, they may be relying on support from a combination of savings and income from other family members including children.
4. One of the differences between employment extension and re-employment is that the latter is more likely to entail a drop in the wage rate.
5. Given the opposition of firms to any extension of the mandatory retirement age, it is unlikely that mandatory retirement will be abolished in the near future since business interests would weigh heavily against such a policy.
6. White-collar workers in large firms are also likely to be recruited directly by other firms and about 20% find their new employment in this manner.
7. The shares of self-employed and family workers are somewhat lower in this table than in the previous table as these figures are taken from the Labour Force Survey in 2001 (PMO2 2001) while the former were taken in MHWL5 (2000).

9

The Labour Market for Youth

THE 1990s ICE AGE

No single part of the labour market has been affected as much by the slowdown of the 1990s as the labour market for youth. The unemployment rate for 20–24 year olds more than doubled from 3.7% in 1990 to 8.6% in 2000 (MHLW4). The press is full of accounts of the difficulty that young people have in finding secure regular employment. In the period of the mid-1990s the situation was so bad that it was popularly referred to as the Ice Age for the labour market. Furthermore, as I have shown in Chapter 4, there has been a sharp trend away from regular employment for those who are working and much of this is concentrated among youth. This trend is fundamentally changing the market. Before discussing the trends in the market, I will explain the process whereby new school graduates go about finding jobs, as it differs substantially from that found in other countries.

FINDING JOBS FOR MIDDLE-SCHOOL, HIGH-SCHOOL, AND TECHNICAL SCHOOL GRADUATES

High-School Graduates

The labour market for new high-school graduates is organized in a systematic fashion conveniently timed to provide employment after the end of the school year and the fiscal year on 1 April. Firms can begin to project their future budget needs well in advance of the new fiscal years and personnel divisions can anticipate the number of new graduates that they would like to hire. Typically, large firms have decided on their hiring a year in advance of 1 April. Most then assign a quota for each school that they wish to target, usually basing the division on past experience of the school's graduates (Okano 1993). In turn, the school understands the needs of the firm in terms of the personal character and abilities of the graduates that would be desired. They then encourage the corresponding students to apply for these positions, and strongly discourage other students from applying to the same firm.[1] In this way the school honours the tacit agreement with the firm to provide a set number of applicants. The firm will administer hiring tests, and interview the applicants, but in virtually all cases it will rely on the school's judgement in the provision of the candidate. The school's incentive to provide the appropriate candidate to each firm lies in the prospects for future graduates. If the company should become dissatisfied with the graduates that it is getting, it will stop hiring from the school in the future. The whole process is tightly regulated by the *shokuan* or public employment offices which prevent firms from openly advertising their jobs directly to high-school graduates (Ariga 2004).

This kind of market, where the school acts as a matchmaker, is reasonably effective, but we should note that roughly half of high-school graduates leave their first employer after only three years. Nevertheless, those graduates that find their jobs with the assistance of their high school are observed to have lower turnover rates. Genda and Kurosawa (2001) believe that this is strong evidence that the system works effectively to find better matches for high-school graduates, but it may also be the case that those students who get referrals (that they find acceptable) from their high schools are precisely the hard-working and motivated graduates who are less likely to switch jobs.

Most high-school graduates do not enter the labour market for full-time employment, however. More than 40% proceed on to a two-year college or four-year university. Another 30–35% attend a *senshū gakkō* or vocational training school. The top tier of these schools, regulated by the Ministry of Education, are known as *senmon gakkō* or specialized training schools. These schools generally offer courses of one to three years' duration, including training for health professionals such as nurses, the teaching profession, industrial design, and information technology. Firms often recruit directly from these schools, as their graduates have skills that can be put to immediate use (Dore and Sako 1998).

The Market for University Graduates

The market for university graduates is timed so that hiring takes place in the same way as for secondary school graduates. The main difference is that, except for those studying in science and engineering, students do not rely on the recommendations of the school or their professor to get work. Instead, they actively apply to the companies that interest them and hope to get through a series of tests and interviews. In this case, the most important screening device for the firm is the university's admission standards, or more specifically, the standards of the university faculty. University faculties have different standards for admitting their students and firms target those faculties that are most likely to yield the students that they want to hire. In some cases, quotas are set for particular university faculties. More commonly, however, the firm simply considers all applications from a range of faculties in order to get some diversity in its hires.

The hiring season for a given year actually begins more than one year prior to the graduation year during the autumn of the student's third year. Figure 9.1 shows the rough sequence of events. Universities hold guidance sessions to discuss the up-coming job-search process and provide students with their own internal guidebooks. Companies are also invited to come and make presentations. Students typically send in postcards asking for brochures and related materials

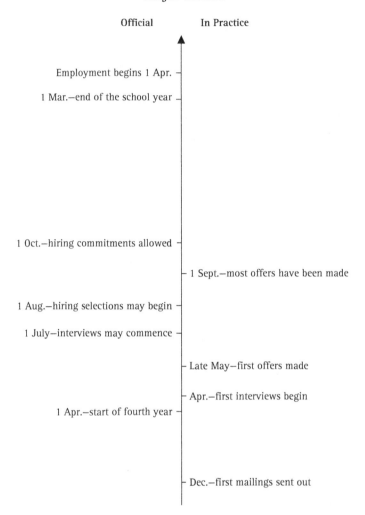

Figure 9.1. *Schedule for the hiring process for Japanese university graduates, 1992*

from the various companies that interest them. They usually receive these brochures around December of their third year.

They then set about trying to gain an initial interview with the firm. In many cases there are too many applicants for the firm to be able to interview all candidates and so some kind of screening test may be used. In the case of science and engineering graduates, firms rely heavily on the professor's or departmental recommendation to narrow down their list of students, much as in the case of secondary schools. For non-science graduates, alumni networks are used and the firm relies on its own employees who are graduates of particular faculties to find new recruits. In some cases alumni return to their old extracurricular clubs in order to find suitable candidates. Most students belong to a *zemi* or seminar group in their final year in university and alumni may show a preference for students in their old professor's *zemi as* well. In recent years, however, employers have been paying more attention to the kinds of skills that new graduates can bring to the firm. As a result, participation in clubs at university is falling, and many students are using their time for additional schooling, taking extra courses, sometimes from *senmon gakkō*, that provide skills that will be attractive to employers. It is likely that the importance of clubs and other alumni networks will decline in the future.

The Naitei   Whatever the method used, candidates begin their interviews for the largest companies roughly one year prior to the hiring dates. Prior to 1997 there were informal agreements, more often than not honoured in the breach, not to make offers to candidates prior to a particular date, usually around 1 October. There were also agreements not to begin interviewing prior to 1 July, but, as we have already seen, these obligations were not taken seriously. An offer to a candidate is known as a *naitei* or 'internal decision', reflecting the fact that any agreement (acceptance) by the candidate is not actually binding, although companies will always honour their offers. Companies actually make offers well before the period in which the *naitei* are formally sent out, however, and they are sometimes referred to as *nainaitei* to reflect the notion that these are even more informal agreements. Again, *nainaitei*, made verbally to the candidate, are honoured by firms, but may be broken by candidates without legal consequences.

There has been a well-defined pattern to the setting of *nainaitei*, with the large firms in the most popular industries such as banking (popular because of its higher wages) making their offers earlier in the season. During the bubble period of the late 1980s the competition for new graduates could be so intense that firms would sometimes insist that prospective candidates attend a 'retreat' to learn about their firm during the week when the industry offers were being made. Thus they could be sure that their prospective employee would not be available to receive an informal verbal offer during this period from other companies, who would then move on to offer the same position to other students. Although this kind of practice has not been prevalent since the early 1990s, there is still a fairly rapid market clearance that takes place in a narrow time slot for given industries.

The agreements among firms not to 'jump the gun' on the hiring season was never adhered to. Instead, the dates in the agreement acted as benchmarks or reference points to prevent the process from continuing to move to earlier and earlier dates. In 1997 the system was finally abandoned for the graduating class of 1998. It appears that the abolition of the agreement led to activity being advanced by roughly one month in late 1996, so the agreements had some impact on the market. Despite the fact that early decisions are made each year, a large proportion of graduates do not conclude their agreements until they graduate.

For example, for the graduating class of 2003, only 67% of men and 60% of women registered with government employment offices had *naitei* by 1 October, with the proportions rising to around 93% for both genders by the graduation date the following April (MHLW15).

The ranking of firms in the labour market by students is likely to vary from year to year, but in general the large firms are given the highest rating. This is not surprising since, on average, the larger firms have more to offer in the way of career prospects, job security, and ultimately, higher salaries. University faculties are also well-ranked in this kind of market, and, as is the case in the USA, there is a considerable amount of published information about admissions standards. Faculties are often rated according to a *hensachi* system, which is a measure of the variance of applicant ability. A *hensachi* of 50 reflects the median applicant according to standardized tests run by the various private schools known as *juku* that prepare students to take university entrance examinations. The university faculty can then be rated on that *hensachi* that gives an applicant a 50% chance of being accepted. This is referred to as the 'borderline *hensachi*'. Borderline *hensachis* for university faculties range from about 40 to 70. The lack of symmetry about the median *hensachi* value of 50 reflects the fact that the weakest *juku* students are not accepted at any university.

The hiring for the public sector takes a slightly different form in that civil service examinations play a central role. The principal ministries of the government hire graduates into one of three classes. The top class is the career path that can ultimately lead to the senior positions in the ministry. The second class is also provided for career bureaucrats, but it is understood that these individuals will never advance to the top positions. For example, in the foreign ministry, those who are sent abroad tend to be posted to less prestigious and important embassies and consulates. Finally, the third class, mainly filled by women, is reserved for the more basic secretarial and clerical functions. The civil service examinations for the top class are notoriously difficult and are most easily passed by those graduates who have already passed the entrance examination to Tokyo University (especially the Faculty of Law) and other top-ranked public universities. The government also interviews prospective applicants, so passing the civil service examination is necessary, but not sufficient, to gain admission to the top ranked career tracks.

In recent years the extent to which firms have restricted their intake to the beginning of April has begun to diminish. Many firms are now hiring for more than one starting date and some are hiring year-round. The reasons for this shift are varied, but in general reflect a loosening up of personnel management in the firm. The growing number of Japanese who are receiving their undergraduate education abroad is one of the major influences on this shift. The university year runs on a different timetable in most other countries and firms wish to be able to accommodate these graduates. The move to a more flexible hiring schedule also makes it easier to hire older workers, who may be willing to take up work in a new firm at a date other than the beginning of April.

Different Career Tracks　Private sector firms also run different career tracks. Chapter 7 drew attention to the distinction between secretarial and managerial career tracks, which are used to sort women into different categories. Similarly, large firms make distinctions between those individuals who are hired into the central office (usually in Tokyo) and those who are hired into local offices with more limited career prospects. There are also distinctions based on the division to which one may be hired. For example, being hired into operations (*eigyōbu*) will generally limit one's career prospects within the firm. As a result of these distinctions, one observes that most large firms hire from a wide range of university faculties even if graduates of a small number of prestigious universities dominate the top managerial positions.

Hiring Patterns of Firms　Despite the fact that firms hire from a wide range of university faculties, there are noticeable tendencies for the larger firms and top government ministries to hire predominately from the higher-ranked faculties. Table 9.1 gives a breakdown of the first destinations of graduates in Japan according to the size of the firm, the importance of the ministry, and the rank of the faculty according to its borderline *hensachi*. More than half of the graduates of the highly ranked universities are likely to enter very large firms with more than 5,000 employees or government employment, but the graduates of even the

Table 9.1. *Job placement of university graduates by faculty standard and employer type, Japan 1992*

Faculty standard	Employer					
	Medium-small firms	Large firms	Very large firms	Government	Elite ministries	Row total (% overall)
Low	29	34	29	8.1	0.25	100 (28)
Medium	21	33	39	6.6	0.25	100 (49)
High	15	28	51	5.0	0.14	100 (12)
Elite	8.1	19	66	5.8	0.55	100 (9)
Tokyo University	4.4	11	66	9.0	9.8	100 (1)
Average	21	31	41	6.8	0.36	100

Notes: Employer definitions: very large firms: over 5,000 employees; Large firms: 1,000–4,999 employees; Medium-small firms: less than 1,000 employees; Elite ministries: Finance, Foreign Affairs, International Trade and Industry, Home Affairs, Posts and Telecommunications, Labour, Education, Agriculture, Construction, Justice, Economic Planning Agency.

Faculty standard definitions: low: borderline *hensachi* * < 50 medium: 50 < borderline *hensachi* <60; high: borderline *hensachi* > 60 but no elite university faculties; elite: graduates of Hokkaido, Tohoku, Tokyo Industrial, Hitotsubashi, Nagoya, Kyoto, Osaka, Kobe, Kyushu, Keio, and Waseda, but excluding Tokyo University.
* See text for definition of borderline *hensachi*.

Source: Recruit Research, Survey of Job Placement of University Graduates, 1992; Kawai Juku, *Nihon no Daigaku*.

lowest-ranked university faculties were still able to find jobs with the largest firms and the government in 1992. Tokyo University is also notable for the large share of its graduates who were hired by elite ministries. Ono (2004) shows that university quality has a major effect on future earnings, even after controlling for ability using ninth grade marks. Graduates of colleges ranked one standard deviation above the mean are likely to have 30% higher earnings than graduates of colleges ranked one standard deviation below the mean, other things equal.

Information in the Market   There is a large amount of information made available to new graduates in Japan. Job-seeker guides produced by companies such as Tōyō Keizai will often list the numbers of new graduates that have been hired in past years and the numbers that will be hired in the next year. They also provide other information about the firm, including their fringe benefits, hours of work, and so on. In order for companies to make their offers so far in advance, they must also commit themselves to their hiring plans in advance. Entry-level wages are not used to attract better candidates, as the firm is interested in attracting candidates for the long run. Consequently, this kind of market will clear according to the utility or value that the organization offers to a graduate over a long-term career. In general, the government and large firms are the most attractive, and consequently, when hiring plans are cut back, we should expect to see a fall in the average rate at which graduates attain these 'good jobs'.

RECENT TRENDS

The deterioration of the labour market in the 1990s affected the nature of the placements in exactly this sort of manner. In particular, the ability of graduates of the lower-ranked universities to find jobs in the more highly ranked firms was compromised during the recession. If we graph the percentage of newly hired university graduates that are hired by either the government or by large firms against the borderline *hensachi* of the faculty we can observe in Figures 9.2*a* and 9.2*b* that there was a marked deterioration in the prospects for the graduates of the lower-ranked universities between 1991 (still a good year for the labour market) and 1996.[2] This tendency has been most noticeable for science and engineering graduates. One effect of this is that more students are seeking postgraduate education, as I will explain later in the chapter.

One other place where we see the effects of labour market conditions for university graduates is in the numbers of prospective graduates who take civil service examinations. Figure 9.3 shows the proportion of new graduates who are sitting the principal examinations for the civil service. In general, university graduates take the examinations for the top two grades, while high-school graduates take the examination for the third grade. The figure indicates that the popularity of the examination changes substantially over time. In particular, the period of the bubble in the late 1980s was a period when there was intense competition to hire new graduates into private sector firms, and there

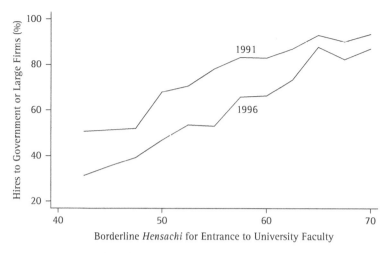

Figure 9.2*a*. *Percentage of newly hired university law, economics, or business graduates in large firms or government jobs: by difficulty of entrance to university faculty, 1991, 1996*
Source: Computed from Recruit.

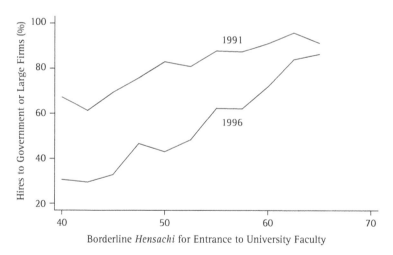

Figure 9.2*b*. *Percentage of newly hired university science graduates in large firms or government jobs: by difficulty of entrance to university faculty, 1991, 1996*
Source: Computed from Recruit.

was a fall in the applicant rate. With the downturn of the 1990s, however, civil service jobs with their guarantees of job security to the age of retirement (60) have become much more attractive and applicant rates rose rapidly. Inoki and Yugami (2001) use time-series analysis to show that the intensity of competition

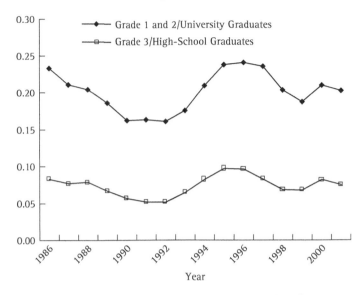

Figure 9.3. *Examination applicants as share of graduates*
Source: NPA (2000).

for civil service jobs is positively correlated with the previous year's unemployment rate and the previous year's rate of involuntary dismissals in the private
sector, as measured in the Employment Trends Survey. They interpret the last of
these three correlations as implying that downsizing by private sector firms does
make the security of civil service employment more attractive.

As would be expected from the experience of other OECD countries in the past
20 years, it is high-school and middle-school graduates who have borne the brunt
of the downturn in the 1990s. In 1991, over 90% of high-school graduates seeking
work through government employment offices had concluded *naitei* by the end
of November in the year prior to graduation. In November 2003, only 61% had
concluded agreements, despite the fact that the cohort size had dropped dramatically (MHLW16). Unemployment statistics tell a similar story. Table 9.2 shows that
youth unemployment rates are not so high for junior college or university graduates, but become much higher as educational attainment drops.[3] As Chapter 6 on
unemployment indicated, it is the less educated who are hardest hit by the poor
economic conditions in Japan. This is typical of the pattern seen in other OECD
countries where the education differential for unemployment rates is often more
severe (Higuchi 2001). The unemployment statistics tell only part of the story,
however, as there is a large discouraged worker effect in this age group as well.
Genda (2001) observes that the numbers of those who wish to work and actually
searched for work in the previous year (but not in the survey week) is at least 50%
of the number of unemployed, giving some idea of the dimensions of the problem.

The recession of the 1990s hit the youth labour market at a particularly bad
time in terms of demographic circumstances. The second-generation baby boom

Table 9.2. *Unemployment rates by age, education, and gender, 2000*

Age group	Education level			
	Middle school	High school	Junior college or specialist school	College, university, or graduate course
All				
15–19	32.9	14.6	–	–
20–24	16.8	10.2	6.7	7.1
25–29	11.3	6.9	5.3	4.4
30–34	9.5	5.5	4.4	2.7
Men				
15–19	32.1	14.6	–	–
20–24	17.2	10.1	8.3	8.3
25–29	11.2	6.4	4.9	4.2
30–34	9.5	5.1	3.7	2.4
Women				
15–19	34.5	14.6	–	–
20–24	16.1	10.2	6.1	5.6
25–29	11.5	7.6	5.5	4.8
30–34	9.7	6.2	4.9	3.9

Source: PHPT (2000).

(i.e. the children of the postwar baby boom) was reaching the labour market at around the time that the recession began. As Figure 9.4 indicates, the number of high-school graduates reached a peak in 1992 before declining. The situation of university and two-year college graduates is somewhat different. The increase in numbers of graduates began in the late 1980s as the Ministry of Education made a conscious decision to expand the number of places in higher education, partly in anticipation of the upcoming surge in high-school graduates. Although the overall number reached a peak in 1996, the decline has been much slower, and the overall number of university graduates has actually increased since then, as many two-year women's colleges have been converted to four-year universities in the hope of improving the employment prospects of their graduates. Whatever the causes of the shifts in enrolments, one thing is clear—the surge of graduates onto the labour market came at a particularly bad time given the recession of the 1990s.

Genda and Kurosawa (2001) make a number of interesting observations about the labour market experience of this generation of graduates. They note that the turnover rates for this group have increased in the 1990s despite the poor condition of the labour market. While some observers have claimed (with no real evidence) that this is a sign that youth are increasingly affluent and carefree, Genda and Kurosawa find evidence that the high turnover rates are caused by mismatches in the labour market. They observe that turnover rates are higher, other things equal, if the unemployment rate was high during the year prior to

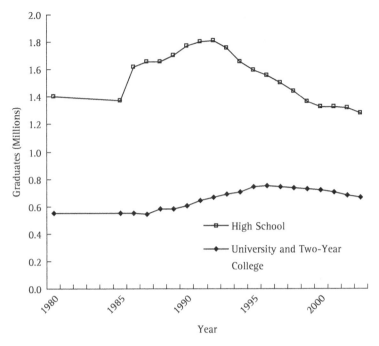

Figure 9.4. *Trends in the number of graduates in Japan*
Source: MOE1 (2001).

graduation, that is, the period when graduates are looking for work. They argue that, under these circumstances, graduates feel compelled to take jobs that they would otherwise not have considered, and that the high turnover rates reflect this dissatisfaction.

A second point made by Genda (2001) is that the freeze on hiring of new graduates has meant that the workers of the youngest cohort in firms have not moved up in the corporate hierarchy as rapidly as in the past. He argues that the work that younger workers are given is generally the least interesting work in the firm and that the older workers keep the more interesting and more highly skilled jobs to themselves. As a result, the youngest groups become dissatisfied as they discover that they have 'done their time' at the low levels, but are not being rewarded with career advancement, training opportunities, and more interesting work.

TRENDS IN THE LEVELS OF EDUCATIONAL ATTAINMENT

At the same time that the entry labour market has been affected by the slowdown in the Japanese economy, there have been major changes in the supply of well-educated graduates. Educational attainment has been rising since the 1980s, and the 1990s have seen a very rapid rise in the numbers of students taking more advanced degrees. I have already mentioned that women are now increasingly likely to enrol in a four-year degree programme rather than a two-year programme. Facing a possible decline in numbers, some of the two-year colleges have reorganized their curriculum to provide a four-year programme and relabelled themselves as universities. One other area where the increase in years of education is particularly noticeable is in the enrolment in graduate programmes by science and engineering students. As Figure 9.5 suggests, for both men and women, the proportion of graduates going on to graduate school in the sciences has tripled. The same trend is not seen in the humanities and social sciences. The upward trend for the sciences begins in the 1980s, but there is a notable acceleration in the upward trend in the 1990s. By the year 2000, nearly a third of all male, and a fifth of all female graduates in science courses went on to graduate-level education. Nevertheless, by the standards of the USA, graduate-level education is still relatively undeveloped in Japan. According to the US Department of Education (2002), in the year 2000 some 13% of students with American citizenship or permanent residency at American universities were in graduate programmes including professional schools. The corresponding figure for Japan was 7% (MOE 2000), although this has been rapidly rising.

Much of the increase in the advancement rate to graduate school of the 1990s must be due to the demands of industry for more highly educated technical staff,

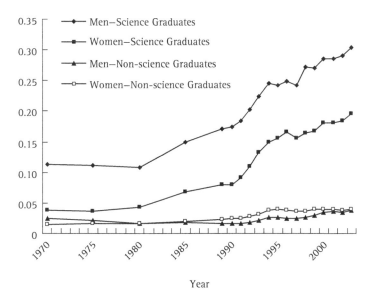

Figure 9.5. *Proportion of university graduates who proceed directly to graduate school*
Notes: Science graduates include graduates of engineering, agricultural studies, and health. Non-science graduates include social sciences, humanities, education, and home studies.
Source: MOE2.

but the Ministry of Education also plays an important role by determining the limits for the numbers of students that may enrol. Nevertheless, the downturn in the labour market may also be playing an important role, as university graduates decide that their employment prospects will be improved with a higher degree. As Figure 9.2 suggests, the downturn of the 1990s has hit science graduates the hardest.

There has also been a major increase in the rates of educational attainment at lower levels. Figure 9.6 shows that the percentages of both men and women that have gone on to tertiary education have increased over the 1990s. As noted earlier, there has been a drop in the share of women taking two-year degree programmes while the share taking a four-year programme has increased rapidly. Figure 9.6 also shows that there has been a gradual increase in the proportion of high-school graduates who are attending specialized training schools. In addition to the high-school graduates, university graduates are now attending these schools to develop some practical skills not offered in their university curriculum. To some extent, these trends may be a statistical artefact due to the upgrading of schools that were formerly in the 'other training schools' category, which has been in decline (Dore and Sako 1998). Nevertheless, the upgrading may reflect the demand for better vocational training.

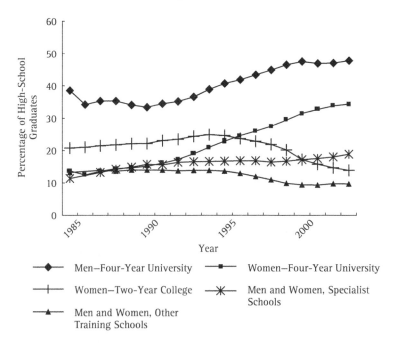

Figure 9.6. *Percentage of high-school graduates advancing to higher education*

Note: The figure shows the percentage of high-school graduates proceeding to different types of higher education.

Source: MOE1 (2001).

At the school leaving age, there has been an increase in the rate at which middle-school students progress on to secondary school. The percentage of those who stopped immediately after their compulsory education at age 15 has never been high in the last 20 years, but it dropped from 7% to 5% of men between 1984 and 1999 and from 5% to 3% of women in the same period (MOE 2000). Fortunately, the poor labour market conditions for middle-school graduates only affect a small proportion of the population of youth at this point, or the youth unemployment problem in Japan would be much more serious than it is.

One effect that increased educational attainment may have is that the average ability of those who do not go on to further education may fall, as the more able students decide to continue with schooling. Ariga (2004), for example, argues that the principal cause of the deterioration in labour market conditions for high-school graduates has been the diminishing quality of these graduates, rather than the recession of the 1990s.

THE '*FRIITAA*' PHENOMENON

The 1990s have seen a doubling of the rate of non-standard employment for the 15–24 year-old age group (Table 4.4). I have already mentioned that this group is frequently referred to by the term *friitaa*–a recently coined term combining 'free' and *arubaitaa* (from the German). The latter term is most often used to describe students who take up part-time jobs. The term *friitaa* is used mainly in discussion of young school graduates under age 30 to describe the fact that they are not bound up in the long-term contracts and responsibilities that attend standard employment. There is intense interest in Japan in this phenomenon, both from the government and from the media industries that cater specifically for this group. Although I have avoided the use of this term in my analysis in Chapter 4, it is worth examining the debate about this phenomenon.

Parasite Singles?

Masahiro Yamada (1999) attracted a great deal of publicity with his book, *The Age of the Parasite Single*. The book begins by observing that there has been an increase in the numbers of young people who continue to live with their parents into their late twenties or early thirties. He notes that, given the costs of housing and the willingness of parents to allow their children to live at home, there is no incentive for them to move out.[4] Yamada takes moral issue with the 'indulgence' of parents who allow their children to remain at home as 'parasite singles'. There is no necessity for these youth to work hard at a standard job. Instead, they can move around freely, choosing to work when they need money for their expenses or if they can find work that is interesting to them. As Genda (2001) points out, there is no reason to believe that this pattern should suddenly have taken root in the 1990s.

In contrast to Yamada, Genda (2001) argues that most of the blame should not be placed on youth and that new graduates have been pushed into non-standard work in the 1990s simply because firms have cut back on hiring new graduates. He places the blame for this on job protection for older workers. He believes that older workers should be more easily dismissed when firms are under economic duress. Analysing firm-level data, he shows that firms with higher shares of older employees tended to hire fewer graduates in the late 1990s. He also notes that firms that have extended their retirement age beyond 60 are less likely to commit themselves to the hiring of new graduates on an annual basis. Although both of these observations are interesting, they do not prove that job protection for older workers is necessarily disadvantageous to youth. The fact that firms tend to hire fewer graduates if they have higher shares of older employees also suggests that they have been cutting back on hiring new graduates for a long period of time, not just in the 1990s. The fact that firms with retirement ages over 60 tend to hire fewer graduates may simply be a reflection of the tendency for such firms to be smaller and to have more 'individualized' personnel management. Such firms may also be less likely to hire on an annual basis since they do not operate with an age-based hierarchical employment and pay structure. Finally, even if firms were able to dismiss their older employees more freely, it is not certain that they would then recruit more young graduates into regular employment.

Concerns about Career Development of Youth

The Japanese Ministry of Health, Welfare and Labour is concerned about the increase in the rate of part-time work. Their own research into the issue suggests that, while some 45% of young part-time workers are having a 'moratorium' on starting their careers and will eventually successfully find regular employment, there are another 40% who are taking part-time work because they cannot find anything better. The remaining 15% are taking part-time jobs while they pursue some other ambition, perhaps in the arts (JIL 2001*b*). The government is particularly concerned about the latter two groups. There are legitimate reasons for the concern of the Ministry. First, many of the part-time workers will not be working enough hours to be included in the pension system. A second concern relates to training. Since much of the training provided to employees is concentrated among the regular, permanent staff, there is concern that youth are not acquiring the skills needed in the future. I have suggested in Chapter 4 that the needs for a highly skilled workforce may be lower in the future as a larger share of the workforce will be employed in those services which do not demand such high skills. Nevertheless, highly developed skills will still be needed in the workplace (Koike *et al.* 2000). What is less certain is whether as large a share of high-skilled employees will be needed as in the past. In the meantime, the MHLW is considering ways to promote more training for part-time workers.

CONCLUSIONS

Japanese youth have had a difficult decade in the labour market. In particular, those graduates without post-secondary education have either found it difficult or chosen not to find full-time regular employment. Although many of those who work at part-time jobs are able to manage by living with their parents, they may be losing out on the opportunity to start a career and develop the skills that will help them in the future. It is possible that this state of affairs is only a temporary one, based on the poor state of the economy. Then, at worst, there would be a cohort scarred by having had the misfortune to enter the labour market during this period. It is also possible, as I have argued, that this state of affairs is here to stay. In this case there will gradually be a long-term bifurcation of those better-educated individuals with regular employment and those less-educated individuals who do not have access to jobs with the kinds of skill development for which Japan has been so widely praised. The future of Japanese society depends to a large extent on which of these two scenarios is realized.

NOTES

1. This is sometimes referred to as the 'one person, one firm' system.
2. Unfortunately, the survey of first destinations conducted annually by the Recruit Corporation has been discontinued, so we don't have information for the most recent years, but it is unlikely that this trend has been reversed.
3. Unfortunately, there are no statistics for the unemployment rates of graduates of vocational training schools such as the *senmon gakkō* mentioned earlier.
4. It is quite possible for young adults to carry on sexual relationships, with the widespread availability of 'love hotels', which provide for short stays of an hour or more and complete anonymity in transactions relating to one's stay.

10

The Declining Labour Force
and Immigration

The major issue facing the Japanese economy over the long run is the rapid ageing of Japan's population. The rapid ageing of the workforce has already been referred to in the context of the labour market for older workers in Chapter 8. Here I take up this issue in a broader perspective.

THE AGEING SOCIETY

Japan is the most rapidly ageing society in the OECD as measured by the rate at which the proportion of the population over the age of 65 is increasing. Figure 10.1 shows projections of the dependency ratio (i.e. those under the age of 15 and over the age of 65 as a share of those aged 15–65), along with total population and the proportion of those over the age of 65. The dependency ratio in the year 2004 is approximately at the same level that it was in 1980, when the members of the postwar baby-boom generation were having their families. From now on, the dependency rate is going to rise rapidly, reaching almost 70% in the year 2020. Furthermore, Japan has the highest life expectancy of any nation and the proportion of those over the age of 80 is also growing rapidly and already constitutes 4.5% of the population. It should also be noted that any reversal of the decline in the fertility rate would also increase the dependency rate in the short run.

The reasons why Japan is in this situation are well understood. Although Japan had the typically pyramidal population/age structure of a developing country in the 1930s, it underwent a rapid demographic transition in the late 1940s, followed by a gradual reduction in fertility beginning in the mid-1970s that has lasted to the present. At the same time the life expectancy of the Japanese rapidly increased so that Japan has been a world leader in this particular measure of development since the 1980s.

The ageing and decline in the population will have a major impact on Japan's total labour supply. Mori (1997) uses age-specific labour force participation rates and the population projections for each age group made by demographers to predict the future size of the labour force. His work suggests that the labour force would decline from its peak of 68 million in 1998 to 64 million in 2010 and then to 59 million in 2025.[1] These estimates are only reasonable in so far as one assumes that the labour force participation rate of women remains at its present

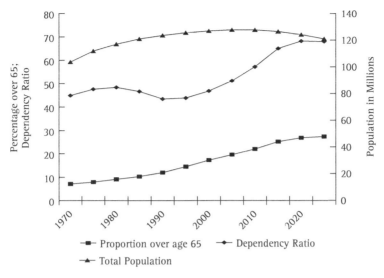

Figure 10.1. *Demographic trends*
Source: National Institute of Population and Social Security Research, Japanese Census.

level. Later in this chapter, I will examine what could happen if we relax this assumption.

PROBLEMS RAISED BY THE AGEING OF THE POPULATION

The ageing of the population presents a number of challenges to the Japanese, including the management of its pension system and other aspects of intergenerational transfers as well as its economic growth. There are also a number of labour market issues, the most serious being the high dependency rate that will develop in some regions of the country.

Fiscal Problems

One of the most serious problems facing Japan is the increased level of payroll taxes that will be needed to finance the welfare state. The Japanese fund their public pensions mainly through payroll taxes. The recent reform to the public pension system lowered future benefit levels and thus reduced future tax levels. Nevertheless, the rate of payroll tax for employees' pensions alone is expected to increase from its level of 13.6% of total earnings in 2004 to 18.3% in 2017. Adding in other income taxes and corresponding increases in health insurance premiums, the total tax burden rises to some 50% of income for the average employee. This kind of burden will increase the pressure on firms to use part-time workers in order to avoid these extra costs. It may also lead to the development of a growing sector in the economy that avoids the tax burden entirely through informal activities. Ultimately, it is likely to depress labour supply, especially through the decision of women to work part time, but also through earlier retirement.

For these reasons, it is possible that the Japanese government will increase the consumption tax from its current level of 5% to at least 10% to help keep income or payroll taxes as low as possible. In this case, many of the compliance problems that exist with the direct tax on labour may be avoided. This is not something that the government is willing to do during the current recession, but the government's advisory panel on tax has already stated that it believes the consumption tax should be raised and the pressure on government to raise the tax will only increase over time (*Asahi Shinbun*, 18 June 2003).

Labour Shortages in Specific Fields

A second problem that Japan will face with the fall in the labour force is that it is more likely that there will be shortages for some technical jobs. The METI survey on employment mismatch cited in the previous chapter suggests that there are shortages in some technical areas. It is possible that Japan can train its own citizens for some of these jobs, but in other cases it may be necessary to bring in foreign skilled workers. One of the main areas of growth in labour demand, however, will be for health and old-age care.

For the most part the Japanese government has promoted the idea that older Japanese are best cared for by their families. Beginning in the 1980s the Japanese government instituted a series of 'Gold Plans' designed to deal with the problems of the ageing society. Although these plans provide for an increase in the number of nursing homes, the plans concentrate on such things as increasing the provision of home helps, home nurses, and short stays in nursing homes. The main provider of care for the elderly is presumed to be the family, especially women, with the state playing a supportive role. In this sense, Japan is much like Southern Europe with its extended family living arrangements, where the elderly live with or in close proximity to their children and do not rely either on the state or the market to provide care. In 2000, the Japanese government instituted Long-Term Care Insurance to ensure that those who need the most care are able to get it. One of its aims has been to diversify the kinds of care that the elderly receive, so that they need not be reliant on their families. The number of elderly that live with their families has dropped in recent years.[2] In 1980, 69% of those over the age of 65 lived with their children, while only 48% did so in 2003 (MHLW10 2002). Nevertheless, about 60% of the elderly receive their care at home (Shinotsuka 1998).

The Role of Women

The ageing of the population, combined with the extent to which daughters or daughters-in-law undertake care, will put some constraints on the labour force participation of women in the future. The Economic Planning Agency estimates that 5 million elderly will need care in 2025, up from 2,650,000 in 2000 (Shinotsuka 1998). Nevertheless, it should still be possible for Japan to increase labour inputs from women in the future, continuing an ongoing trend. A more difficult and serious problem for the labour market comes from the fact that the increase in the dependency rate shown in Figure 10.1 is not evenly distributed around the country. There are regions and specific locales where the number of working-age persons available to help look after the elderly at home is very low (the support ratio is low) and in these cases the labour market will face severe local shortages. For example, in 2000, 25% of the population of Shimane prefecture was over the age of 65 compared with the national average of 17%, and the dependency rate had already reached 65% (PHPT 2000). Since the Long-Term Care Insurance plan puts the responsibility for provision of care on local municipalities, it may not be viable in the regions with the highest dependency rates (Shinotsuka 1998).

As labour supply declines in Japan, the rising price of labour will increase the potential demand for immigrant labour, especially in those industries that must compete internationally. Most of the OECD is responding to the problem of an ageing population by allowing substantial inflows of immigrants. Japan, however, is unlikely to do so in the foreseeable future, except for a limited number of occupations.

IMMIGRATION

Defining Immigrants

Immigrants make up a very low share of Japan's population in comparison with most other OECD countries. The definition of who is foreign in Japan is complicated by the fact that there is a large group of roughly 530,000 permanent residents of Korean nationality, who are in most respects similar to Japanese nationals. That is, their first language is Japanese, most do not speak Korean, or at least not fluently, and virtually all were born in Japan. They are the descendants of groups of Koreans brought to Japan during the Imperial period from 1910 to 1945. They were denied Japanese citizenship with the signing of the San Francisco Peace Treaty of 1952 that ended the American Occupation. Since 1992 a 'special permanent residents' category was created for these Koreans and a smaller group of Chinese. Although a small number (around 10,000) choose to become Japanese citizens each year, the majority maintain their Korean or Chinese nationality. For the purposes of this discussion, I will treat the 'special permanent residents' as if they were Japanese, except to note, in passing, that they suffer discrimination in the labour market because of their ethnic identity. The resident Korean community also provides family links that enable Koreans from Korea (including clandestine workers) to find work in Japan. References to Koreans or Chinese foreigners in the remainder of this chapter are to those individuals who do not fall into this category of Imperial period immigrants and their descendants. For that reason, the statistics that I report will sometimes differ from those published in other sources.

The Immigration Control Act of 1990

Table 10.1 shows the proportion of the population that is foreign along with the proportion of the labour force for selected OECD countries. Japan is near the bottom in terms of the proportion of foreigners in its population. In general, the Japanese state has been opposed to having larger numbers of foreigners resident in Japan, and this is also reflected in popular opinion. With the exception of foreigners who were married to, or the children of, Japanese workers, and certain categories of skilled workers, the labour market was officially closed to the outside world until 1990. Skilled workers could only enter on a fixed-term basis. The tight labour market of the late 1980s brought a large influx of undocumented foreign workers, most of them visa overstays. The Japanese government's response to this was the 1990 Immigration Control Act, which brought in the following measures (Papademetriou and Hamilton 2000):

1. The children of Japanese who had migrated to other countries, known as *Nikkeijin*, were allowed to take up residence in Japan and to work without restriction. Although residence was limited in the first instance to three years, many then applied and obtained permanent residency. This ruling was brought in with the belief that the *Nikkeijin* would fit in better with Japanese society. In reality, the *Nikkeijin* have found it difficult to mix in Japanese society due to language and other cultural differences. The majority of the *Nikkeijin* come from Brazil and Brazilians are now the second largest group of foreigners resident in Japan, after Chinese.

Table 10.1. *Proportion of the population or labour force that is foreign in selected OECD countries, 1999*

Country	Percentage of total population	Percentage of labour force
Japan	0.8	1.0
Korea	0.4	0.4
UK	3.8	3.9
Germany	8.9	8.7
France	5.6	6.1
Italy	2.2	3.6
USA	10.3[1]	11.7[2]

Notes:
[1] Foreign-born share in 1996.
[2] Foreign-born.

Source: OECD3 (2001), chart 1.5, table 1.13; includes resident Koreans and Chinese.

2. A limited number of 'trainee' workers could be brought in for the purpose of teaching them skills that they would then use in their home countries. Large firms have always been able to bring in a number of workers to be trained for their overseas subsidiaries. The new regulations allow small and medium-sized enterprises to hire these unskilled workers also for a three-year period. A Technical Internship Training Programme (TITP) allows trainees that pass a skill test to change their status from trainee to 'designated activities', thereby allowing them to stay in the country for an additional three years. As Table 10.2 shows, the numbers of foreigners who fall into this category is quite limited. The majority of the participants in the TITP have been from China and Indonesia. Although some firms may abuse the trainee system in order to obtain unskilled labour, the government monitors the conditions of employment closely and there are high costs, estimated to be around 1.2 million yen in employing a trainee (Iguchi 1998).

3. Except for the categories mentioned in (1) and (2) it is illegal to employ unskilled workers from overseas. The new legislation also provides penalties for both workers and employers. Workers who enter the country illegally may be fined or imprisoned, and any illegal worker may be deported if apprehended. In 1999, 55,000 were deported. Since 2000, there has been a five-year ban on re-entry into Japan. There are also penalties including fines (up to 2 million yen) or imprisonment (up to three years) for employers that hire illegal workers or for agents that bring them in.

Despite these prohibitions the government still estimates that in the year 2000 there were roughly 220,000 undocumented workers representing more than a quarter of the foreign labour force. This estimate is conservative as it is based on inflows and outflows of foreigners. Any migrant who enters Japan unofficially will not be counted and there has been a sharp rise since 1996 of illegal immigrants coming in unofficially. More than 7,000 were apprehended in 1998 and others must have escaped detection. People-smuggling is now a global

Table 10.2. *Foreign labour force according to classification, 1999*

Category	Number (1000s)
Total foreign labour force	670
Foreign residents with permission based on specialist occupation	125.7
Trainees and working holiday-makers	23.3
Estimated number of students in part-time jobs	47.0
Nikkeijin	220.5
Estimated number of illegal workers	252
Spouse or child of Japanese national or permanent resident[1]	277.2

Note:
[1] Not all of this group will be in the labour force.

Source: OECD3 (2001), table III.20. Excludes resident Koreans and Chinese.

enterprise and Japan is affected, although not perhaps to the extent found elsewhere in the OECD.

4.   There was an expansion of the number of categories under which skilled workers were allowed to work. There are very strict provisions and qualifications are needed for many of these jobs, however, and the new law actually prohibits some individuals who would have been allowed under the old law (Mori 1997).

5.   Students were allowed to work part-time, including students on 'Working Holidays'.

Japan also makes little effort to give assistance to refugees or asylum-seekers. In 2001, only 353 persons applied for asylum, but the government rejected 316 of these initially.[3]

Although the number of undocumented workers in Japan has undoubtedly fallen, the numbers of foreigners who are officially registered in Japan rose by 700,000 between 1990 and 2001 (PMO4 2003). The majority of these are from Latin America (*Nikkeijin*) and from other Asian countries, especially China. Some of this increase in foreigners comprises children or other non-employed family members, so this figure is larger than the net contribution of foreigners to the working population. Nevertheless, we can assume that the drop in the labour force would have been much larger had it not been for this increased immigration. Since the overall labour force has dropped since 1998, these increases have clearly not been able to keep up with the decline of Japanese in the labour force.

WHERE DO FOREIGN WORKERS WORK AND HOW ARE THEY TREATED?

The employment of foreign workers tends to be divided between those (primarily from Europe, North America, and so on) who are highly skilled and work in the service sector, and those coming from poorer countries, often with fewer skills or qualifications, who work in manufacturing, construction, and services. Table 10.3 shows the distribution of documented foreign workers and illegal workers according to industry. Documented foreign workers are mainly found in manufacturing (trainees and *Nikkeijin*) and in the services (highly skilled workers). Male undocumented workers tend to be found in manufacturing and construction. Women who are undocumented tend to be hostesses, waitresses, and factory workers. Many of those who are classified as hostesses or waitresses are engaged in prostitution. There is also a large population of documented Asian women working as prostitutes or hostesses brought in by special agents on cultural visas. Most of the 25,000 Filipinos in Japan on entertainment or show business visas must fall into this category.

Much of the employment of the less skilled is in areas where it is difficult to attract labour at a low wage rate (i.e. the elasticity of supply with respect to the wage is very high). The *Nikkeijin*, being fully documented, are in limited

Table 10.3. *Foreign workers by industry, 2002*

Industry/occupation	Documented workers	Undocumented workers[1]	
		Men	Women
Construction	1.3	27	–
Manufacturing	71.5	41	16
Services	14.1	16	70
Hostess		–	40
Waitress/bartender		5	11
Repairs		7	5
Dishwashing		–	6
Other service		4	8
Other	13.1	16	15
Transport and communications	2.9		
Trade and restaurants	8.5		
Finance and insurance	1.2		

Note:

[1] Based on apprehended illegal workers.

Source: MHLW13 (2002) and MOJ1 (2002).

supply and great demand. Consequently, their wage rates tend to be much higher, and they also tend to work in middle-sized companies that will avoid hiring undocumented workers. The smallest companies generally provide the poorest working conditions and pay and this is where most undocumented workers (primarily from Asia) are to be found. In general, the hourly wage rates for unskilled foreign workers tend to be comparable to those of native workers, but since they usually don't receive bonuses, their annual earnings, and the costs to their employer, are considerably lower. They are usually not enrolled in social insurance programmes, so again, the cost of their labour will be lower to the employer (Mori 1997). Workers who find their employment through kinship networks (*Nikkeijin* and Koreans) also get better treatment than those who go through brokers. There also seems to be a fairly well-defined stratification in terms of nationality among the less-skilled, with *Nikkeijin* and Koreans at the top, followed by nationals of other East Asian countries and then other Asians.

Undocumented workers are subject to various forms of abuse, at least until they establish a personal network that will provide them with better information about job opportunities. Unsafe working practices and failure of their employer to pay their wages are some of the problems that they experience. Ignorance of Japanese law, and fears of being apprehended, also prevent them from voicing complaints about mistreatment. Undoubtedly the worst treated will be women in the sex industry who are often controlled by gangsters and work in conditions close to slavery.

PUBLIC POLICY AND ATTITUDES TO IMMIGRATION

The national government maintains a position that is opposed to large-scale immigration, especially of unskilled workers.[4] For example, in the 2000 Basic Plan for Immigration Control we find the following: 'if you trace back the history of Japanese society and give thought to the Japanese people's perception of society and their sensitivity, it would not be realistic to suddenly introduce a large number of foreign workers' (MOJ2 2000). On the other hand, local governments are more flexible, partly by necessity—immigrants tend to be concentrated in certain regions, and local authorities need to deal with the problems of accommodating them, educating their children, and providing social services. For example, in 2002 nearly one-third of the 265,000 Brazilians living in Japan were located in the two heavily industrialized prefectures of Aichi and Shizuoka (MOJ1 2002). Local governments have also been the first to allow foreigners (permanent residents) the right to vote in some circumstances (Kashiwazaki 2002).

Private employers have, understandably, been more willing to accept foreign workers than the government. For example, Nikkeiren, the Federation of Japanese Employers, noted in its position paper of 2000 that:

The issues of visa status, expanding the number of occupations covered under training and skill development programs, and *also of accepting immigration*, should begin to be studied soon and preparations made to provide job opportunities appealing to foreigners and better living conditions for them. (Nikkeiren 2000; emphasis added)

Similarly, in its *Japan 2025* vision paper of 2004, Keidanren, the Japan Business Federation (with which Nikkeiren merged in 2002), called for greater tolerance for diversity and for the government to 'open its doors to people from around the globe' (Keidanren 2004). Nevertheless, Keidanren has not gone so far as to call for the employment of unskilled foreign workers. Small and medium-sized enterprises see the matter differently, however, and in this sense the tension between local and centralized interests mirrors that of the public sector.

THE ECONOMIC ARGUMENT AGAINST LARGE-SCALE IMMIGRATION

It is usually taken as axiomatic that Japan's declining workforce will create major problems for the country. While it is undoubtedly true that the increase in the dependency ratio will call for imaginative solutions to the problem of caring for the elderly, and while there are likely to be major regional problems, Japan's outlook need not be as bleak as some predict. The first point to make is that a smaller workforce will require a smaller capital stock (other things equal) so that actual consumption need not fall. Dekle (2000), for example, uses a model with perfect foresight to calculate one future scenario using Japanese government projections of the size of the labour force. In his model, consumption per capita continues to grow at 1.2% per year. This is accomplished through a fall in the savings rate from its present level of more than 30% to levels around 20% by mid-century. Net exports remain positive until 2010 after which they become negative. The current account, however, remains positive until 2020 as repatriated earnings remain large. Only after 2025 does the net external debt held by Japan start to fall.

Although Dekle's model only represents one possible scenario, it does imply that the Japanese need not suffer great losses in their quality of life as a result of the demographic change. Dekle's model depends on a rate of total factor productivity growth of 2%. This seems to be plausible once we recognize that there are opportunities to raise productivity outside of manufacturing to much higher levels. This issue will be addressed below.

Even if the Japanese public was more open to the prospect of immigration, it is still worth asking whether it would be a good idea for Japan to accept larger numbers of immigrants. The issue is complex, as capital will generally benefit, while labour can be affected according to the skill levels of the immigrants. Chiswick (1998) points out that the scarcity of land in Japan may present a further complication. Using a simple macroeconomic model, he argues that a land-poor country such as Japan should not take in immigrants, even if a land-rich country such as the United States finds it in its interest to do so. The costs to the Japanese in terms of sharing the land resource with immigrants may be greater than the net benefits that they would bring to the economy. Last, but not least, there is simply the question of the effect that large-scale immigration would have on Japanese culture, which is essentially not quantifiable. Even if we ignore this issue, there will be costs (as in all societies) in assimilating new immigrants.

ALTERNATIVES TO IMMIGRATION

There are several alternative ways in which Japan can deal with its declining population. The first of these is to raise the labour inputs of women in the market economy. A second is to export capital and use foreign labour overseas, while a third is to raise labour productivity at home. All of these are likely to be important in the future, and the second is already of great significance. I will look at each of these in turn.

Increasing the Labour Contribution made by Women

Changes in the taxation of spouses' earnings (under consideration by the Japanese government) as well as the additional provision of day-care facilities through the second Angel Plan and the promises of the Koizumi government could raise the participation rate of women substantially.[5] If we assume that women can achieve the levels of labour force participation found in the USA then it is possible to compensate for some of the drop in the labour force.

Following Ono and Rebick (2003) I divide the problem into two components—increasing hours of work, and increasing the participation rate.[6]

Increasing the Labour Input of Part-Time Workers   Around 42% of employed Japanese women work part time. As a result, Japanese women only work 136 hours per month on average compared to men, who work 165 hours per month. If employed Japanese women all worked as many hours as the men they would increase their labour input by 21%. This is an unrealistic expectation, but it does serve as an upper bound for what is possible. For the purposes of my overall estimate I look at what would happen if the rate at which women aged 25–64 in Japan worked part time was at the US level of 20% rather than 42%.[7] These women work about half as many hours as their full-time counterparts. If half of them were now to work full time, this would increase the female labour input by roughly $0.5 \times 0.4 \times 0.5$ or 10%.

Increasing the Labour Force Participation Rate of Women   Again, I use the USA as a benchmark, and assume that Japan is able to raise the labour force participation rate of women from its level of 67% to the US level of 77%. In this case, there is an increase of about 15% in the female labour force input. Adding the two effects together (and compounding) gives a total increase in the labour input of women of 26.5%, which would result if Japanese women had participation and part-time employment rates comparable to those in the USA. In terms of the overall labour force this represents an increase of 0.265×0.41 or around 11%.[8] Mori (1997) uses contemporary labour force participation rates to forecast the future labour supply and finds that the labour force can be expected to fall by roughly 9 million persons or by 14%. If increased use of women in the labour force could increase labour inputs by 11%, then this would help to compensate for the projected losses.[9]

Exporting Capital

As discussed in Chapter 6, the period from 1992 to 2003 has seen employment in manufacturing drop by over 3 million. Japan is adapting to its labour 'shortage' in the expected manner—exporting capital to make use of foreign labour. Japan has been making large direct foreign investments ever since current account surpluses became established in the 1980s. We are most interested in the movements taking place in manufacturing since this is the activity that can most easily use foreign labour. The actual number of investments rose rapidly in the 1980s, with the USA and ASEAN (Association of South East Asian Nations) being the regions in which most investments were made. In the 1990s, most of the investment activity shifted to China and in general, the number of new investments fell in the late 1990s after the Asian financial crisis. Nevertheless, both output and employment of Japanese-owned businesses in Asia increased by some 50% between 1996 and 2001, with a doubling taking place in China

(METI 2002). This must reflect the fact that many investments are still expanding their production levels. Direct foreign investment in manufacturing does have some positive impacts on employment in the capital goods industries and for some intermediate goods. Nevertheless, one government estimate based on the analysis of input—output tables suggests that roughly 800,000 jobs have disappeared in manufacturing due to foreign investment, of which more than half have been in the small and medium enterprise sector. The greatest impact has been felt in the electronics and communications equipment industries (METI 2002).

Fukao and Amano (1998), however, argue that foreign production may not be as substitutable for domestic production as suggested by METI estimates. If foreign investment provided a 100% substitute for exports then they estimate that over 2 million jobs would have been lost in manufacturing. However, if foreign investment only substitutes for domestic investment at a rate proportional to the share of this investment in total world production, job losses would be much lower, at 40,000. To some extent the outcome depends on what Japanese firms would have done if they had not invested overseas. If Japanese firms would have continued to use domestic sources for intermediate goods and so on, then the job losses are very great. What Fukao and Amano are suggesting, however, is that domestic Japanese producers would have lost business in any case, due to the high costs of labour and land. Whatever view one takes on this issue, the effect is the same—Japan is moving out of manufacturing very rapidly. This is an inevitable consequence of the increased labour costs and substitution of capital for labour and is no different from the experience of many other developed countries.

Improving Productivity

The third way in which Japan can compensate for its declining labour force is by raising productivity. Table 10.4 shows productivity growth rates in labour productivity for a number of sectors in the economy, comparing the rates of productivity growth in the 1980s with the 1990s. Labour productivity growth has fallen in most of the sectors.[10] In general, the fall in average labour productivity can be attributed to slower growth in total factor productivity rather than a slowdown in rates of investment. The OECD estimates that annual TFP growth declined over the 1990s falling from roughly 3% to 1.25% (OECD2 2001). Hayashi and Prescott (2002) claim that the decline has been even greater. After taking account of working hours, they claim that TFP grew at 3.7% between 1983 and 1991 and then only at the rate of 0.5% between 1991 and 2000. Either way, the drop has been large enough to have a great impact on Japanese growth.

The most careful study of differences between the USA and Japan in the rate of growth of total factor productivity (TFP) was undertaken by Jorgenson and Kuroda (1990), who controlled for the quality of inputs. These series have been

Table 10.4. *Productivity growth in Japan, 1980–1999*

Industry	Annual productivity increase 1980–1989	Annual productivity increase 1990–1999
Agriculture, forestry, fishing	4.9	0.5
Manufacturing	3.9	3.3
Food products	−0.8	2.1
Textiles	−1.0	2.7
Pulp and paper	3.8	0.5
Chemicals	10.2	3.6
Ceramics	5.1	1.5
Basic metal	−0.8	1.1
Fabricated metal	5.6	1.0
Machinery	5.5	−0.1
Electrical machinery	12.8	10.5
Transport equipment	3.6	3.0
Precision instruments	7.8	1.7
Construction	3.0	−3.0
Utilities	1.1	2.0
Trade	4.2	3.6
Finance and insurance	8.5	4.2
Transport and communications	3.6	3.0
Other services	1.0	1.5

Note: Productivity growth is measured as value added divided by employment and hours worked.

Source: OECD2 (2001), table 5.

updated by Weinstein (2001) using OECD data to show trends in TFP growth from 1960 to 1993 and his results are shown in Figure 10.2. The main point to note is that although Japanese productivity in manufacturing converged towards that of the USA between 1960 and 1982, reaching approximately 94% of US levels, the gap in productivity between the USA and Japan in other sectors has actually widened. Only in finance and insurance is there an appreciable convergence and Weinstein believes that this is mainly due to ongoing deregulation. Performance in agriculture and transportation and communication is particularly weak. Productivity in transportation and communication has risen in Japan, but not as rapidly as in the USA where deregulation in the 1980s helped maintain rapid TFP growth (Weinstein 2001). Figure 10.2 also suggests that deregulation in the utilities industries could raise productivity substantially since Japan's levels of TFP are very low.

How much can improvements in productivity compensate for the drop in the labour force? Weinstein (2001) argues that regulations are the main reason why Japanese productivity is very low. If deregulation allowed Japanese productivity

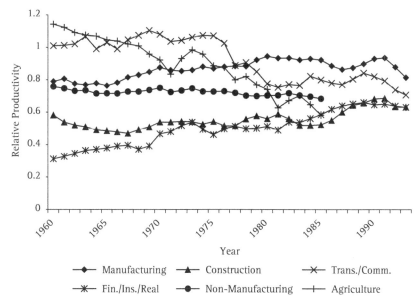

Figure 10.2. *Japanese productivity relative to the USA, 1960–93*
Source: Weinstein (2001).

to rise to US levels, then Japanese GDP would rise by roughly one-third (since Japanese levels of TFP are on average 75% of US levels). This would more than compensate for the decline in the labour force in terms of its impact on the standard of living. It may be unreasonable to expect Japan to reach US levels of productivity, but these estimates do suggest that raising TFP is a way for Japan to deal with its declining labour force.

CONCLUSION

In conclusion, although Japan will almost certainly continue to see a decline in its labour force over the next 25 years, the prospects are not necessarily as bleak as first suggested. Immigration is unlikely to fully compensate for the drop in the labour force, but it is likely that immigrant labour will be encouraged for skilled occupations. The increased reliance on foreign sourcing in manufacturing, increased use of women as paid labour, and improvements in productivity through deregulation can ensure that Japan can cope with its demographic problems without suffering a drop in living standards relative to other OECD countries. The main problems that Japan faces will be (1) ensuring that a fair means of transferring wealth between generations is obtained through the tax and welfare systems and (2) dealing with problems specific to locales or to particular sectors such as the provision of care for the elderly.

NOTES

1. Mori's estimates are actually restricted to the labour force between the ages of 18 and 69, and I have assumed that the labour force below 18 and over 69 stays constant at roughly 4 million.
2. It should be noted that as a substitute for co-residency, residence in the neighbourhood, often next door in a sub-divided lot or in a separate self-contained apartment, has become more prevalent (Brown 2003).
3. Comparable figures for the UK, France, and Italy were 11,000, 2,400, and 2,000 respectively (USCR 2003).
4. Nevertheless, in 2003 METI stated in its White Paper that Japan will need more immigration in the future.
5. The MHLW is also considering lowering the threshold where part-time workers would be required to contribute to pension benefit programmes (Fukawa and Yamamoto 2003) from three-quarters of standard working hours to one-half of standard working hours and earnings from 1.3 million to 650,000 yen. It is not clear how this would affect the choice of hours of work.
6. This section borrows directly from Ono and Rebick (2003).
7. We exclude women younger than 25 as many are still in school. Women over 64 are more likely to wish to work part time regardless of impediments to working full-time.
8. This figure might be slightly smaller if the growth in the women's labour input was adjusted for being of lower quality than male labour input.
9. Some of the gains presented here will improve GDP levels without necessarily improving welfare. An example of this is the case where unpaid family-based child-care or nursing care for the elderly moves out of the home and is provided by paid labour in child-care centres or old-age homes. There may be some improvements in labour productivity as economies of scale are realized, but to a large extent these gains will not increase net social welfare.
10. The fall to negative values in construction is especially notable and can be attributed to the large number of employees in idle or 'zombie' construction companies, which are being kept afloat by creditor banks.

11

Conclusions and Prospects

At the start of this book, I referred to the debate about the extent to which the Japanese economy is changing. I hope that through these pages I have shown that the Japanese labour market and its institutions have undergone some substantive changes over the past 10 to 20 years. These changes have not been able to solve all of Japan's labour market problems, but they seem to be leading in a direction that may be appropriate for Japan's needs. At this point I would like to briefly survey the changes that have taken place and comment on how they may be rational solutions to Japan's problems.

First, although there has been an increase in the rate of involuntary dismissals, especially since 1998, the view that firms should offer job protection for their employees still seems to hold.[1] It is true that employees' expectations and ambitions have changed over the past 20 years. Most young employees today do not expect that they will work for the same company until mandatory retirement and many of them say that they would prefer not to do so (MHLW7 2003: 173). Nevertheless, overall mobility rates remain low by international standards and tenure has shown only a slight decline for men, and an increase for women. Instead of encouraging greater mobility for regular employees, Japanese firms are finding that greater use of non-standard employees such as part-time workers, contract workers, and dispatched workers can provide much of the flexibility that they need.

While the Japanese firm may not be drastically altering its policy on dismissal, pay systems are undergoing changes. Performance-related pay has been widely introduced and age- and tenure-earnings profiles have become flatter during the 1980s and 1990s. In the future, it will be less likely that a firm will have to pay an older employee much more than he or she is worth to the company. These moves are also consistent with a move towards corporate governance that puts greater emphasis on profitability and control of labour costs.

Women's position in the Japanese labour market is also undergoing change. On the one hand, most women will continue to work in the secondary part of the labour market, but increasingly as part-time employees rather than as family workers. On the other hand, for a select group of career-oriented women there are greater opportunities to develop a satisfactory career within what is still a heavily male-dominated work environment. In no small part this is based on the increased educational attainment of women, but the increased provision of child-care is also a factor. Japan used to be noted for having a relatively low variance in the age of marriage and childbirth (Brinton 1993). That rigidity seems to be breaking down and there is a sense of greater individual choice in lifestyle. Social attitudes are slowly changing, especially in the younger generation. Younger men are more likely to say that they wouldn't mind working for a female boss or that they believe that women are as capable as men. It is unlikely that Japan will attain the level of gender equality found in some European countries or in Australia in the near future. Nevertheless, many women seem to be satisfied to work at part-time jobs after marriage (Sato 1998).

Overall, one has the sense that the employment system is loosening up. Entrance ceremonies for new hires are somewhat less important than in the past. Hiring is spread through the year to a greater extent and the youth labour market is more mobile. Fast-track promotions are being introduced. The pay system is becoming more flexible and companies are considering offering their employees some choice over their fringe benefit packages, where none existed in the past. The distinction between regular and non-regular workers is also becoming somewhat more blurred, with many firms offering their more skilled part-time workers the opportunity to switch to regular status.

To see what the future holds for the Japanese firm, we might look at the foreign-owned firm. Higuchi (2001), using a survey by the former MITI, notes that foreign firms are no more likely than Japanese-owned firms to dismiss their workers. This is, of course, partly due to the fact that they are typically new, growing enterprises, but it is also a reflection of the fact that they, too, need to be concerned about their reputation. Where foreign firms do behave differently is in their pay systems, their working hours, and their treatment of women. Their pay systems are likely to be more flexible than those of Japanese firms, and more individualized. Promotion is less likely to be dependent on seniority, and young employees are able to rise faster in the firm. Foreign-owned firms have shorter working hours and employees are more likely to take their allotted vacation. Women are more likely to be treated as equals. This all seems consistent with the direction in which Japanese-owned firms are heading.

At the same time that larger firms have been moving towards a more individualized contract, and greater use of part-time workers, we have seen a decline in the numbers of family-owned firms. Less than 20 years ago Patrick and Rohlen (1987) were able to point to the importance of Japan's small business and family enterprise sector as a distinguishing feature of the economy. Today, one is more likely to remark on the fact that Japan is one of the few OECD countries where the self-employed sector is actually shrinking (Genda and Kambayashi 2002). To a large extent, this is the result of deregulation in the distribution sector, as smaller, less efficient firms are being squeezed out. While this may pose difficulties for the owners of such businesses, improving the efficiency of the distribution sector is one of the ways in which Japan will cope with the shrinking of its labour force.

Not all of the changes taking place in the labour market are benign. Perhaps the most serious problem is found in the labour market for youth. The rise in the unemployment rate has hit youth particularly hard and is concentrated among those with less than tertiary education. Many of the young men and women entering the labour force today will find it difficult to find satisfactory full-time employment as regular employees. They will have limited access to training in the part-time jobs that they hold. Over the long run, this may lead to the development of greater social inequality.

For much of the period since the 1950s, Japan has managed to avoid most of the problems that have been faced by other industrialized countries. The 1990s mark a point at which Japan has started to experience many of the same economic and social problems seen elsewhere, and policy-makers will naturally look to the experience of other countries to devise solutions to its problems. In the past, Japan has looked to other countries for models to use in the development of its political and economic institutions. Today, Japanese policy-makers are actively looking at the experience of other countries in dealing with problems such as youth unemployment. One field where Japan is not likely to follow the lead of other OECD countries is in the use of foreign labour. The Japanese are wary of establishing a large guest-worker population in the country akin to that seen in Germany. The Japanese have already run a limited experiment with immigration in the case of the *Nikkeijin* and found that it has not been easy to accommodate this group socially. There have been no calls for a large-scale revision of immigration policy, and it is likely that the use of foreign workers will remain restricted to skilled workers in areas where there are acute shortages. While there will continue to be an inflow of undocumented workers, it is unlikely that this will reach the levels seen in the USA or Europe, simply because of Japan's geographical position.

In order for Japan to cope with its declining workforce, it will need to improve productivity in the non-manufacturing sectors of the economy. As we have seen, there is plenty of scope for this improvement. The government can play a positive role in this process through the appropriate competition policy. In order to do this, however, there must be a swing away from the kind of interest group politics that has served to protect low productivity sectors from competition. In the labour domain, the Japanese government should make it easier for firms to adjust their labour force. One way that they can do this is through the provision of more generous unemployment benefits and retraining programmes. Japan still spends a relatively small proportion of its GDP on such programmes and there is ample room for expansion.

The government should also encourage firms to develop personnel management systems that allow for greater use of mid-career hires. The difficulty that middle-aged workers have in finding jobs is one of the reasons why firms are reluctant to fire their surplus employees. One moderately encouraging sign has been the greater willingness of firms to hire mid-career employees. One government survey shows that one in three firms is now thinking of increasing the number of mid-career hires that it makes (MHLW7 2003: 176).

The case law that has developed to protect Japanese employees is too restrictive and arbitrary. It would be better if the law was determined through a political process, rather than through the courts. In particular, firms should be able to dismiss workers if they can provide an appropriate severance payment. Legislation could be devised to determine just what level of severance payment would be appropriate based on age and years of service to the firm.

The greatest challenge posed by the decline in the workforce is the great need for flexibility in employment. When the labour force and industrial sectors were growing, it was easier to make adjustments to shifts in demand through the entry labour market for new school graduates. In the future, it will be harder to do this, and it is precisely for this reason that greater mobility in the labour market for middle-aged workers should be encouraged.

Finally, I believe that many of the features of Japanese employment institutions will remain intact. Blue-collar workers will continue to be among the best skilled in the world, and they will continue to have 'careers' in the workplace. The gender gap in earnings is likely to remain at a high level by international standards. Firm size will continue to be an important determinant of earnings. Even if the mobility of middle-aged Japanese men increases, it is likely that most of it will be voluntary, and employment protection will remain at high levels in the middle-sized and large companies. Despite the emergence of greater individualism, Japanese will continue to identify strongly with their company, rather than their occupational specialization.

The dual structure of the labour market will also persist, with distinctions between regular and non-regular work becoming more significant than the division according to enterprise size. Just as the distinctions along firm-size lines tend to be blurred, so the distinctions between regular and non-regular workers may become more blurred as firms try to develop the skills of their non-regular employees. Nevertheless, dualism will continue to be a striking feature of the Japanese labour market, and one that enables firms to offer high levels of job protection to their core employees. The employment system is not breaking down, just remodelling itself to cope with a new economic and demographic environment.

NOTE

1. MHWL7 (2003: 170–173) reports on attitude surveys of firm managers and employees that support this view.

References

Abe, M. (2002). 'Corporate Governance Structure and Employment Adjustment in Japan: An Empirical Analysis Using Corporate Finance Data'. *Industrial Relations*, 41/4: 683–702.

Abe, Y. (2002). 'Does the Y1.03 Million Tax Exempt Limit Depress the Hourly Wage of Part-Time Workers?' *Japan Labor Bulletin*, 41/9: 6–8.

— and F. Ohtake (1997). 'The Effects of Income Tax and Social Security on the Part-Time Labor Supply in Japan'. *Review of Social Policy*, 6: 45–64.

Abegglen, J. (1958). *The Japanese Factory: Aspects of its Social Organization*. Glencoe: The Free Press.

Abraham, K. G., and S. N. Houseman (1989). 'Job Security and Work Force Adjustment: How Different are U.S. and Japanese Practices?' *Journal of the Japanese and International Economies*, 3/4: 500–21.

AEDSC (Association of Employment Development for Senior Citizens) (1997). *Teinen Tōtatsusha nado no Shūgyō to Seikatsu Jittai ni kansuru Chōsa Kenkyū (Survey Research on the Working and Living Conditions of those who have Reached Mandatory Retirement or Equivalent)*. Tokyo: the Association of Employment Development for Senior Citizens.

Aoki, M. (1988). *Information, Incentives and Bargaining in the Japanese Economy*. Cambridge: Cambridge University Press.

Ariga, K. (2004). 'From Golden Eggs to Rotten Apples: Changing Landscape of the Market for New High School Graduates in Japan'. Interfaces for Economic Analysis Discussion Paper 021, Kyoto University.

—, G. Brunello, and Y. Ohkusa (2000). *Internal Labour Markets in Japan*. Cambridge: Cambridge University Press.

Benson, J. (1996). 'A Typology of Japanese Enterprise Unions'. *British Journal of Industrial Relations*, 34/3: 371–86.

Brinton, M. C. (1993). *Women and the Economic Miracle: Gender and Work in Postwar Japan*. Berkeley: University of California.

Brown, C., Y. Nakata, M. Reich, and L. Ulman, eds. (1997). *Work and Pay in the United States and Japan*. Oxford: Oxford University Press.

Brown, N. (2003). 'Under One Roof: The Evolving Story of Three Generation Housing in Japan', in J. W. Traphagan and J. Knight (eds.), *Demographic Change and the Family in Japan's Aging Society*. Albany, NY: SUNY Press.

Brunello, G., and F. Ohtake (1987). 'Bōnasu, Chingin no Kettei Mekanizumu to Koyō: Kigyōbetsu Deta ni yoru Saikō'. *Osaka Daigaku Keizaigaku*, 37/1: 28–41.

Chiswick, B. R. (1998). 'The Economic Consequences of Immigration: Application to the United States and Japan', in M. Weiner and T. Hanami (eds.), *Temporary Workers or Future Citizens? Japanese and U.S. Migration Policies*. New York: NYU Press, 177–208.

Chuma, H. (2002). 'Employment Adjustments in Japanese Firms during the Current Crisis'. *Industrial Relations*, 41/4: 653–82.

Clark, R. (1979). *The Japanese Company*. New Haven: Yale University Press.

Clark, R. L., and N. Ogawa (1992a). 'The Effect of Mandatory Retirement on Earnings Profiles in Japan'. *Industrial and Labor Relations Review*, 45/2: 258–66.

Clark, R. L., and N. Ogawa (1992*b*). 'Employment Tenure and Earnings Profiles in Japan and the United States: Comment'. *American Economic Review*, 82/1: 336–45.

Cole, R. (1979). *Work, Mobility and Participation: A Comparative Study of American and Japanese Industry*. Berkeley: University of California.

Cusumano, M. A. (1985). *The Japanese Automobile Industry: Technology and Management at Nissan and Toyota*. Cambridge, Mass.: Harvard University Press.

Darby, J., R. A. Hart, and M. Vecchi (2001). 'Wages, Work Intensity and Unemployment in Japan, UK and USA'. *Labour Economics*, 8/2: 243–58.

Dekle, R. (1990). 'Do the Japanese Elderly Reduce their Total Wealth? A New Look with Different Data'. *Journal of the Japanese and International Economies*, 4: 309–17.

— (2000). 'Demographic Density, Per-capita Consumption, and the Japanese Saving–Investment Balance'. *Oxford Review of Economic Policy*, 16/2: 46–60.

Doi, T. (1981). *The Anatomy of Dependence*. Tokyo: Kodansha.

Dore, R. (1973). *British Factory–Japanese Factory: The Origins of National Diversity in Industrial Relations*. Berkeley: University of California.

— and M. Sako (1998). *How the Japanese Learn to Work*, 2nd edn. London: Routledge.

Edwards, L. N., and M. K. Pasquale (2003). 'Women's Higher Education in Japan: Family Background, Economic Factors, and the Equal Employment Opportunity Law'. *Journal of the Japanese and International Economies*, 17/1: 1–32.

Flath, D. (2003). 'Regulation, Distribution Efficiency and Retail Density', in M. Blomstrom, J. Corbett, F. Hayashi, and A. Kashyap (eds.), *Structural Impediments to Growth in Japan*. Chicago: University of Chicago.

Freeman, R., and M. Rebick (1989). 'Crumbling Pillar: Declining Union Density in Japan'. *Journal of the Japanese and International Economies*, 3/4: 578–605.

— and M. B. Weitzman (1987). 'Bonuses and Employment in Japan'. *Journal of the Japanese and International Economies*, 1/2: 168–94.

Fujimura, H. (2003). 'Changes in the Spring Wage Offensive and the Future of the Wage Determination System in Japanese Firms'. *Japan Labor Bulletin*, 42/5: 6–12.

Fukao, K., and T. Amano (1998). 'Taigai Chokusetsu Tōshi to Seizōgyō no Kudōka (Foreign Direct Investment and the Hollowing out of Manufacturing)'. *Keizai Kenkyu*, 49/3: 259–75.

Fukawa, T., and K. Yamamoto (2003). 'Japanese Employees' Pension Insurance: Issues for Action'. *Journal of Population and Social Security*, 2/1: S6–S13.

Genda, Y. (1998). 'Japan: Wage Differentials and Changes since the 1980s', in T. Tachibanaki (ed.), *Wage Differentials: An International Comparison*. London: Macmillan.

— (2001). *Shigoto no naka no Aimai no Fuan (A Vague Unease at Work)*. Tokyo: Chuo Koron Shinsha.

— and R. Kambayashi (2002). 'Declining Self-Employment in Japan'. *Journal of the Japanese and International Economies*, 16/1: 73–91.

— and M. Kurosawa (2001). 'Transition from School to Work in Japan'. *Journal of the Japanese and International Economies*, 15/4: 465–88.

Gill, T. (2001). *Men of Uncertainty: The Social Organization of Day Laborers in Contemporary Japan*. Albany, NY: State University of New York Press.

Gordon, A. (1985). *The Evolution of Labor Relations in Japan*. Cambridge, Mass.: Harvard University Press.

Hanami, T. (2000). 'Equal Employment Revisited'. *Japan Labour Bulletin*, 39/1.

Hart, R. A., and S. Kawasaki (1999). *Work and Pay in Japan*. Cambridge: Cambridge University Press.

Hashimoto, M. (1990). *The Japanese Labor Market in a Comparative Perspective with the United States*. Kalamazoo, Mich.: Upjohn.

— and J. Raisian (1985). 'Employment Tenure and Earnings Profiles in Japan and the United States'. *American Economic Review*, 75: 721–35.

Hayashi, F., and E. Prescott (2002). 'The 1990s in Japan: A Lost Decade'. *Review of Economic Dynamics*, 5: 206–35.

Higuchi, Y. (1995). 'Sengyō-shufu hōgō seisaku no keizai-teki kiketsu (The Economic Consequences of Policies to Protect Full-Time Housewives)', in T. Hatta and N. Yashiro (eds.), *Jakusha hōgō seisaku no keizai bunseki (Economic Analysis of Policies to Protect the Weak)*. Tokyo: Nihon Keizai Shinbunsha.

— (2001). *Koyō to Shitsugyō no Keizaigaku (The Economics of Employment and Unemployment)*. Tokyo: Nihon Keizai Shinbunsha.

—, M. Abe, and J. Waldfogel (1997). 'Nichi-bei-ou ni okeru ikuji kyūgyō shussan kyūgyō seidoto josei shūgyō (Childcare and Maternity Leave Policies and Women's Employment in Japan, the United States and the United Kingdom)'. *Jinko Mondai Kenkyu (Journal of Population Problems)*, 53: 49–66.

— and M. Kawade (2003). *Kojin no Kyaria Keisei ni taisuru Kigyō to Gyōsei no Shien (Firm and Government Support for Career Development of Individuals)*. Tokyo: PRI.

Hildreth, A. K. G., and F. Ohtake (1998). 'Labor Demand and the Structure of Adjustment Costs'. *Journal of the Japanese and International Economies*, 12/2: 131–50.

Hirschman, A. O. (1970). *Exit, Voice and Loyalty: Responses to Decline in Firms, Organizations and States*. Cambridge, Mass.: Harvard University Press.

Horioka, C. Y. (2001). 'Japan's Public Pension System in the Twenty-First Century', in M. Blomstrom, B. Gangnes, and S. La Croix (eds.), *Japan's New Economy: Continuity and Change in the Twenty-First Century*. Oxford: Oxford University Press, 99–119.

Hoshi, T., and A. Kashyap (2001). *Corporate Financing and Governance in Japan: The Road to the Future*. Cambridge, Mass.: MIT Press.

Hōsō Jihō (Monthly). Tokyo: Hōsōkai (Lawyers' Association).

Houseman, S., and M. Osawa (1998). 'What is the Nature of Part-Time Work in the United States and Japan?' in J. O'Reilly and C. Fagan (eds.), *Part-Time Prospects: An International Comparison of Part-Time Work in Europe, North America and the Pacific Rim*. London: Routledge, 232–51.

Ichinose, T. (2001). 'Tenshoku ni yoru shōgai chingin no genshō to sōki taishoku yūgū seido (Early Retirement Plans and the Decline of Lifetime Income Resulting from Job Changes)'. *Rōsei Jihō*, 3484: 27–34.

Ichniowski, C., T. A. Kochan, D. Levine, C. Olson, and G. Strauss (1996). 'What Works at Work: Overview and Assessment'. *Industrial Relations*, 35/3: 299–333.

Iguchi, Y. (1998). 'Challenges for Foreign Traineeship Programs in Japan'. *Japan Labor Bulletin*, 37/10.

Imano, K. (1998). *Kachinuku Chingin Kaikaku (Successful Wage Reform)*. Tokyo: Nihon Keizai Shinbun Press.

Inoki, T., and K. Yugami (2001). 'Kokka Kōmuin e no Nyushokukōdō no Keizai Bunseki (Economic Analysis of the Job-Attainment Activity for Civil Servants)', in T. Inoki and F. Ohtake (eds.), *Koyō Seisaku no Keizai Bunseki*. Tokyo: Tokyo University Press.

Ishida, H. (1993). *Social Mobility in Contemporary Japan*. Stanford, Calif.: Stanford University Press.

JIL (Japan Institute of Labour) (1998). *Kanrishokusō no Koyōkanri shisutemu ni kansuru sōgōteki kenkyū (shita) hiseizōgyō anketto chōsa sōkatsuhen (General Research concerning the Employment Management Systems for the Managerial Class: Part 2, Compilation of Surveys of Non-Manufacturing).* Tokyo: Japan Institute of Labour.

JIL (Japan Institute of Labour) (2001a). *Shitsugyō kōzō no kenkyū (Research on the Structure of Unemployment).* Tokyo: Japan Institute of Labour.

— (2001b). *Daitoshi Wakumono no Shūgyō kōdō to Ishiki: Hirogaru Furiitaa Keiken to Kyōkan (The Employment Activity and Conciousness of Youth in Large Cities: The Widening Experience and Response of Freeters).* Tokyo: Japan Institute of Labour.

— (2002). *Japan Labor Flash,* 15 Oct., vol. 29 (ezine).

— (2003). *Rōdō Jōhō,* 16 May, No. 302 (ezine).

— (various years). *Japan Labour Bulletin.* Tokyo: Japan Institute of Labour.

Jorgenson, D. W., and M. Kuroda (1990). 'Productivity and International Competitiveness in Japan and the United States, 1960–1985', in C. R. Hulton (ed.), *Productivity Growth in Japan and the United States.* Chicago: University of Chicago Press.

JPC (Japan Productivity Centre) (Annual). *Katsuyō Rōdō Tōkei* (Practical Labour Statistics). Tokyo: Japan Productivity Centre.

Kashiwazaki, C. (2002). *Japan: From Immigration Control to Immigration Policy?* www.migrationinformation.org: Migration Policy Institute.

Kato, T. (2001). 'The End of Lifetime Employment in Japan? Evidence from National Surveys and Field Research'. *Journal of the Japanese and International Economies,* 15/4: 489–514.

— (2003). 'The Recent Transformation of Participatory Employment Practices', in S. Ogura, T. Tachibanaki, and D. Wise (eds.), *Labor Markets and Firm Benefit Policies in Japan and the United States.* Chicago: University of Chicago Press, 39–80.

— and M. Morishima (2002). 'The Productivity Effects of Participatory Employment Practices: Evidence from New Japanese Panel Data'. *Industrial Relations,* 41/4: 487–520.

Katz, L. F., and A. L. Revenga (1989). 'Changes in the Structure of Wages: The United States vs Japan'. *Journal of the Japanese and International Economies,* 3/4: 522–53.

Kawai Juku (Annual). *Nihon no Daigaku* (Japan's Universities). Tokyo: Tōyō Keizai.

Keidanren (2004). *Japan 2025.* Tokyo: Keidanren.

Koike, K. (1988). *Understanding Industrial Relations in Modern Japan.* London: Macmillan.

—, H. Chuma, and S. Ohta (2000). *Monozukuri no kinō to sono keisei (Skills for Making Things and their Development).* Toyota City: Toyota Chūbu Sanseiken.

— and T. Inoki, eds. (1990). *Skill Formation in Japan and Southeast Asia.* Tokyo: University of Tokyo.

Koshiro, K. (1983). 'Development of Collective Bargaining in Postwar Japan', in T. Shirai (ed.), *Contemporary Industrial Relations in Japan.* Madison: Wisconsin, 205–58.

Kurosaka, Y. (1988). *Makuro Keizaigaku to Nihon no Rōdō Shijō: Kyōkyūsaido no Bunseki (Macroeconomics and the Japanese Labour Market: A Supply-Side Analysis).* Tokyo: Tōyō Keizai.

Kuruvilla, S., and C. Erickson (2002). 'Change and Transformation in Asian Industrial Relations'. *Industrial Relations,* 41/2: 171–228.

Lazear, E. (1979). 'Why is there Mandatory Retirement?' *Journal of Political Economy,* December 87: 1261–84.

Lincoln, E. J. (2001). *Arthritic Japan: The Slow Pace of Economic Reform.* Washington: Brookings Institution Press.

Lincoln, J. R., and A. L. Kalleberg (1990). *Culture, Control and Commitment: A Study of Work Organization and Work Attitudes in the United States and Japan.* Cambridge: Cambridge University Press.

Marshall, G., A. Swift, and S. Roberts (1997). *Against the Odds?: Social Class and Social Justice in Industrial Societies.* Oxford: Clarendon Press.

METI (Japan, Ministry of Economics and Trade) (Annual). *Chūshō Kigyō Hakusho* (White Paper on Medium and Small Enterprises).

METI-Recruit (Ministry of Economics, Trade and Industry and Recruit Works Research Center) (2001). *Koyō no misumattchi no jittai bunseki* (Empirical Analysis of Mismatch in Employment). Tokyo: METI and Recruit Works Research Center.

MHLW1 (Japan, Ministry of Labour/Health, Labour and Welfare) (Annual). *Chingin Sensasu* (Wage Census) (1999–2002 available at www.mhlw.go.jp). Tokyo: Rodo Horei Kyokai.

MHLW2 (Annual). *Rōdō Kumiai Kihon Chōsa* (Basic Survey of Labour Unions). Tokyo: Ministry of Finance.

MHLW3 (Annual). *Employment Trends Survey.* Tokyo: Ministry of Finance.

MHLW4 (Annual). *Rōdō Tōkei Yōran* (Handbook of Labour Statistics). Tokyo: Kokuritsu Insatsu Kyoku.

MHLW5 (2000). *Kōnenreisha Jugyō Jittai Chōsa Hōkoku* (Report on the Survey of Employment of Older Persons) (available at www.mhlw.go.jp).

MHLW6 (Annual). Yearbook of Labour Statistics. Tokyo: Statistics and Information Department, Minister's Secretariat, Ministry of Health, Labour and Welfare.

MHLW7 (Annual). *Rōdō Hakusho/Rōdō Keizai Haksho* (White Paper on Labour/Labour Economy). Tokyo: Japan Institute of Labour/Japan Ministry of Health, Labour and Welfare.

MHLW8 (Annual). *Taishokkin Seido no Genjō to Kadai* (The Current Situation and Issues in the Retirement Payment System). Tokyo: Rōmu Gyōsei Kenkyūsho.

MHLW9 (2004). *Kakutei kyōshutsu nenkin renraku kaigi dai 9 kaigi jiroku, 26.3.04* (Record of the Fifth Conference on Defined Contribution Pensions), published at http://www.mhlw.go.jp/shingi/2004/06/txt/s0628-1.txt.

MHLW10 (2002). *Kokumin Seikatsu Kiso Chōsa* (Basic Survey of Citizens' Lives) (2002 available at www.mhlw.go.jp).

MHLW11 (2004). *Heisei 16 nen 3 gatsu kōkō-chūgaku shinsotsusha no shūshoku naitei jōkyō nado (Heisei 15 nen 11 gatsu miman genzai) ni tsuite* (March 1994 report on middle/high school graduating students' conditions of *naitei*, etc. (as of the end of November 2003)).

MHLW12 (2000). *Tenshokusha no jittai (heisei 10 nen chōsa) (The Current Situation of Job Changers—1998 Survey).* Tokyo: Ministry of Finance.

MHLW13 (2002). *Gaikokujin koyō jōkyō hōkoku kekka (Heisei 14 nen 6 gatsu 1 nichi genzai)* (Report on the Employment Conditions of Foreigners (as of 1 June 2002)). Tokyo: Ministry of Health, Labour and Welfare.

MHLW14 (various years). *Shūgyō Keitai no Taiyōka ni kansuru Sōgō Jittai Chōsa (Survey on the Diversification of Employment Status).* Tokyo: Ministry of Health, Labour and Welfare.

MHLW15 (2004). *Heisei 15 nendo daigaku nado sotsugyō yōteisha shūshoku naitei jōkyō nado chōsa (Heisei 15 nen 10 gatsu 1 nichi genzai) ni tsuite* (The Conditions of Employment Agreements for Prospective Graduates of Universities, etc. in Financial Year 2003). Tokyo: Ministry of Health, Labour and Welfare.

MHLW16 (2004). *Shinki gakusotsusha no shūshoku naitei jōkyō nado ni tsuite* (The Conditions of Employment Agreements for New-Graduate Job-Seekers). Tokyo: Ministry of Health, Labour and Welfare.

Mincer, J., and Y. Higuchi (1988). 'Wage Structures and Labour Turnover in the United States and Japan'. *Journal of the Japanese and International Economies*, 2: 97–133.

Miyamoto, D., and Y. Nakata (2002). 'Seiki Jūgyōin no Koyōsakugen to Hiseiki Rōdō no Zōka: 1990 Nendai no Ōgata Kourigyō wo Taishō ni (Cuts in Employment of Regular Workers and the Increase in Nonregular Labour: Large Scale Retailers in the 1990s)', in Y. Genda and Y. Nakata (eds.), *Risutora to Tenshoku no Mekanizumu* (*The Mechanism of Restructuring and Job-Changing*). Tokyo: Tōyō Keizai Shinposha, 81–102.

MOE1 (Japan, Ministry of Education) (Annual). *Monbu Tōkei Yōran* (Handbook of Education Statistics). Tokyo: Ministry of Education.

MOE2 (Japan, Ministry of Education) (Annual). *Gakkō Kihon Chōsa* (Basic Survey of Schools). Tokyo: Ministry of Education.

MOJ1 (Japan, Ministry of Justice) (2002). *Heisei 14 Nen migenzai ni okeru gaikokujin tōrokusha tōkei ni tsuite* (Statistics on Registered Foreigners in 2002), available at www.moj.go.jp.

MOJ2 (2000). *Basic Plan for Immigration Control* (available at www.moj.go.jp).

Mori, H. (1997). *Immigration Policy and Foreign Workers in Japan*. Basingstoke: Macmillan.

Morishima, M. (1991*a*). 'Information Sharing and Firm Performance in Japan'. *Industrial Relations*, 30/1: 37–61.

— (1991*b*). 'Information Sharing and Collective Bargaining in Japan: Effects on Wage Negotiation'. *Industrial and Labor Relations Review*, 44/3: 469–85.

— (1992). 'Use of Joint Consultation Committees by Large Japanese Firms'. *British Journal of Industrial Relations*, 30: 405–24.

— (1999). 'Role of Labor Unions in the Recent Change in White-Collar HRM Practices in Japan'. *Japan Labour Bulletin*, 38/12: 6–11.

— (2002). 'Pay Practices in Japanese Organizations: Changes and Non-changes'. *Japan Labour Bulletin*, 41/4: 8–13.

Motonishi, T., and H. Yoshikawa (1999). 'Causes of the Long Stagnation of Japan during the 1990's: Financial or Real?' *Journal of the Japanese and International Economies*, 13/3: 181–200.

Mouer, R., and Y. Sugimoto (1986). *Images of Japanese Society*. London: Kegan Paul International.

Mulgan, A. G. (2002). *Japan's Failed Revolution: Koizumi and the Politics of Economic Reform*. Canberra: Asia Pacific Press.

Murakami, Y. (1981). 'The Age of New Middle Mass Politics: The Case of Japan'. *Journal of Japanese Studies*, 8/1: 29–72.

Nagase, N. (2001). 'Paato no chingin ni 103 man en no kabe wa juyōka (Is the Upper Limit of 1.03 Million Yen Significant in Determining a Wage Rate for Part-Timers?)'. *Japanese Journal of Labour Studies*, 489: 60–1.

— (2002). 'Wife Allowance and Tax Exemption behind Low Wages for Part-Time Workers'. *Japan Labour Bulletin*, 41/9: 8–10.

Nakakubo, H. (1996). 'Procedures for Resolving Individual Employment Disputes'. *Japan Labour Bulletin*, 35/6: 5–8.

— (2002). 'Should the Treatment of Regular and Part-Time Workers be Equalized? Discrepancies in Conditions and Focused Legal Regulations'. *Japan Labour Bulletin*, 41/10: 6–7.

Nakamura, K., H. Sato, and T. Kamiya (1988). *Rōdō Kumiai wa Hontō ni Yaku ni Tateiru no ka?* (*Do Labour Unions Play a Useful Role?*). Tokyo: Sōgō Rōdō Kenkyūjo.

Nakane, C. (1970). *Japanese Society.* Berkeley: University of California Press.

Nickell, S. J., L. Nunziata, W. Ochel, and G. Quintini (2003). 'The Beveridge Curve, Unemployment and Wages in the OECD', in P. Aghion, R. Frydman, and J. E. Stiglitz (eds.), *Knowledge, Information and Expectations in Modern Macroeconomics: Papers in Honor of Edmund S. Phelps.* Princeton: Princeton University Press.

Nikkeiren (2000). *Toward a Market with a Human Face: Nikkeiren Position Paper 2000.* Tokyo: Nikkeiren.

Nitta, M. (1992). 'Intrafirm Communication at Small- and Medium-Sized Enterprises'. *Japan Labor Bulletin,* 31/11: 5–8.

—— (2003). *Henka no naka no koyō shisutemu (The Employment System in a Changing Japanese Society).* Tokyo: Tokyo University Press.

Nomura, M. (1992). '1980 Nendai ni okeru Nihon no Rōdō Kenkyū: Koike Kazuo shi no Shosetsu no Hihanteki Kento (Japanese Labour Research in the 1980s: Critical Comments on the Theory of Kazuo Koike)'. *Nihon Rōdō Kenkyū Zasshi,* 34/12: 3–21.

NPA (Japan, National Personnel Authority) (2000). *Kōmuin Hakusho* (White Paper on Civil Servants). Tokyo: Ministry of Finance.

Ochiai, E. (1997). *The Japanese Family System in Transition: A Sociological Analysis of Family Change in Postwar Japan.* Tokyo: LTCB International Library Foundation.

OECD1, Organization for Economic Cooperation and Development (Annual). *Employment Outlook.* Paris: OECD.

OECD2 (2001). *Economic Survey: Japan.* Paris: OECD.

OECD3 (2001). *Trends in International Migration.* Paris: OECD.

Ogawa, N., and R. D. Retherford (1993). 'The Resumption of Fertility Decline in Japan: 1973–92'. *Population and Development Review,* 19/4: 703–41.

Ogura, K. (2002). 'Hitenkeiteki koyō no kokusai hikaku: Nihon, Amerika, Ōshūshokoku no gainen to genjō (International Comparison of Atypical Employment: Concepts and Current Situation in Japan, US and European Countries'. *Nihon Rōdō Kenkyū Zasshi,* 44/8: 3–17.

Ohta, K. (2000). 'Kokusai Hikaku kara mita Nihon no Shotoku Kakusa (Japanese Income Differentials Seen in International Perspective)'. *Nihon Rōdō Kenkyu Zasshi,* 42/7: 33–40.

Ohta, S., and Y. Genda (1999). 'Shūgyō to Shitsugyō (Employment and Unemployment)'. *Nihon Rōdō Kenkyū Zasshi,* 41/4: 2–13.

Ohtake, F. (1998). 'The United States', in T. Tachibanaki (ed.), *Wage Differentials: An International Comparison.* London: Macmillan.

—— (2000). '90 Nendai no Shotoku Kakusa (Income Differentials in the 1990s)'. *Nihon Rōdō Kenkyū Zasshi,* 42/7: 2–11.

Okano, K. (1993). *School to Work Transition in Japan.* Clevedon: Multilingual Matters Ltd.

Okunishi, Y. (1998). 'Kigyōnai Chingin Kakusa no Genjō to sono Yōin (In-house Wage Differentials and Determining Factors'. *Nihon Rōdō Kenkyū Zasshi,* 22/10: 2–16.

Ono, A. (1987). 'Jukuren Kasetsu Ka, Seikatsu Kasetsu ka (Two Competing Hypotheses for the Nenko Wage System)'. *Keizaigaku Kenkyū,* 28: 1–25.

Ono, H. (2004). 'College Quality and Earnings in the Japanese Market'. *Industrial Relations,* 43/3: 595–617.

—— and M. E. Rebick (2003). 'Constraints on the Level and Efficient Use of Labour', in M. Blomstrom, J. Corbett, F. Hayashi, and A. Kashyup (eds.), *Structural Impediments to Growth in Japan.* Chicago: University of Chicago.

Papademetriou, D. G., and K. A. Hamilton (2000). *Reinventing Japan: Immigration's Role in Shaping Japan's Future.* Washington: Carnegie Endowment for International Peace.

Patrick, H. T., and T. P. Rohlen (1987). 'Small-Scale Family Enterprises', in K. Yamamura and Y. Yasuba (eds.), *The Political Economy of Japan: Volume 1, The Domestic Transformation*. Stanford, Calif.: Stanford University Press, 331–84.

Pempel, T. J. (1998). *Regime Shift: Comparative Dynamics of the Japanese Political Economy*. Ithaca, NY: Cornell University Press.

PHPT (Department of Public Management, Home Affairs and Post and Telecommunications) (2000). *Population Census* (available at www.stat.go.jp). Tokyo: Nihon Tōkei Kyōkai.

PMO1 (Japan, Prime Minister's Office/Department of Public Management, Home Affairs and Post and Telecommunications) (Annual or Semi-Annual). *Special Survey of the Labour Force Survey*. Tokyo: Nihon Tokei Kyokai.

PMO2 (Annual). *Annual Report of the Labour Force Survey*. Tokyo: Nihon Tokei Kyokai.

PMO3 (various years). *Employment Status Survey* (2002 available at www.stat.go.jp). Tokyo: Nihon Tōkei Kyōkai.

PMO4 (Annual). *Japan Statistical Yearbook* (recent years available at www.stat.go.jp).

Posen, A. S. (1998). *Restoring Japan's Economic Growth*. Washington: Institute for International Economics.

Rebick, M. (1992*a*). 'The Japanese Approach to Finding Jobs for Older Workers', in O. S. Mitchell (ed.), *As the Workforce Ages: Costs, Benefits and Policy Challenges*. Ithaca, NY: ILR Press, 103–24.

—— (1992*b*). 'The Persistence of Firm-Size Earnings Differentials and Labor Market Segmentation in Japan'. *Journal of the Japanese and International Economies*, 7: 132–56.

—— (1994). 'Social Security and Older Workers' Labor Market Responsiveness: The United States, Japan, and Sweden', in R. M. Blank (ed.), *Social Protection and Economic Flexibility: Is There a Trade-Off?* Chicago: University of Chicago Press, 189–222.

—— (1995). 'Rewards in the Afterlife: Late Career Job Placements as Incentives in the Japanese Firm'. *Journal of the Japanese and International Economies*, 9/1: 1–28.

—— (1998). 'The Japanese Labour Market for University Graduates: Trends in the 1990s'. *Japan Forum*, 10/1: 17–30.

—— (2000). 'Japanese Labour Markets: Can We Expect Significant Change?' in M. Blomstrom, B. Gangnes, and S. J. La Croix (eds.), *Japan's New Economy: Continuity and Change in the Twenty-First Century*. Oxford: Oxford University Press.

Retherford, R. D., N. Ogawa, and S. Sakamoto (1996). 'Values and Fertility Change in Japan'. *Population Studies*, 50: 5–25.

Roberts, G. S. (2002). 'Pinning Hopes on Angels: Reflections from an Aging Japan's Urban Landscape', in R. Goodman (ed.), *Family and Social Policy in Japan*. Cambridge: Cambridge University Press.

Rohlen, T. (1974). *For Harmony and Strength: Japanese White-Collar Organization in Anthropological Perspective*. Berkeley: University of California.

Rōmu Gyōsei Kenkyūsho (1998). *Rōsei Jihō*, no. 3356.

Saint-Paul, G. (1996). *Dual Labor Markets: A Macroeconomic Perspective*. Cambridge, Mass.: MIT Press.

Sato, H. (1997). 'Labour–Management Relations in Small and Medium-Sized Enterprises: Collective Voice Mechanisms for Workers in Non-unionised Companies', in M. Sako and H. Sato (eds.), *Japanese Labour and Management in Transition: Diversity, Flexibility and Participation*. London: Routledge.

—— (1998). 'Hitenkei Rōdō no Jittai (Atypical Employment: Does it Offer Flexible Work?)' *Nihon Rōdō Kenkyū Zasshi*, 40/12: 2–14.

—— (2000). 'The Current Situation of "Family-Friendly" Policies in Japan'. *Japan Labour Bulletin*, 39/2: 5–10.

Sato, T. (2000*a*). *Fubyōdo Shakai Nihon (Japan, the Unequal Society)*. Tokyo: Chūkō Shinsho.

—— (2000*b*). ' "Shin Chūkan Taisho" Tanjō kara 20 Nen (Twenty Years after the "New Middle-mass" '. *Chuō Kōron*, May: 68–82.

—— (2003). 'Use of On-Site Contract Workers in the Manufacturing Sector and Revision of the Worker-Dispatching Law'. *Japan Labor Bulletin*, 42/4: 7–11.

Shinotsuka, E. (1985). 'Koyō Chōsei to Koyō Chōsei Joseikin no Yakuwari (Employment Adjustment and the Role of Employment Adjustment Subsidies)'. *Nihon Rōdō Kyōkai Zasshi*, 27: 2–18.

—— (1998). 'The Supply of Manpower for Care Services from the Viewpoint of Care Insurance'. *Review of Population and Social Policy*, 7: 15–43.

Shirai, T., ed. (1983*a*). *Contemporary Industrial Relations in Japan*. Madison: University of Wisconsin.

—— (1983*b*). 'A Theory of Enterprise Unionism', in Shirai (1983*a*), 117–45.

Sorrentino, C. (1984). 'Japan's Low Unemployment Rate: An In-Depth Analysis'. *Monthly Labor Review*, 107/3: 18–27.

Strom, S. (1998). *Rethinking Lifetime Jobs and their Underpinnings*. New York: *New York Times*, D1.

Tachibanaki, T. (1996). *Wage Determination and Distribution in Japan*. Oxford: Oxford University Press.

—— (1998*a*). 'Introduction to Wage Differentials: An International Comparison', in T. Tachibanaki (ed.), *Wage Differentials: An International Comparison*. London: Macmillan Press.

—— (1998*b*). *Nihon no Keizai Kakusa: Shotoku to Shisan kara kangaeru (Japan's Economic Differentials in Income and Assets)*. Tokyo: Iwanami Shoten.

—— (2000). 'Nihon non Shotoku Kakusa wa Kakudaishiteiru ka (Are Japan's Income Differentials Widening?)'. *Nihon Rōdō Kenkyū Zasshi*, 42/7: 41–52.

—— and T. Noda (2000). *The Economic Effects of Trade Unions in Japan*. London: Macmillan.

—— and S. Ohta (1994). 'Wage Differentials by Industry and the Size of Firms, and the Labour Market in Japan', in T. Tachibanaki (ed.), *Labour Market and Economic Performance: Europe, Japan and the US*. London: Macmillan.

Taira, K. (1983). 'Japan's Low Unemployment: Economic Miracle or Statistical Artifact?' *Monthly Labor Review*, 106/7: 3–10.

Tanisaka, N., and F. Ohtake (2003). 'Impact of Labor Shedding on Stock Prices'. *Japan Labor Bulletin*, 42/1: 6–12.

Tomita, K. (2000). 'Sekushuaru Harasumento no Jittai to Bōshi no tame no Hairyo Gimu (The Status of Sexual Harassment and Obligatory Measures to Prevent it)'. *Nihon Rōdō Kenkyū Zasshi*, 42/5: 16–22.

Tsuru, T., and J. B. Rebitzer (1995). 'The Limits of Enterprise Unionism: Prospects for Continuing Union Decline in Japan'. *British Journal of Industrial Relations*, 33/3: 459–92.

Upham, F. K. (1987). *Law and Social Change in Postwar Japan*. Cambridge, Mass.: Harvard University Press.

USCR (United States Committee for Refugees) (2003). *Worldwide Refugee Information* (available at www.refugees.org).

US Department of Education, National Center for Education Statistics (E.D. Tabs), Laura G. Knapp, Project Officer (2002). *Enrollment in Postsecondary Institutions, Fall 2000 and Financial Statistics, Fiscal Year 2000.* Washington: US Department of Education.

Vogel, E. (1979). *Japan as Number One.* Cambridge, Mass.: Harvard University Press.

Wakisaka, A. (1997). 'Women at Work', in M. Sako and H. Sato (eds.), *Japanese Labour and Management in Transition: Diversity, Flexibility and Participation.* London: Routledge.

— (2002). 'Ikuji Kyūgyō seido ga Shokuba de riyōsareru tame no jōken to kadai (Conditions and Issues Involved in Utilizing Childcare Leave in the Workplace)'. *Nihon Rōdō Kenkyū Zashi*, 44/6: 4–14.

Weathers, C. (2001*a*). 'Changing White-Collar Workplaces and Female Temporary Workers in Japan'. *Social Science Japan Journal*, 4/2: 201–18.

— (2001*b*). 'The Last Gasp of Labor's Dual Strategy? Japan's 1997 Wage-Setting Round'. *Japan Forum*, 13/2: 215–32.

Weinstein, D. E. (2001). 'Historical, Structural and Macroeconomic Perspectives on the Japanese Economic Crisis', in M. Blomstrom, B. Gangnes, and S. La Croix (eds.), *Japan's New Economy: Continuity and Change in the Twenty-First Century.* Oxford: Oxford University Press, 29–47.

Wolff, L. (2003). *Sexual Harassment Law in Japan.* Sydney: Faculty of Law, University of New South Wales.

Yamada, M. (1999). *Parasaito Shinguru no Jidai (The Age of the Parasite Single).* Tokyo: Chikuma Shinsho.

Yamauchi, N. (1997). 'The Effects of Aging on National Saving and Asset Accumulation in Japan', in M. D. Hurd and N. Yashiro (eds.), *The Economic Effects of Aging in the United States and Japan.* Chicago: University of Chicago, 131–52.

Index

Note: Numbers in **bold** type indicate a figure or table.

9 780199 247240